Media Racism

This book is dedicated to my children, Jalia, Justin, and Amiri. May you see your authentic selves in the world all around you.

Media Racism

The Impact of Media Injustice on Black Women's Lives

Marquita M. Gammage

MEDIA RACISM

Printed in the United States of America

24 25 26 27 28 10 9 8 7 6 5 4 3 2 1

Mailing/Submissions:
Universal Write Publications, LLC
421 8th Avenue, Suite 86
New York, NY 10116

Website: UWPBooks.com

ISBN: 978-1-942774-07-5

Library of Congress Control Number: 2023921454

This book has been partially supported with a financial grant from SAGE Publishing.

S Sage

Contents

Acknowledgments

I would like to acknowledge the work of Black women advocates throughout the world who seek to advance justice and liberation for African people globally. To Black women in the academy, you are invaluable. I also want to recognize my family and their unwavering love and support.

List of Tables and Figures

INTRODUCTION

Outfitted in a dark pink dress with ruffle sleeves that contrast her brown skin, an adolescent African American girl's image is plastered down the sides of high-rise buildings, across billboards, at bus stops, and on public transportation across the nation. Against a light-blue backdrop, a white head bow flanks her natural curls, which frame her face. Her lips are pinched closed as if she is forbidden to speak. Just above her head of curls is a warning: "The most dangerous place for an African American is in the womb." The first installments of this billboard were displayed outside high-rise buildings and the Holland Tunnel in New York City during Black History Month in 2011. The advertisements were part of a national campaign by the Life Always group, intended to charge Planned Parenthood with racially targeting African Americans for abortion services. These controversial antiabortion advertisements have been termed a form of reproductive injustice by civil rights and reproduction rights activists. The advertisements falsely represent African American women as the face of abortion and abortion as the leading cause of death among African Americans. Consider the fact that in 2009 the Centers for Disease Control and Prevention (CDC) reported that between 1997 and 2006 the majority of women who obtained an abortion were White. "Among women from the 39 areas for which race was reported for 2006, white women (including both Hispanic and non-Hispanic white women) accounted for the largest percentage (55.8%) of abortions; black women accounted for 36.4% and women of other racial groups for 7.8%" (Pazol et al., 2009). Based in illogical distortions of facts, several images of wide-eyed perfectly innocent Black children have been obstructed with racist assaults against Black womanhood.

Images such as these, which encapsulate African American babies' mortality rate into a singular determent, are gross perversions of African American health inequalities in America. African Americans' lives have been significantly negatively affected by exploitative systems, medical

1

and biological terrorism, and unethical experimentations. As noted by Harriet Washington (2006) in *Medical Apartheid*:

> Blacks have dramatically higher rates of nearly every cancer, of AIDS, of heart disease, of diabetes, of liver disease, of infectious diseases, and they even suffer from higher rates of accidental death, homicide, and mental illness. Before they die young from eminently preventable diseases, African Americans also suffer far more devasting but equally preventable disease complications, such as blindness, confinement to wheelchairs, and limb loss. Studies continue to demonstrate that, far from sharing the bounty of American medical technology, African Americans are often bereft of high-technology care, even for life-threatening conditions such as heart disease. (p. 20)

The elimination of these realities in discourse on African Americans' lives, and more specially in media representations of African Americans, erroneously places the burden of health and life disparities among Blacks on the Black woman.

Historically, media representations of African Americans have not been based on factual evidence but instead have overly employed culturally racist stereotypes of Blackness. In fact, racialized media of African Americans were the norm for much of America's history. The racist bias against African Americans in the media emanates from the racial bias that exists in American society. The treatment of African Americans in the media was and is an important part of institutional racism and must be dissected to fully understand African Americans' overall well-being in the United States.

Media Racism: The Impact of Media Injustice on Black Women's Lives examines the calculus of media racism's effect on the sustainability of anti-African racist ideologies. The significance of this text is to establish criteria by which we can begin to examine the role of media in the lives of Black females and, more specifically, the impact of this role on their lived experiences. Currently there is limited research available that considers the significance of media as an important issue in life disparities. Consequently, this text considers the effects of media racism on Black females' physical, mental, cultural, political, and social well-being. By generating research on this subject matter, we may be able to lay the foundation for addressing the contemporary realities of issues impacting Black women's lives.

PROBLEMATIZING MEDIA RACISM

Media racism is the creation of broadcasting entities (i.e., news outlets, including newspapers, television and film, radio, print advertisements, and social media) to market race-based ideologies, biases, prejudice, and discrimination about a particular racial group. Media racism was birthed out of the historic use of racialized categorizing of Africans as inferior and is based in the institutional power to control the public image of an entire group of people. A byproduct of *institutional racism*, or the power to marginalize an entire population in the structures of society based solely on race, media racism serves the political, cultural, and social interest of White supremacy. Media racism also serves racist political agendas, for it has provided imagery that parallels anti–African American political climates and policies that helped rationalize the targeting of African Americans as noncitizens in the 18th and 19th centuries, second-class citizens in the 20th century, and criminally unfit for citizenship in the 21st century.

Media racism expanded its scope as broadcast technologies were advanced and the industry of cinema and film was created. The prevalence of racist representations of African Americans sparked outrage among the African American community. Many Black activists lobbied and campaigned for censorship of racist content. In the 1915 case *Mutual Film Corporation v. Industrial Commission of Ohio*, the United States Supreme Court ruled that the production of films was not protected under the First Amendment, citing film production as a commercial industry not entitled to free speech protections. Film censorship laws and local censorship boards were established and controlled the discourse on what was considered acceptable media content. Many of the restrictions developed focused on immoral, violent, and sexual content and largely addressed concerns of religious constituents, mainly the Catholic Church. Thus, because of the racism embedded in American institutions, public policies supported racist images and did not seek to create censorship laws that would prohibit media racism.

The Motion Picture Producers and Distributors of America (MPPDA) was established in 1922 by William Hays and in 1945 became known as the Motion Picture Association of America (MPAA). The Motion Picture Production Code, or "Hays Code," provided a set of production guidelines that was adopted in 1934 and required all films released on or after July 1, 1934, to obtain a certificate of approval before their release. The Catholic layman Joseph Breen was one of the primary code enforcers, chosen by Hays, to ensure that motion picture production studios adhered to the code in the United States (MPAA, 2018, p. 7). Hence, it is not surprising to find the Catholic Church's concerns took priority in censorship regulations.

Governmental censorship was completely turned on its head in the 1952 case of *Joseph Burstyn, Inc. v. Wilson* when the United States Supreme Court ruled that First Amendment protection extends to motion picture production. This decision, which overturned the court's 1915 ruling, meant that censorship boards no longer possessed the power to approve the distribution of films. The threat of government regulation that justified the Production Code was greatly reduced, and the Production Code Administration (PCA) authority in the film industry was diminished. Racially biased content continued to eclipse the image of African Americans, and little was done structurally to alter the racist representations of Blackness. Also, racial epithets were determined to be acceptable language content in movies, and descriptors were developed by the MPAA to cite the content in films.

Racially abusive media against Africans and African Americans have existed since the beginning of Black subjugation in America (Balkaran, 1999; Bennett, 2010; Davenport, 2009). In 1967, the Kerner Commission documented the heightened presence of racism in media and how media used racially biased reporting and production practices that validated racist ideologies about African Americans. The *Kerner Commission Report on the Causes, Events, and Aftermaths of the Civil Disorders of 1967* details the social and civil realities faced by African Americans and provides critical review of the media coverage and reporting of racial problems and civil disorders concerning African Americans (National Advisory Commission on Civil Disorders, 1967). Chapter 15 of the report discusses the impact and role of news media in inflaming racial tensions and intensifying public demand for state-sanctioned control over and violence against African Americans. News media coverage of anti-Black civil discourse and riots by Whites versus African American civil discourse differs significantly. This divergence can be discussed in terms of righteous struggle, where White anti-Black public assaults and violence received coverage legitimizing these actions, yet, on the other hand, African Americans' public response to anti-Black terrorism, policy, and policing received news coverage that condemned and actively worked to delegitimize the concerns of Black communities. Positioning African Americans' protest and civil discourse as irrational and not justified led to inaccurate impressions, and, according to the Kerner Commission report, news media "failed to report adequately on the causes and consequences of civil disorders and the underlying problems of race relations" (National Advisory Commission on Civil Disorders, 1967, p. 201). Additionally, media's framing of anti-Black terrorism as righteous coincided with White supremacist views and further validated the deeply rooted anti-Blackness ideologies, beliefs, and practices in American society. The historic use of media against Black communities signifies a structural investment in anti-Black media and has laid the foundation for media racism.

Racialization of media did not occur simply as a result of racist media producers, journalists, and writers. In the same way that racism is intrinsically woven in other institutions in America, racism is inseparable from

American media. The media is a mass communication device that is designed to deliver information to large audiences. America has systematically used the media to broadcast racist ideologies about multiple racial groups. While the media has been used to promote the inferiority of Blacks, it has simultaneously been used to endorse White supremacy. Thus, the media operates as a system of oppression against African Americans, and any study of African Americans' marginalization must include an examination of media racism.

WEAPONIZING BLACK WOMANHOOD

Examining the role of media in creating barriers to sustaining positive life outcomes among African Americans has proven pivotal over the past few centuries. While media productions have evolved technologically, media racism remains embedded in the fabric of American media productions, including television and film, news, radio broadcasts, and social media. Twenty-first-century media productions on Black womanhood mirror past centuries' stereotyped portrayals of Blackness, and media injustice against African Americans persists. The content of contemporary media, and television shows starring Black women in particular, is entrenched with the systematic promotion of unhealthy and socially corrupt lifestyles and negative images of Black womanhood. There is alarming evidence that politics, scholarship, and media contribute to the stereotype that African Americans, and Black women in particular, are chronically unhealthy and in need of social control.

Racist representations of Black women in the media are used to weaponize their existence and therefore justify the injustices Black females experience in health care, social programs, American institutions (both educational and economic), the criminal justice system, and the larger general public. Media images of Black womanhood are inflated with messages of criminality and social unruliness. Reality television shows in particular seem to be infatuated with showcasing Black women as chronically violent, animalistic, and threatening. These racialized portrayals of Black women work collectively to situate their womanhood as one of the primary dangers facing the American public. In *Representations of Black Women in the Media* (M. Gammage, 2015), I argue that media representations of African American women employ and advance stereotypical portrayals of Black womanhood:

> Black women in particular have endured a long legacy of one-dimensional news reporting. Stereotypes such as the welfare queen, illegitimate baby-mama, and jezebel have infiltrated the news media and are the primary storylines about Black women. The First Lady Michelle Obama is no

exception. She has been reported as an aggressive, power hungry terrorist and slave. News media broadcasting has damaged the image of Black women and is often left unchallenged. Reporting practices such as these directly influence public opinions and may affect public policies. (p. 11)

The influx of television dramas and reality television shows starring Black women has created a new breeding ground for broadcasting racist ideologies about African Americans. And while Black media producers, writers, and directors are engaged in the construction of Black images, most of the mainstream media on Blackness is still primarily owned and/ or distributed by White-owned media broadcasting companies. Consider reality television. Currently, two network television stations house the majority of "unscripted" reality television shows starring Black females: VH1 and Bravo. Combined, the two networks maintain the majority control over Black women's images in reality television. Dissecting the impact of these racially informed images of womanhood on Black women's lives is a critical component of race and media studies. According to Gandy (1998),

racial projects are both discursive and symbolic, in that they are oriented toward the creation of meaning, as well as influencing the allocation of economic and political resources. This perspective suggests that a discursive strategy is often designed to normalize and justify a racial imbalance in the distribution of capital and other social value. (p. 37)

The media has closely associated Black womanhood with pathological dysfunction, self-deification, and criminality. The mass media continues to operate as anti–Black women and anti-Black by publicizing messages and images of Blacks as pathologically threatening to the sovereignty of the nation.

The American public, American institutions, and the American government have isolated the Black woman and have targeted her as a threat to the public and White supremacy. Media have helped fuel these perceived threats by overly broadcasting and promoting images and messages about Black women as unsafe and unfit for existence in society. Although this threat is artificial, Black women have faced real consequences that have further subjugated them and marginalized their presence in America. By positioning the Black woman as a dangerous weapon, America has ushered in a host of political, judicial, legislative, medical, social, and economic attacks against her. Media have advanced and promoted these racial ideologies and oppressive tactics to justify these systematic assaults. Understanding the function of weaponizing Black womanhood through the media can help us better fight the current and anticipate the further policies and strategies against Black people. This book attempts to expose the contemporary use of media racism in advancing racist ideologies about African Americans, and Black women in particular, and how racist representations negatively affect the lives and well-being of African American women.

CHAPTER OVERVIEW

Chapter 1, "Anti-Blackness and Media Racism: A Cautionary Tale," chronicles the historic use of media in advancing racist sentiments against African Americans in politics, scientific research, and social policies. I argue that media is an instrument of communication that when paired with racism perpetuates national anti-African ideologies that have negatively impacted the lives of African Americans yet are still utilized in the 21st century.

Chapter 2 is titled "From Crack Mamas to Baby Mamas: Black Women, Media, and Public Policy." This chapter explores how media images directly impact public perceptions of Black womanhood. This chapter will discuss how media have greatly affected public opinions about Black women and how their continued presence in the media further validates public policies that render Black womanhood a criminal act. Over the past three decades, media-promoted stereotypes have directly impacted public perceptions of Black womanhood and have validated public policies that negatively impact the well-being of Black women. This chapter explores the 1980s "welfare queen," the 1990s "crack mama," and the 2000s "baby mama" stereotypes as a calculated political media attack on Black motherhood in the post–civil rights era. I argue that there exists a pattern of media racism against Black women to validate public policy reforms, and this approach is predictive of future policy initiatives. If we pay close attention to the current representations of Black women in the media, we may be able to anticipate the next wave of social reforms that endanger the health and safety of African Americans.

Chapter 3, "Unhealthy Representations of Black Women in Television Dramas," details the lifestyles among lead Black female characters in television dramas. Three shows—*Scandal* (Rhimes et al., 2012–2018), *How to Get Away With Murder* (Rhimes et al., 2014–2020), and *Being Mary Jane* (Akil et al., 2013–2019)—portray the lead Black females exhibiting high-risk behaviors in their everyday lives, without health consequences. Given the popularity of these shows, it is imperative that we investigate the content and messages that these shows promote. For example, Black women are shown battling high levels of stress in their jobs and personal lives, experiencing physical harm or threat, engaging in high alcohol consumption, and exhibiting high-risk sexual behaviors, all of which lead to increased health and life risk.

Chapter 4, "Reality Television as a Public Health Crisis for Black Women," investigates the antihealth images presented of Black women in contemporary reality television shows starring Black women. The social impact of violence, alcohol and drug abuse, and high-risk behaviors will be detailed as these are the primary images broadcasted of Black womanhood in shows such as *Love and Hip Hop: Hollywood* (Scott-Young et al., 2014–2019), *Basketball Wives LA* (O'Neal et al., 2010–present), *The Real Housewives of Atlanta* (Hersh et al., 2008–present), and *Married to Medicine* (Huq et al., 2013–present). This chapter explores how reality television starring African American women has been designed to further marginalize African Americans by representing them as chronically unhealthy and dysfunctional. It also highlights the economic value placed on portraying Black women as a danger to the American public's health and safety.

Chapter 5, "Black Lives Matter? Devaluing the Health and Safety of Blacks in the Media," investigates representations of Black humanity and the Black Lives Matter movement as a form of media injustice. From broadcasting a depraved neglect for Black motherhood to delegitimizing Black parents' protection of Black youth, current popular media have been used to endorse racist ideologies about Black humanity being inferior and even intraculturally lacking any value. This chapter features evidence that media aid in the justification of the systematic oppression of and assaults against Blacks. In addition, this chapter critically analyzes the use of scripted and unscripted television shows, starring Black women, that have attempted to engage aspects of the Black experience with police brutality and the Black Lives Matter movement. Here, I explore television dramas and reality television shows that have incorporated content revolving around the value of Black lives and the Black Lives Matter movement. Evidence demonstrates that television dramas starring African American women have placed the Black woman at the center of this fight for justice and equality. However, these series have yet to abandon the stereotypical portrayals of Black womanhood, and thus the representations of the Black Lives Matter movement have been swallowed up by selfishness, corruption, and criminality.

Chapter 6, "Black Women's Lives Versus Black Women's Representations," examines attitudes and opinions about media representations of Black women's lifestyles in comparison to Black women's real-world personal lifestyles. African American women were surveyed to determine their overall attitudes about their lifestyles and behaviors. In addition, participants were asked to evaluate the representations of Black women in reality television shows and television dramas starring Black women, in order to determine if Black women rate the lifestyles of lead Black female characters as healthy or unhealthy and whether they adopt such behaviors. Data from this chapter will be used to further assess the accuracy of media images regarding Black women's health choices and lifestyles.

The concluding chapter of this book explores the significance of Black women media ownership and productions and how contemporary Black women media creatives are transforming the media into a tool of empowerment.

CHAPTER 1

Anti-Blackness and Media Racism
A Cautionary Tale

Africans in America have endured a lasting legacy of injustice that has altered the state of Black life in America. Since the arrival of Africans under the system of enslavement in North America, Africans' biological and psychological health has been disrupted, deconstructed, and terrorized. Slavery removed Africans from their native homelands and forced them into an alternative ecological system. Not only was the climate and environment dissimilar, but the food and dietary systems were drastically different. Also, the conditions of enslavement—the dehumanization process of turning the African into the negro, which provided a free surplus labor supply—created the foundation for unhealthy work and living environments among enslaved populations.

Enslavement denied the masses of Africans nutritional food options, exposed Africans to foreign illnesses, treated Africans inhumanly, brutally battered and abused Africans, and unleashed horrific experimental medical practices on Africans. Africans under enslavement did not enjoy the basics of eating the same meals as their enslavers, nor did they exercise the right to prepare their Indigenous cuisine. Instead, much of the food supplied to enslaved Africans consisted of scrap meats such as chitterlings (the small intestines of a pig); turkey necks; pig feet, tails, and lips; and gizzards (an organ found in the digestive tract of some animals). Additionally, Africans would grind corn and flour, and some were able to grow their own vegetables and herbs. In preparing their own meals, Africans applied their knowledge of spices and herbs to season foods and make flavorful meals. Their knowledge and skill in rice cultivation also aided them in preparing meals that were more germane to their cultural diets.

Africans attempted to counter the dangerous and unhealthy conditions of enslavement by utilizing their medical and spiritual knowledge informed by their cultural heritage. However, the change in environment hampered their access to medical herbs and supplies. Additionally, African medical practices were attacked by Whites and demonized. Enslaved Africans' healing practices were considered unscientific and unsafe and were frequently termed witchcraft. Plantation owners banned the use of herbs and other African medicines out of distrust and fear of the use of poisons against them. Even still, Africans applied and passed on their medical and healing knowledge to survive throughout enslavement.

Enslaved Africans' interaction with health care and medical professionals was far less than moral; it was terroristic. According to Harriet Washington (2006) in *Medical Apartheid*, Africans were subject to a host of experimental medical procedures and were frequently misdiagnosed and mistreated:

> The records reveal that slaves were both medically neglected and abused because they were powerless and legally invisible; the courts were almost completely uninterested in the safety and health rights of the enslaved. The practice of hiring slaves out further endangered enslaved workers by removing much of an employer's incentive to keep the slave healthy and safe. Some humane plantation owners were careful to choose less risky work venues, but a great danger of slave death or disability was inherent in some forms of mining, tobacco production, rice farming, and most plantation work. In these settings, the slave's possible death became part of his owner's commercial calculations. (p. 30)

Medical practitioners would frequently support the uninformed diagnoses of White plantation owners who accused Africans of faking illnesses and malingering in order to avoid work (Washington, 2006). Many enslaved Africans reported the use of one-cure treatments of all African illnesses, which were hazardous and deadly. The distrust of White medical professionals caused enslaved Africans to pretend to consume medicines they were given, and to hide their illnesses. Thus, African healing practices proved to be more holistic and effective, and enslaved Africans would routinely rely on the healing women and men in their community to address their health care concerns.

African midwives were also vital for the care and well-being of pregnant women during enslavement. From providing nutritional supplements to delivery of the child, African midwives were instrumental in lessening the impact of the harsh conditions of enslavement on pregnant women.

According to Washington (2006), "Midwives used African techniques, herbs, and medicines so successfully—without dangerous tools of the day, such as forceps—that many white women called them to attend births" (p. 49). Although some Whites expressed appreciation for African medical procedures, many considered African healing practices as inferior and unorthodox, despite the fact that there was competition among the two groups of medical healers. The fear of African healers would often result in punishments and even death for those suspected of using herbs and African medical techniques. Midwifery among African women in America continued post-enslavement and in many cases was the only access to medical care for African Americans, especially in the South, as Blacks were denied access to medical professionals and hospitals across the nation.

Medical professionals would also use enslaved Africans for medical experimentation and testing of medicines and vaccines. Doctors purchased enslaved Africans solely for experimentation, which often resulted in increased illness, disfigurement, and death. Without any legal rights and the lack of ethical guidelines in medical research, African men, women, and children were examined, infected, and dissected without their consent. As noted in *Medical Apartheid*, "Physicians' recollections, medical journals, and institutional records limn a pattern of abusing African Americans that was supported by custom and sometimes by law" (Washington, 2006, p. 57). Consider former president Thomas Jefferson's use of enslaved Africans' bodies to test unproven remedies for infectious diseases. Jefferson infected 200 enslaved Africans with cowpox to inoculate against smallpox. From disfigurement to death, Black women were objects of gruesome medical fascination. The medical advancements of famed "Father of Gynecology" James Marion Sims were a result of the horrifying experiments he conducted on enslaved African women without anesthesia or consent. African women did not possess medical authority over their bodies; instead, their rights were controlled by their enslavers. Sims and other medical professionals benefited from the system of slavery, which allowed them to conduct any experiments they deemed fit without consequences. Thus, African women's bodies under enslavement became an inherent part of medical testing, procedures, and experimentations and informed medical practices in the United States and globally.

In the 17th and 18th centuries, print advertisements and newspapers were used to justify enslavement and the oppression of Africans. United States presidents promoted ideas of Blacks' innate inferiority to Whites and attacked the mental capacity and physical health of African Americans. Thomas Jefferson (1787), for example, stated:

Comparing them by their faculties of memory, reason, and imagination, it appears to me that in memory they are equal to the whites; in reason

much inferior, as I think one could scarcely be found capable of tracing
and comprehending the investigations of Euclid; and that in imagination
they are dull, tasteless, and anomalous. (p. 231)

Media were also used to broadcast the auction of enslaved Africans and
to notify the public of runaways, Africans who would emancipate themselves from the system of slavery by escaping their enslavers' control and
living as free individuals. Ironically, when financial interest overrode
scientific racism, newspaper advertisement publications more accurately
reflected the intelligence and skills of Africans (Washington, 2006). As
noted by Harriet Washington (2006), newspaper advertisements of runaways were "replete with references to 'artful,' 'well-spoken,' 'crafty,' and
intelligent'" (p. 42). However, the bulk of advertisements represented
Africans as illiterate hard laborers.

An iconic use of media to maintain Black subjugation is illustrated in the
mythology and use of the Willie Lynch letter. Recorded as a speech by
William Lynch in 1712 reportedly delivered in Virginia on the bank of
the James River, this letter is told to have been printed and advertised to
southern plantation owners as an instructional guide to slavery and
property management. Lynch proposed an infallible method to controlling enslaved Africans that was rooted in fear and internal divisions
among enslaved populations. Lynch cautioned owners to limit the killings of Blacks and instead break Black women so that they would
socialize their children to accept their oppression. Lynch's letter also
encouraged the destruction of Black marriages and male–female relationships in order to eliminate interdependence. The narrative of the massive
distribution of this letter and similar racist media served as an educational tool to further oppress enslaved Africans and has had severe
psychosocial effects on the African American family.

PUBLIC HEALTH POLITICS
AND RACIST LABELING

By the turn of the 20th century, media representations of African
Americans began to parallel politics and public policies that racially targeted Africans in America. During the early 1900s, media (i.e., radio
broadcasts, newspapers, and films) were used to promote the idea of
genetically unfit humans, and Africans were a primary victim of this scientific racism. Pioneers of the eugenics movement and the founder of
Planned Parenthood, Margaret Sanger, used medical research journals
and news media outlets to advertise Black existence in the general public
as a public health issue to a global audience. The now discredited
Eugenics Project was a race-based scientific movement designed to

enhance the health of humanity by selectively breeding humans deemed fit for reproduction and by sterilizing those considered genetically defected. Sanger was an avid supporter of the eugenics movement and also sponsored ideas of undesirable human populations. Mass media, journals, and public advertisements were used by Sanger and her supporters to advance anti-Black reproductive injustice, which portrayed Black Americans as unfit to contribute to the growth of the human race and in need of state-sanctioned reproductive control.

Racist injustice in society was legitimized through politics, research discourse, and scholarship. Politicians and courts were not immune to this discriminatory conditioning of Blacks. In the 19th century, political figures used their political power to promote racist ideologies about Africans and their access to freedom. In the 1850s, Chief Justice of the United States Supreme Court Roger Taney wrote an opinion rationalizing the disrespect and dehumanization of Blacks by Whites due to Blacks' assumed inferiority to Whites. On March 6, 1857, the Supreme Court ruled on the *Dred Scott v. Sandford* case, also known as the Dred Scott decision, concluding that Scott and Africans in general were not entitled to freedom, even in non-slavery-practicing states, or citizenship rights and privileges. Newspapers quickly spread word of the court's ruling, and Africans in the North and South, free and enslaved, immediately felt the rippling effects.

The controversial discourse around Abraham Lincoln and his promotion of racist ideas about African Americans is often overshadowed by his signing of the Emancipation Proclamation. On January 1, 1863, Lincoln signed into law the proclamation that declared all enslaved persons free from enslavement in the rebellious states. In modern history, this act to unite the union has eclipsed Lincoln's racist sentiments about African Americans. However, his racist ideas shaped the state of racial affairs before and after the end of slavery. Lincoln (1858) stated:

> I will say then that I am not, nor ever have been in favor of bringing about in any way the social and political equality of the white and black races, [applause]—that I am not nor ever have been in favor of making voters or jurors of negroes, nor of qualifying them to hold office, nor to inter-marry with white people; and I will say in addition to this that there is a physical difference between the white and black races which I believe will for ever forbid the two races living together on terms of social and political equality. And inasmuch as they cannot so live, while they do remain together there must be the position of superior and inferior, and I as much as any other man am in favor of having the superior position assigned to the white race. (pp. 145–146)

Lincoln's promotion of a segregated society and Black marginalization in 1858 would be long-standing as Jim Crow laws made segregation and discrimination legal until 1965. These racist commentaries were to have momentous impact on the health and wellness of African Americans. From physical health to the social and psychological well-being of African Americans, national anti-African ideologies were the predictor of Blacks' experiences in education, employment, and society in general. And media became the channel to transmit these messages to the larger American public.

Early cinematic productions catapulted the use of media to advance racist ideologies in America. In 1915, D. W. Griffith released the American drama film *Birth of a Nation*. Adapted from Thomas Frederick Dixon Jr.'s novel *The Clansman: An Historical Romance of the Ku Klux Klan*, the film blatantly depicts racist ideas about African Americans and helped rationalize the trending political and racist scientific discourse. *Birth of a Nation* uses silent acting and monographed inserts to chronicle the state of racial affairs in 19th-century America, and the film's only sound is musical instrumentation. The lives of two White families and their engagement with racial politics are trailed during the Civil War and in post–Civil War America. African Americans are only represented through the lens of Blackface—a caricature enactment of Blackness performed by Whites with black theatrical makeup over their face to signify Blackness—and are characterized as simple-minded servants who upon freedom become ruthless and dangerous. During the film's enactment of Reconstruction, African Americans are represented as politically corrupt and oppressive to White voters. Gus, a White male actor in Blackface, is described as "a renegade negro" in the film's opening credits and portrayed as an aggressive and sexually violent vigilante. When Gus encounters Flora Cameron, the youngest daughter of one of the primary families, he is depicted as aggressively soliciting her. Flora fights him off and runs away through the woods. Preferring death over a sexual assault by Gus, she jumps off a cliff to end her life. Discovering what happened to Flora, the White community calls for the birth of the Ku Klux Klan to avenge Flora's attacker and to protect White womanhood and White supremacy. A war ensues between the Ku Klux Klan and the Blacks, to the Klan's victory. The success of the Klan sent a message to all Blacks to remain in their place, as inferior beings with no power. The National Association for the Advancement of Colored People (NAACP) and African American activists petitioned for the film to be banned and for film censorship on racist content, and the film was successfully banned in several cities. Censorship codes were created to govern the standard of moral and suitable content for films in America. Earlier codes contained provisions banning portrayals of immoral content and interracial relationships (Motion Picture Association of America, 2018); however, these codes did not curtail the racist representation of Blacks in films.

Until the 1950s, in the aftermath of the *Brown v. Board of Education* (1954) decision declaring segregated schools unconstitutional, African Americans were confined to stereotypical roles in television and film. The permanency of media racism in television and film was cemented by the commercial success of *Birth of a Nation* and the resulting rise of the Ku Klux Klan. The film is hailed as a masterpiece and groundbreaking and, in 1992, was selected for preservation in the National Film Registry by the United States National Film Preservation Board. Rotten Tomatoes (n.d.a), one of the "world's most trusted recommendation resources for quality entertainment," credits the film as "a landmark film whose achievements and pioneering techniques remain fully relevant today" (Rotten Tomatoes, n.d.b). The film not only created a picture of African Americans as uncivilized and sexually violent but also established African Americans as untrustworthy to the American public.

Injustice in research ranged from racist scientific publications about the African race as innately inferior to grotesque experiential studies that altered the biological health of African Americans. In 1911, the *Encyclopedia Britannica*, a leading scientific periodical, published racist articles on African Americans' mental aptitude by Walter F. Willcox, citing diminished intellectual capacity in Blacks through maturity and Black mental inferiority compared to Whites (Willcox, 1911, p. 344; see also Aldrich, 1979). The developer of the Stanford–Binet IQ test, Lewis M. Terman, an American psychologist and prominent eugenicist, argued that African Americans lacked the mental capacity to understand concepts and are intellectually deficient. In his 1916 publication, Terman writes, "They cannot master abstractions but they can often be made into efficient workers" (pp. 91–92). His global popularity catapulted the use of scientific racism to justify racial discrimination. Such prominent philosophers and scholars as David Hume, Voltaire, Immanuel Kant, Louis Agassiz, and Georg Wilhelm Friedrich Hegel all advanced unproven racist ideologies about African people. And racist scholarly literature dominated the discourse on African humanity and citizenship, shaping the mistreatment of Africans globally.

Nightmarishly racist experimentations provided data that helped justify systematic racism at governmental levels and validated racist social sentiments about Africans' social being and rights. Tuskegee, Alabama, endured one of the most egregious medical research experimentations of the 20th century in the United States. The Tuskegee Syphilis Study, also known as the Tuskegee Experiment, was a research study conducted by the United States Public Health Service in 1932. In the study, 600 low-income Black males from Macon County, Alabama, were subjects in an experimental procedure to document the effects of syphilis if left untreated on the human body. Four hundred of the participants were diagnosed with the disease, and although the treatment for syphilis, penicillin, became available in 1950, the men were denied access to treatment. By 1940, mortality rates were higher among the African American population as a result of the disease. Even so, the study went on for a total of 40 years, and while it was finally forced to end in 1972, the disease had directly negatively impacted Black families and communities for decades. Faulty health data gathered from racist scientists and researchers were utilized to market African Americans as social degenerates, and media became the outlet to spread these racist assaults nationally.

African Americans' second-class citizenship was legally formalized under the system of Jim Crow (1877–1965), and legal discrimination against Blacks was federally instituted. Under the Jim Crow laws, oppression of African Americans was once again legal, and inequalities in health care would continue to impede African Americans' health. African Americans were denied access to quality health care facilities, which were reserved for Whites only, and subjected to untrained health providers, while African medical practices were demonized. In addition, African American patients continued to be subjected to inhumane and horrific medical abuses, including experimentations (Washington, 2006). According to Kerri L. Hunkele (2014) in "Segregation in United States Healthcare: From Reconstruction to Deluxe Jim Crow," racist medical laws and practices not only marginalized African Americans' access to health care but also directly negatively affected the overall quality of life that could be achieved by African Americans:

> The limitation of healthcare severely decreased both the quality of life and life expectancy. Therefore, by denying African Americans equal access to healthcare, Whites were denying Blacks an equal quality of life. These types of segregation laws deeply affected the African American community. Accounts of deaths because of such laws exist throughout the time period. Not only were these laws legally atrocious, but also they were deadly in some cases. These segregation laws were allowed, by the United States Supreme Court, to continue in the form of Jim Crow Laws until 1954, when the Court's 1954 decision in *Brown v. Board of Education* integrated schools and reversed the 1896 decision in *Plessy v. Fergusson* [sic], which was the Supreme Court decision that allowed segregation to occur as long as facilities were equal for both races. (p. 4)

The systematic oppression of African Americans was a calculated assault against Black humanity and further crippled the state of Black life in America. Racial discrimination in medical care disallowed White doctors and nurses the responsibility of providing medical care to Black patients, segregated patients based on race, and supplied inadequate medical treatment and facilities to African Americans. African American women continued to service their communities with medical care based on their knowledge of African medicines, and they also became midwives and community nurses. However, medical professionals often attempted to discredit Black midwives as incompetent, and religious ideologies were used against African medical practices, which were deemed ungodly and malevolent. As noted by Hunkele (2014), "The American Medical Association targeted midwifery for extermination during the early twentieth century, spreading misinformation about the supposed inabilities and malpractices of traditional midwives. African American midwives thus were discriminated against, not only because of their race, but also because of their skill" (p. 21). Medical publications would cite Black midwives as untrained and unlicensed, and these publications were used to invalidate the usefulness of Black midwives in African American communities. Despite these contentions, Black women health care providers were instrumental in extending the overall wellness of Black communities as they provided a much-needed resource that was denied otherwise. Private African American hospitals also attempted to fill the void in quality medical care for African American patients. The first African American–owned hospital, Provident Hospital and Training School, was established in 1891 in Chicago by Dr. Daniel Hale Williams, and many more would soon follow. African American–owned hospitals offered safety and security of medical services in a culturally responsible environment (Foster, 2012). However, amidst a growing population, many suffered from racist profiling, inadequate funding, and limited staffing. Nathaniel Wesley (2010) documents the history of over 500 Black hospitals that were operational in the 20th century but unfortunately met their demise as legislative changes reshaped health care services nationally.

The fight for change through the civil rights movement of the 1950s and 1960s led to increased access to health care facilities and a growth in public health care facilities in Black communities as a result of Title VI of the Civil Rights Act of 1964 (Quigley, 1965). However, the challenges were not completely removed as many hospitals instituted new ways to discriminate against patients, and racial disparities in health care continued to persist (Friedman, 2014; Quigley, 1965). Media surrounding these controversial circumstances often focused on alleged factors contributing to the lower quality of health of Black local residents such as gang violence and drug abuse, while not addressing the system failure to uphold the civil rights ordinances. Often named after civil rights pioneers and leaders, the new medical facilities were supposed to offer safe and convenient medical services in local communities regardless of the patient's race. However, insufficient funding and staffing resulted in increased negative health outcomes despite hospitalization. Yet, media treatment of these hospitals promoted narratives of incompetence in terms of hospital operations and medical care, especially in the case of African American–managed facilities. Martin Luther King Jr./Charles R. Drew Medical

Center of Los Angeles (1972–2007) was a county hospital in an economically impoverished Black community. King/Drew hospital would be the first of its kind, a county-funded hospital operated by primarily Black medical professionals, and would train future medical professionals with Drew Medical Society, a local medical organization made up of Black doctors, playing an essential role in the governance of the hospital and training programs (Hunt & Ramon, 2010). From the onset, national support and high expectations surrounded the establishment of the hospital; however, within the first few years of its opening, news outlets began chronicling an array of concerns that were largely racially biased (Hunt & Ramon, 2010). King/Drew gained the reputation of failing to provide effective medical care to patients in a timely fashion and was iconically called "Killer King." Local news outlets alleged that residents reported that family members were admitted to the hospital for life-threatening and non-life-threatening illnesses but unfortunately did not receive medical attention or the appropriate medical attention, which resulted in their loss of life. According to Darnell Hunt and Ana-Christina Ramon (2010) in "Killing 'Killer King': The *Los Angeles Times* and a 'Troubled' Hospital in the Hood," the *Los Angeles Times* journalistic treatment of King/Drew unfairly presented the problems in the hospital as a result of mismanagement, fraud, and medical malpractices, and "racial framing worked to divert attention away from other important determinants of the hospital's performance" (p. 284). As noted in their research, the *Los Angeles Times*'s articles on the hospital reported that the facility "had 'squandered' ample resources through inefficient operations, excessive legal settlements, and widespread employee fraud" (Hunt & Ramon, 2010, p. 306). Controlling the narrative around this Black-operated medical institution, news outlets such as the *Los Angeles Times* selectively covered stories of incompetence and maladministration and ignored structural issues with the county's oversight of the hospital. The news reports would frequently allude to the race of the medical professionals and administrators at the hospital as the catalyst for the imploding troubles the hospital faced (Hunt & Ramon, 2010). The *Los Angeles Times* news coverage of King/Drew was highly applauded and awarded with the highest award in journalism, the Pulitzer Prize for Public Service. King/Drew was forced to close its doors in 2006, and the local community was once again left without medical care, or an emergency medical facility, in their surrounding area. Residents were once again subject to long-distance medical care, which would prove detrimental to the health and wellness of Black local residents. Media racism played a pivotal role in the framing of the hospital and directly contributed to its closure according to Hunt and Ramon (2010), who argue:

> To be sure, mainstream news media like the *Times* typically serve as the "managers of public opinion" by emphasizing voices newsworkers believe

should be heard, "while muffling of silencing others." The *Times*—like most large metropolitan newspapers—enjoyed a symbolic relationship with the local power structure, which more often than not motivated its newsworkers to toe the official line on the major issues of the day. (p. 291)

The racist news coverage of Black-operated and Black-owned hospitals was widespread, and it directly contributed to the dismissal of the ideology that Black medical institutions could provide high-quality care and services and maintain an ethical and sociocultural commitment to Black communities. This ideology was birthed out of classical African medical practices, as in the case of Imhotep, whose medical sanctuaries were the earliest forms of hospitals, and continued to prove effective among African Americans who would operate over 500 private Black hospitals. Media racism helped shape the discourse on Black medicine in the 19th century, was once again used to frame the narrative on Black medical institutions in the 20th century, and has had grave consequences on the access to health care for African Americans.

Racist media framing was also used to validate changes in public assistance benefits that would alter the state of African Americans' well-being and access to governmental assistance. Welfare programs underwent major reform as Black Americans were characterized as the face of poverty in America and as illegitimate recipients of governmental aid. Martin Gilens (2003) discusses the systematic misrepresentation of Blacks and poverty in mass media. Gilens illustrates how news media coverage shifted from a predominantly White focus on poverty to racialized discourse despite data illustrating Blacks' minority status in relation to poverty and governmental aid. Analysis from his research contradicts the representations of Blacks: "Combining the coverage of poverty from three magazines, over half (53.4 percent) of all poor people pictured during these four-and-a-half decades were African American. In reality, the average percentage of African Americans among the poor during this period was 29.3 percent" (Gilens, 2003, p. 110). Gilens states:

> But starting in 1965 the complexion of the poor turned decidedly darker. From only 27 percent in 1964, the proportion of African Americans in pictures of the poor increased to 49 percent and 53 percent in 1965 and 1966, and then to 72 percent black in 1967 . . . African Americans have dominated news media images of the poor since the late 1960s. In the period between 1967 and 1992, blacks averaged 557 percent of the poor people pictured. (p. 110)

The racialization of the American poor continued to frame Americans' perception and treatment of African Americans. As new president Ronald Reagan came into office in 1981, he also linked poverty and welfare as a problem impacting the country. He was a major critic of welfare and targeted the Black woman as a chronic criminal abuser of the welfare system. On the campaign trail in 1976, Reagan introduced his "welfare queen" caricature and popularized the welfare queen label as the face of Black womanhood. He falsified a story of an alleged Black woman with 80 different names and 30 addresses, which she used in an elaborate scheme to collect welfare benefits. This stereotyped caricature of Black women was used to rationalize the public perception of Black aid recipients and to justify Reagan's welfare reform proposal. Despite his false claims, Reagan was elected president and significantly cut funding from the Aid to Families with Dependent Children (AFDC) federal assistance program. Black women would forever bear the label of welfare queen. In August 1996, President Bill Clinton signed into law the Personal Responsibility and Work Opportunity Reconciliation Act, which completely restructured Americans' access to government family support aid. Before the news audience and the American public, Clinton announced his welfare reform policy with two Black women surrounding him on stage as he signed his reform into law. Lillie Harden, a 42-year-old African American mother who once received welfare benefits, is pictured with the president and then gives a speech supporting the new welfare policy. Through Lillie Harden, Black women were once again the face of welfare. Although Clinton did not verbalize the term *welfare queen*, the image of his platform during his speech transmitted the message that Black women were the face of welfare and that African Americans needed to take "personal responsibility" in addressing their issues with poverty.

Coupled with the overemphasis of African Americans as illegitimate recipients of governmental aid, media entities spotlighted drug use and gang violence as primary detriments of poor health outcomes among African Americans. Racist media framing not only echoed political and scientific labeling of Blacks as inferior to Whites but was also used to validate public policies aimed to further marginalize Blacks in America. In the post–civil rights era, media entities spotlighted drug use, gang violence, and welfare dependence as primary cultural characteristics of African Americans. News media and movies showcased African Americans as chronic abusers of crack cocaine, which was also linked to increased health disparities in Black communities. African American women were termed "crack mamas," and news media would actively pursue Black mothers to broadcast images of the so-called crack mama. In addition, several movies were created that portrayed the Black male as a violent drug lord and young Black men and women as chronic abusers of alcohol and drugs. Movies such as *New Jack City* (Van Peebles, 1991), *Boyz n the Hood* (Singleton, 1991), and *Menace II Society* (Hughes & Hughes, 1993) portrayed African Americans as ruthless criminals and dangerous addicts. Scenes from this film genre depicted Black men and women using machine guns, snorting drugs, and covered in blood as they lay dead on public streets. Dionne Bennett (2010) in her article "Looking for the 'Hood and Finding Community: South Central, Race, and Media" argues that media representations of Black urban communities glamorize fictional pretensions of hyperviolence among Blacks and are highly awarded. According to Bennett, "Media representations of South Central have exaggerated, racialized, and distorted the social ills of the area and constructed Black Los Angeles as a site of grotesque cultural pathology" (p. 216). This hypercriminal treatment of African Americans resulted in a public health scare and harsher legal penalties for Black drug users and distributors.

The rise of hyperviolence among Blacks in hip-hop music and videos along with the increasing use of extremely violent films showcasing Black life created the momentum used to enforce stricter legal sanctions against violent and drug offenders. In August 1994, President Bill Clinton signed into law the Violent Crime Control and Law Enforcement Act, which mandated harsher sentencing practices for repeat offenders and life sentences for individuals convicted of two or more crimes and a violent felony, known as the three-strikes law, and provided funding for law enforcement and courts. The three-strikes provision was part of the United States Justice Department's Anti-Violence Strategy and led to severe sentencing enhancements of 25 years to life for convicted persons, including self-convictions known as pleas. In addition, more aggressive policing practices increased in Black communities. And Black communities are still faced with increased levels of police brutality today.

While these images were used to validate the need for harsher policing and sentencing practices against repeat offenders, they also provided an alternative narrative to the growing health disparities among African Americans. The rise in mortality rates among Blacks in the 1990s could be assumed to be a primary result of the pathologically violent Black culture without any connection to poor medical services, violence against African Americans, and impact of racism on African Americans' health. Ironically, while these films have portrayed Black culture as chronically violent, they also managed to capture an unexplored reality of Black communities, marginalized medical care. When the character Ricky is shot in the film *Boyz n the Hood* (Singleton, 1991), he lies in the street in his own blood with his friend Tre attempting to aid him, until his brother and friends arrive. The men carry Ricky to their car and then drive him home to his mother. No ambulance ever arrives, and medical attention is not rendered in the film. The possibility of Ricky receiving medical care is eliminated, yet this image is grossly underscored.

Other medical concerns have been cautioned as a result of mass incarceration; in particular, much concern has risen around the impact of drug policies, mass imprisonment, and HIV. The rise of HIV, or the human immunodeficiency virus, in the Black community, for example, was used to advance the ideology that African Americans are pathological and in need of intervention, especially since health, political, and news authorities framed the rise of HIV among Blacks as a result of drug abuse, specifically crack cocaine, and hypersexual lifestyles. However, research contradicts this stereotype and provides evidence that "African Americans report less risky drug use and sexual behaviors than their White counterparts" (Blankenship et al., 2005, p. 2). The Centers for Disease Control and Prevention (CDC) also began heavily reporting on the status of HIV among African Americans, and Black women in particular. The CDC (2011) states that at some point in their lifetimes, 1 in 32 Black women will become infected with HIV. While all women are impacted by HIV and STDs, Black women represent over 64% of all American women living with HIV/AIDS (Browne-Marshall, 2012). An alarming aspect of improving Black females' health is the lack of available data, especially on Black women's health in relation to the social and political dynamics. The resulting limited data on Black females' health indicators inhibit meaningful interventions. Kim M. Blankenship and colleagues (2005), for their article "Black–White Disparities in HIV/AIDS: The Role of Drug Policy and the Corrections System," investigated the function of drug policies and correctional institutions in affecting the rate of exposure to HIV/AIDS among African Americans. The researchers argue that high rates of exposure to correctional institutions have disproportionately impacted African Americans' health and may impact their risk for HIV. Media representations of incarcerated African Americans have not only portrayed them as hyperviolent and criminal but simultaneously depicted Blacks as sexually risky and prone to contracting HIV/AIDS.

Understanding the historic function of media racism in perpetuating high-risk lifestyles among African Americans, and Black women in particular, is crucial if we are to fully comprehend African American women's portrayals in contemporary media. Media representations of African American women in the 21st century disproportionately characterize Black women as socially, physically, and psychologically destructive. The long-standing racialized framing of Blackness in America, and the media more specifically, must be deconstructed.

21ST-CENTURY MEDIA PORTRAYALS

Examining the role of media in creating barriers to sustaining positive life outcomes among African Americans has proven pivotal over the past few centuries. While media productions have evolved technologically, *media racism* remains embedded in the fabric of American media productions, including television and film, news and radio broadcasts, and social media. Twenty-first-century media productions on Black womanhood mirror past centuries' stereotyped portrayals of Blackness, and media injustice against African Americans persists. The content of contemporary media, and television shows starring Black women in particular, is entrenched with the systematic promotion of unhealthy lifestyles and negative images of Black womanhood.

Consider the media's framing of the first African American presidential family. Since the beginning of Barack Obama's presidential campaign in 2007, racist assaults against him and his family questioned his qualifications and right to run for president. The July 21, 2008, cover of the *New Yorker* framed the Obamas as radical anti-American Black nationalists. Michelle Obama has a machine gun strapped across her back as she fist-bumps Barack Obama, who is stereotypically dressed in what appears to be Muslim attire. In the background rests a picture of Osama bin Laden over the fireplace, which is burning the American flag. Although the published image was considered satire, this media image helped give credence to the racist unsupported sentiments about the Obamas. As First Lady, Michelle Obama received numerous racist and sexist attacks by the public and in the media. In August 2012, the Spanish magazine *de Fuera de Serie* published "Michelle Se Come a Obama," a cover image of Michelle Obama painted as an enslaved woman. As noted in *Representations of Black Women in the Media* (M. Gammage, 2015):

> The cover image is a literal reprinting of French artist Marie-Guillemine Benoist's "Portrait d'une nègresse." The original painting displays Black womanhood as clothed in American slavery and subject to sexual exploitation. The cover image is a painting of First Lady Michelle Obama with her hair pulled back and pinned up with a white headscarf wrapped around her hair. She is wearing a white dress that is hanging off her shoulders, and one of her breasts is completely exposed. She is seated sideways in a chair that is covered with the American flag as she gazes off in the distance. This reprinting places First Lady Michelle Obama as the embodiment of the 21st century damnation of Black womanhood. (p. 31)

Countless other media images and broadcasts of the Obamas disrespected and challenged their position as the First Family. Media racism used against the Obamas was designed to legitimize the racist stereotypes of Blacks in political power and foster a political climate of rejection and backlash, which was the end result.

Black professional athletes have also endured widespread racial discrimination in the media. From portrayals of Black athletes as brutes and animals to the delegitimization of Black athletes' social activism, media has challenged the self-determination and success of Blacks in sports. This opposition to Black athletes in America was not created by the media, for Blacks were once denied the opportunity to play professional sports in America; however, racist media have been used to rationalize the discrimination against Black athletes. In my article "Pop Culture Without Culture: Examining the Public Backlash to Beyoncé's Super Bowl 50 Performance," I argue:

> Similar damned realities have historically and contemporarily existed for Black athletes and celebrities. In 1968, Tommie Smith and John Carlos['s] Olympic medals were removed for raising their fist in solidarity of the demand for equal civil rights for Black Americans (Ratchford, 2012). Fast-forwarding to 2009, LeBron James was ridiculed for exercising his right to switch professional basketball teams (Ratchford, 2012). He was treated as a human commodity with no rights. Although LeBron rejected this treatment and moved to another team, the owner of the Cleveland Cavaliers basketball team, Dan Gilbert, echoed the sentiments of the general American public in stating that James ultimately belonged to the Cavaliers. In 2016, Olympic gymnast Gabriel (Gabby) Douglas was highly ridiculed on social media for her African textured hair, dark lipstick, and not putting her hand over her heart during the medal ceremony playing of the pledge of allegiance. Douglas was called unpatriotic and considered unworthy of representing the United States. This was a similar faith she experienced 4 years prior in the 2012 Olympics when she won both team and individual all-around gold. (M. Gammage, 2017, p. 13)

Not only are African American athletes racially attacked in social media and the news, but controversial magazine and billboard images of Blacks in sports are also a norm. For instance, LeBron James's 2008 cover image for *Vogue* was reminiscent of images of dangerous manlike apes (J. Hill, 2008). James was the first African American male to appear on the cover of *Vogue*, yet his image embodied the stereotypical portrayal of the dangerous Black male. LeBron James and Gisele Bündchen are posed in an eerily similar fashion as the 1917 image from a popular U.S. Army World War I poster used for recruitment. The recruitment poster reads, "Destroy This Mad Brute, Enlist U.S. Army" (Hoops, 1918). Between the words stands an oversized gorilla, mouth wide open and legs spread, with a bat in one hand and a captured White woman wrapped in his other arm. Comparably, the *Vogue* cover shows James with his mouth wide open and legs separated, with a basketball beneath one hand and his other arm wrapped around the waist of Gisele, a White woman. Immediately after the release of the image, *Vogue* was criticized for perpetuating the racist stereotype of Black men as aggressive and violent and after White women. This was the same stereotypical image of Gus in *Birth of a Nation* in 1915.

Black professional athletes have not only experienced racial framing of their images but have also been discriminated against when they have used their platforms for social activism. According to Dr. Justin Gammage (2018), Black athletes' use of social protest in 2017 and 2018 has been racially reframed to reduce the impact of their actions. The movement has been termed disrespectful to persons in the armed services and the American flag, when in fact the movement is about calling attention to the racial injustices experienced by African Americans in the criminal justice system. However, political and media coverage of these athletes has chosen to focus on personal issues in their lives and careers. Also, social media has been used to attack and delegitimize the social activism among Black athletes.

African American politicians and celebrities are not the only set of African Americans who are subjected to racial discrimination in the media; in fact, every day average African Americans are routinely portrayed in a stereotypical manner. Consider the news media coverage of Black Americans versus White Americans during natural disasters. During Hurricane Katrina, which struck the Gulf Coast in August 2005 and flooded larger portions of New Orleans, Louisiana, as a result of the city's levee system failing, the majority of Black citizens who were strained and flooded in were described by the news media as "refugees." A refugee is a person who has been displaced and forced to leave their nation and seek asylum in a foreign country because they cannot return home for their safety. The Black citizens of New Orleans were in effect classified as noncitizens, and the lack of immediate aid rendered by the United States government was reminiscent of legislative conflicts that delay aid to foreign countries in crisis. In addition, news media represented Black citizens who sought self-aid (i.e., food and shelter) as looters who illegally took goods. However, similar coverage of White Americans used less criminal terminology and instead used affirming language such as "the survivors found aid" and "looking for food." An illustration of one of these scenarios is described in the article "Race and Media Coverage of Hurricane Katrina: Analysis, Implications, and Future Research Questions":

> In one of the photos, a Black male was shown in waist-high water, carrying a carton of soft drinks and a full garbage bag. The other photo showed a White couple carrying food and drinks through similar floodwaters. Although nearly identical in composition, the photos were released with markedly different captions. The first caption—for the photo with the Black subject—began with "A young man walks through chest deep flood water after looting a grocery store . . ." The caption for the second photo read, "Two residents wade through chest-deep water after finding bread and soda from a local grocery store." That comparable photos could carry such different captions was attributed by some to the major difference between the images: the race of the parties depicted. (Sommers et al., 2006, p. 4)

The researchers' assessment of the news media coverage of the two demographics illustrates that media disproportionately represent Blacks within the tropes of race, class, and justice. African Americans' will to survive during Hurricane Katrina was marketed as a criminal act, and the racial bias in the media further validated the delayed distribution of aid and the harsh militarized evacuation tactics deployed. When aid and evacuations finally arrived, African American survivors reported horrific mistreatment (S. Lee, 2006). Depictions of African Americans in contemporary news media as criminal and violent do not diverge from coverage of Blacks in past centuries. Instead, the racist media used during the launch of the war on drugs parallels the current treatment of African Americans amidst the Black Lives Matter movement.

Media Racism and the Public Framing of Black Lives[1]

In recent years, the killing of unarmed African American men, women, and children by police officers and individuals acting as neighborhood monitors has sparked outrage across the nation and globally. Many of these incidents have been captured on video and shared on social media and through several news outlets. A disproportionate number of Blacks killed by police officers have been unarmed, yet the majority of these cases have closed without indictments or convictions. According to MappingPoliceViolence.org, Black people are 2.9 times more likely to be killed by police officers than Whites in the United States, based on data collected between 2013 and 2023. In 2022, data indicate that U.S. police killed 280 African Americans. "There were 188 days in 2022 when police killed Black people in the U.S.," reports MappingPoliceViolence.org. The 2022 Police Violence Report highlights the lack of criminal prosecution against law enforcement and the reliance on Black women to prosecute officers. The report states:

> Each year, fewer than 3% of killings by police result in officers being charged with a crime. Officers are disproportionately prosecuted by Black prosecutors—especially Black women. Representing only 1% of the nation's elected prosecutors, Black women were 9% of prosecutors who charged officers for killing someone, 11% of prosecutors convicting officers and 19% of prosecutors charging officers in two or more deadly force incidents from 2013–2022. (Mapping Police Violence, 2022)

The 2021 Police Violence Report also documents the disproportionate impact on people of color, who have the highest incidents of being killed while unarmed; Black people have the very highest rate. In fact, in 2021, while African Americans made up 13% of the U.S. population, "Black people were more likely to be killed by police, more likely to be unarmed, and less likely to be threatening someone when killed" (Mapping Police

Violence, 2021). African Americans made up 38% of unarmed people killed by police in 2021 and 39% of "unarmed and not alleged to be threatening" people killed by police that same year, the largest percentages among all racial groups reported (Mapping Police Violence, 2021). This is documented as a systemic issue, as "police disproportionately kill Black people, year after year" (Mapping Police Violence, 2021).

These unjust policing and judicial practices have resulted in the birth of the Black Lives Matter movement, a systematic movement designed to affirm the value of Black humanity and challenge the criminal justice system's assault on Blackness. Founders Alicia Garza, Patrisse Cullors, and Opal (Ayọ) Tometi created the #BlackLivesMatter hashtag in 2013 as a racially conscious movement dedicated to address the injustices faced by African Americans in the criminal justice system. "Black Lives Matter is an ideological and political intervention in a world where Black lives are systematically and intentionally targeted for demise. It is an affirmation of Black folks' humanity, our contributions to this society, and our resilience in the face of deadly oppression" (Black Lives Matter Global Network Foundation, n.d.). The movement has grown into a global crusade for the humanity of Black people around the world. It has sparked many local and national protests and has worked toward legislative reform. The expansive public participation in the movement has been recorded and discussed by the media. Yet the bulk of the media coverage has been dedicated to the initial phase of street protests and later the criminal proceedings announcements (i.e., indictment decisions and verdict decisions).

In cases of on-duty shootings by police officers, both news media and social media have played a vital role in the promotion of images about the victims and the officers. In effect, an overwhelming majority of the Black victims have been negatively framed in the media as violent, criminal, aggressive, and a perceived threat to the public, while the officers and neighborhood "monitors," who have been predominantly White, have been represented as upstanding public servants. These racially biased messages have informed public perceptions of the victims and have been used to validate states' failure to indict or convict officers in the case of unarmed African Americans. Consider the case of Trayvon Martin, a young African American boy who was killed by George Zimmerman. Images from Martin's social media pages and cell phone were showcased in the news media, which portrayed him as a drug-using violent thug. Photographs of Martin that gave the appearance of him smoking an unknown substance and brandishing what appears to be a weapon, along with messages and images that have been interpreted as bragging about physical altercations, were republished all over social media and broadcasted through multiple news outlets. The media ascribed a stereotypical character, the dangerous Black man, to a

Black boy without any criminal record and before the trial no evidence of drug use. Examining the news media headlines, examples of which are presented in Table 1.1, demonstrates a stereotypical racialized framing of Trayvon Martin as violent and unstable. While additional context is provided in each of these news stories, the headlines speak for themselves and communicate a very clear message about Martin that portray him as a dangerous thug. These media stories along with public comments and social media posts ushered in a wave of assaults against Martin, which influenced the public's perception of the 17-year-old Black boy. The criminalization of Martin and other unarmed African American males reflects the stereotypical classification of Black males as brutes and thugs (Smiley & Fakunle, 2016).

News Headline	Media Company and Date of Publication
Gun, drug texts feature in new Trayvon Martin shooting evidence	CNN, May 26, 2013
Trayvon's thug pix	*New York Post*, May 24, 2013
Trayvon Martin: Typical teen or troublemaker?	*USA Today*, December 11, 2012
Trayvon Martin started confrontation, Zimmerman lawyer says	*The Washington Post*, March 26, 2012
Trayvon Martin shooter told cops teenager went for his gun	ABC News, March 25, 2012

Table 1.1   Media Portrayals of Trayvon Martin as Violent and Unstable

The media diverged significantly in the representations of Martin and Zimmerman. Despite police recordings of Zimmerman using racist language and stereotypes to target others as criminals, coupled with the dispatch audio recording from the night he killed Martin where law enforcement instructed Zimmerman not to follow or pursue Martin, Zimmerman was painted as an innocent victim who had to stand his ground and protect himself. The court ruling mirrored this judgment and found Zimmerman not guilty under Florida's stand-your-ground law. Ironically, the law permits the use of violent force when the person is being pursued and/or attacked. In this case, there was a considerable amount of evidence indicating that the armed Zimmerman pursued and stalked an unarmed child, Martin. If Martin attempted to protect himself, why was his defense not considered standing his ground? Ironically, news media coverage of Zimmerman aids in justifying his "killing" of Martin. News outlets, including those listed in Table 1.2, avoided the

word *murder* when reporting on the case and instead overly sensationalized Zimmerman's minor injuries as potentially life-threatening. Within
United States news coverage, Zimmerman was portrayed as a heroic
neighborhood watch leader, acting within his right to protect and defend
himself and his community. Even public commentary, such as Geraldo
Rivera's claim that Martin was killed because of the hoodie he was wear-
ing, attempted to rationalize the murder of this young Black boy
(Castellanos, 2012).

News Headline	Media Company and Date of Publication
Photo appears to show Zimmerman bleeding after Trayvon Martin killing	CNN, December 4, 2012
George Zimmerman: Trayvon Martin threatened my life	CNN, June 22, 2012
Trayvon Martin shooting wasn't a case of racial profiling	CNN, May 30, 2012
Did Trayvon Martin attack George Zimmerman first?	*The Christian Science Monitor*, March 27, 2012
Cops, witnesses back up George Zimmerman's version of Trayvon Martin shooting	ABC News, May 17, 2012
ABC News exclusive: Zimmerman medical report shows broken nose, lacerations after Trayvon Martin shooting	ABC News, May 15, 2012
Zimmerman to argue self-defense, will not seek "stand your ground" hearing	CNN, May 1, 2013

Table 1.2   News Media Stories of George Zimmerman as Justified

The injustice against Trayvon Martin and other young Black boys over the
past few decades has caused many to draw parallels between 21st-century
violence against Black youth and 20th-century domestic terrorism against
Blacks as in the case of Emmett Till. Till was a 14-year-old African
American boy visiting his family in Money, Mississippi, when he was brutally murdered for allegedly flirting with a White woman. Till's murder left
his body and face so disfigured that he was hardly recognizable. His
mother requested his body be returned to her for burial, and she held an
open-casket funeral to advertise to the country the horrific nature of racial
injustice in America. Over 60 years later, African Americans' brutalized
lifeless bodies still lay on display in public and serve as a constant reminder
of the racial hatred and subjugation of Blacks in America.

A dissimilar media coverage is established in the case of White men in America who have been accused of violent crimes against African Americans. In the majority of the recent cases where White men have been accused of committing hate crimes and mass shootings against African Americans, and have not committed suicide, the police success-fully apprehended the suspects without incident. The media coverage of these cases has been more exploratory and descriptive versus the pre-scriptive approach taken in the case of African American victims. In the case of Dylann Roof, a 21-year-old White male accused of killing nine African Americans in a historic Black church in North Carolina, news forums on the case described the incident and focused on the victims and their families. For instance, when Roof was provided food from Burger King by police officers in Shelby, North Carolina, news outlets simply provided details and did not take a prescriptive stance on the situation. Consider news coverage of the case that read "Cops Bought Burger King for Dylann Roof Following His Arrest" (ABC7, 2015). The headline does not ascribe any character attributes to Roof, nor does the article assume a moral or social position on the actions of the officers. However, when African American news commentator Symone Sanders misspoke and reported that the police brought Roof *to* Burger King, news coverage shifted and began to describe her actions as false reporting. The overfo-cus on her mix-up between the phrases "brought him to" and "brought him" food from Burger King completely ignored the larger point, which was that Roof was provided food from Burger King as a meal by the police department, which was an insult to the victims, their families, and African Americans in general. While the police department attempted to justify their actions by stating that the holding facility did not have ade-quate food to supply him, their actions raised many questions regarding the value of White life versus Black life.

Consider the cases of African Americans who have been killed by law enforcement or have died in the custody of law enforcement after requesting basic human rights. African Americans have made requests for the basic human right to breathe yet have been denied this human neces-sity by law enforcement, which has resulted in their death. George Floyd proclaimed his life was exiting his body. Eric Garner stated over 10 times that he could not breathe as police officers restrained him in an illegal chokehold and restricted his air passage; he was later pronounced dead at the hospital. Several African American women have died in police custody over the years. Sandra Bland, Ralkina Jones, Kindra Chapman, Raynette Turner, and Natasha McKenna were all African American women who died in police custody in 2015. In 2016, Symone Marshall died in police custody in Walker County Jail in Huntsville, Texas, after not receiving medical care despite the fact that she was arrested after a car accident that left her in a ditch. Her family informed law enforcement that she needed medical attention, which according to the police department she refused. Marshall was found having a seizure in her cell and later declared dead at the hospital. The contested and controversial deaths of Black women in police custody have resulted in outrage. After the death of Sandra Bland, a 28-year-old Black activist who died in police custody in Waller County, Texas, the #SayHerName movement was launched to address police brutality and in-custody deaths of Black females and to challenge the media and public perceptions of racial injustice against Black women. These cases provide evidence that the criminal justice system and media are often less sympathetic to the human rights of African Americans and instead once again provide prescriptive reporting where they seem to offer some rationale for the denial of African Americans' human rights by law enforcement.

Justifications for the murders of unarmed African Americans are abundant in United States news media headlines and stories (see Table 1.3). The hypercriminalization of African Americans in the media and American society contributes to these falsified ideas of unarmed African Americans (M. Oliver, 2003). Framing of psychological instability, violent and criminal histories, and aggression is frequently used to characterize African Americans who have been murdered by police officers. Michael Brown, Sandra Bland, Breonna Taylor, George Floyd, and countless others all were represented with these racialized tropes, which consequently were accepted by many as rationales for their deaths. The term *raid* was consistently attached to Taylor's name, and she was repeatedly linked to drug activity. *Robber* and *robbery* were routinely used to describe Brown. The mental health of both Bland and Floyd was consistently questioned, and drug abuse was interwoven with Floyd's name and case.

When offering exploratory reporting, news media often explore the psychological state of Whites significantly differently than they do that of Blacks. In the case of Dylann Roof, news outlets dissected his potential state of mind at the time of his criminal actions as a potential rationale for his behavior. Yet, media analyses were more psychologically forgiving toward Whites than when this approach was used in cases of unarmed Blacks who were killed by police officers. Consider the media treatment of Michael Brown, an unarmed African American boy who was shot to death several times by officer Darren Wilson. The media speculated that Brown's psychological state was unstable because he allegedly had just committed a "strong arm robbery" and therefore may have been on guard when the officer approached him. There is of course no evidence to support this assessment of Brown's mental state. In fact, the police department's strategic release of the video footage of Brown from earlier that day was questioned as a premature rationale for the murder. Even

News Headline	Media Company and Date of Publication
No dice, BLM, Michael Brown was not innocent	*The Washington Times*, March 13, 2017
Sandra Bland previously attempted suicide, jail documents say	*The Washington Post*, July 22, 2015
Failure to be bonded out led Sandra Bland to suicide, jail officials allege	*Chicago Tribune*, November 12, 2015
"Lethal dose": What drugs did George Floyd have in his system?	*The Sun*, March 29, 2021
Floyd's drug use, prior arrest central to murder defense	*Bloomberg Law*, April 13, 2021
George Floyd had "violent criminal history": Minneapolis police union chief	*New York Post*, June 2, 2020
Breonna Taylor case evidence does not "prove a homicide" by police, Andy McCarthy says	Fox News, September 23, 2020
Breonna Taylor is a drug war victim	*Forbes*, September 23, 2020
Breonna Taylor's ex-boyfriend sentenced on drug charges	WAVE 3, November 30, 2021

Table 1.3   News Media Stories of Unarmed African Americans Killed by Police

the term *strong arm robbery*, which was used by law enforcement and later adopted by the media, was a part of the racist justification for Brown's death. Although a monetary transaction was captured on tape—Brown provided money and took a product—this part of the video was overshadowed in the media by the section in the video where Brown appears to force his way out of the exit door of the store, which was being blocked by the store owner. In describing the video, neither the police department nor the media ever used noncriminal terminology, and they did not consider minor crime language such as *misdemeanor shoplifting*; instead, the media more aggressively described Brown's actions as a violent criminal act. Even still, the rule of law is that a person is innocent until proven guilty. Yet Brown, who had never been charged with this crime, was convicted in the court of public opinion without due process, which he could never receive because he was killed. The use of hypercriminal and violent terminology in the media against African Americans killed by law enforcement is another instance of media racism. These injustices in the media have been used to validate law enforcement's use of deadly violence against African Americans even when unarmed, lying on their backs, with hands up in the air.

The humanizing of White male terrorists and murderers in the media conveys an unrelenting investment in White supremacist racist propaganda. This form of racism calls for news outlets, social media, and the general public to champion the innocence and justification of Whites in killing and terrorizing African Americans. News media are used to promote the humanity of Whites as regular people who have somehow fallen victim to the assumed violent nature of Blacks, as in the case of Darren Wilson, or have suffered the consequences of a broken mental health care system, as in the case of Dylann Roof (see Table 1.4). Explorations of who these men are, beyond the immediate headlines, lead the discourse and frame the public narrative around their cases. Thus, news media are more interested in the humanity of White men, which leads to biographic news coverage instead of criminalization.

News Headline	Media Company and Date of Publication
Charleston Church shooting: Who is Dylann Roof?	CNN, Jun 19, 2015
FBI says Dylann Roof should not have been cleared to purchase a weapon	CNN, July 10, 2015
Dylann Roof's past reveals trouble at home and school	*The New York Times*, July 16, 2015
Forgiveness for Dylann Roof after Charleston's mass murder	*The Atlantic*, June 20, 2015
Darren Wilson: Ferguson made me unemployable	*USA Today*, August 4, 2015
What we know about Ferguson officer Darren Wilson	*USA Today*, August 19, 2015
Police officer in Ferguson is said to recount a struggle	*The New York Times*, October 18, 2014
"I felt like a five-year-old holding on to Hulk Hogan": Darren Wilson in his own words	*The Guardian*, November 25, 2014
Ferguson cop Darren Wilson is expecting a child: "I want to live a normal life"	*People*, November 26, 2014

Table 1.4 Media Representations of White Males Who Murder Black Americans

Media racism is a form of structural racism, and it allows the current racial biases to continue to exist in American society. Media racism supplements the embedded institutional forms of racism by providing imagery and news content that gives credence to the systematic oppression of certain groups. In this case, the subjugation of African Americans is bolstered by racialized media content that frames African Americans as dangerous to the health, safety, and sovereignty of America. These victim-blaming media frames have significant impact on the criminal prosecution and verdicts or lack thereof (Dukes & Gaither, 2017). There is alarming evidence that politics, scholarship, and media contribute to the stereotype that African Americans, and Black women in particular, are chronically unhealthy and in need of social control. The distortion of African American reality helps to validate American racism and the marginalization of African Americans in American society. Leading television shows starring African American women continue in the tradition of using media to advance racist and sexist beliefs about Blackness. The following chapters will critically analyze Black women's representations in media and how their media images negatively affect African Americans' lives.

NOTE

1. "Media Racism and the Public Framing of Black Lives" first appeared in the 2022 NCBS Report and is published with the permission of NCBS.

CHAPTER 2

From Crack Mamas to Baby Mamas

Black Women, Media,
and Public Policy

Stereotypes operate as a fictional depiction of a particular group of people. However, popularizing stereotypes to the point where they are believed to be true transforms the stereotype into a social perception, which may be extremely difficult to alter. Consider one of the oldest racist tropes regarding African Americans, the uncultured love of the watermelon. The racist stereotype that African Americans possess an unhealthy and unnatural love for watermelon has plagued the Black community for centuries. What was once a symbol of Black economic self-sufficiency post-enslavement was turned into a damning spectacle of ridicule and racism. After emancipation, newly freed Africans sought various ways to secure self-employment and economic independence. Selling watermelons proved economically savvy and yielded financial rewards. Intimidated by Africans' growing economic stability and independence, Whites began constructing rumors about Africans and watermelons in an attempt to discredit their political and economic power. As noted by William R. Black (2014) in "How Watermelons Became a Racist Trope," media played a pivotal role in sensationalizing the stereotype and normalizing the misguided racist anecdotes about Blacks and watermelons:

> Newspapers amplified this association between the watermelon and the free black person. In 1869, *Frank Leslie's Illustrated Newspaper* published perhaps the first caricature of blacks reveling in watermelon. The adjoining article explained, "The Southern negro in no particular more palpably

exhibits his epicurean tastes than in his excessive fondness for watermel-ons. The juvenile freedman is especially intense in his partiality for that refreshing fruit."

While these propaganda depictions of African Americans helped normal-ize the stereotype, the mythology around Blacks and watermelons carried a much larger purpose. According to Black (2014),

> The primary message of the watermelon stereotype was that black people were not ready for freedom. During the 1880 election season, Democrats accused the South Carolina state legislature, which had been majority-black during Reconstruction, of having wasted taxpayers' money on watermelons for their own refreshment; this fiction even found its way into history text-books. D. W. Griffith's white-supremacist epic film *The Birth of a Nation*, released in 1915, included a watermelon feast in its depiction of emancipa-tion, as corrupt northern whites encouraged the former slaves to stop working and enjoy some watermelon instead. In these racist fictions, blacks were no more deserving of freedom than were children.

The media promotion of the watermelon stereotype along with other racist tropes, such as the dangerous sex-crazed Black man, was used to fuel the campaign for a segregated society. The resulting legislation, Jim Crow, allowed for legal discrimination and disenfranchisement of African Americans, and by the turn of the century, for instance, the majority of African Americans holding public offices were removed from their positions. Thus, racialized stereotypes when backed by media and entrenched in political discourse can erupt into public policies that mar-ginalize the existence of a group despite their lack of merit. More specifically, when racial stereotypes advance White supremacy and political dominance, they are woven into the fabric of America and do not waver regardless of any considerable amount of evidence disproving the racist sentiments.

Over the past three decades, media-promoted stereotypes have directly impacted public perceptions of Black womanhood and have validated public policies that negatively impact the well-being of Black women. This chapter explores the 1980s "welfare queen," the 1990s "crack mama," and the 2000s "baby mama" stereotypes as a calculated political media attack on Black womanhood in the post–civil rights era.

REPRODUCTIVE INJUSTICE AND
THE WELFARE QUEEN LABEL

Following the racialization of poverty in America, which largely con-densed African Americans into the poor citizenry of America, governmental officials began restructuring public assistance programs under the same racial framework. African Americans, and Black women in particular, were represented as illegitimate abusers of governmental aid. Campaigning for president in 1976, Ronald Reagan was a major critic of welfare and targeted the Black woman as a chronic criminal abuser of the welfare system. As discussed in Chapter 1, on the campaign trail, Reagan introduced his welfare queen caricature and popularized the welfare queen label as the face of Black womanhood. He falsified a story of an alleged Black woman, Linda Taylor, with 80 different names and 30 addresses that she used in an elaborate scheme to collect welfare benefits. Taylor was claimed to drive a white Cadillac and live a luxurious lifestyle on governmental aid. This stereotyped caricature of Black women was used to rationalize the public perception of Black females as illegitimate aid recipients and to justify Reagan's welfare reform proposal. Sociologist Patricia Hill Collins (2005) argues that "the Reagan/ Bush administration also realized that racializing welfare by painting it as a program that unfairly benefited Blacks was a sure-fire way to win White votes. This context created the controlling image of the 'welfare queen' primarily to garner support for refusing state support for poor and working-class Black mothers and children" (p. 132). The racial political targeting of Black women proved successful (M. Gammage, 2017). Although there was no evidence to support Reagan's attack on the Black woman, he was elected president in 1980 and significantly cut funding from the Aid to Families with Dependent Children (AFDC) federal assistance program. However, for several years before and after his election, the image of Black women as criminal abusers of the welfare system reigned throughout politics and the media. Carpenter (2012) contends that the welfare queen label became an icon that would forever be inseparable from Black womanhood:

> The welfare queen icon was the target of media sensationalism during the Reagan Era. The image of a black welfare recipient wearing a fur coat and gold jewelry while driving a Cadillac to purchase steak, alcohol, and cigarettes with her food stamps became the poster child for welfare reform. The image of this woman defined all welfare recipients until welfare was synonymous with black motherhood. Purportedly, the behaviors of black mothers, rather than structural issues, social and economic conditions, and political agendas, propagated dependency and economic failure. (p. 268)

The branding of Black women as untrustworthy, illegitimate, and unhealthy mothers skyrocketed in the media. Coverage of the failing economy, poverty, and economic hardship was eclipsed by the overpromotion of lazy criminal Black women. During the Reagan era, the media overpublicized messages of Black female welfare dependency, which undoubtedly influenced the public perception of African Americans.

According to Entman and Rojecki (2000), such images give credence to the false perceptions of African Americans:

> The average White mistakenly believes that Blacks constitute one-third of the American population, a majority of the poor, and the bulk of welfare rolls. No wonder, perhaps, so many Whites resentfully overestimate government attention and spending on poverty. Their misimpressions may be reinforced by images—and voids—in the media. Television news tends to illustrate welfare and poverty by portraying urban Blacks rather than the (actually more numerous) rural Whites, furnishing symbolic resources many Whites use to justify resentments. (pp. 8–9)

Thus, the falsified embellishment of Black women as abusers of welfare in the media has resulted in public backlash against Black aid recipients and nonrecipients.

The welfare queen label operates like a double-edged sword against Black women. On one end, it calls for governmental reform of public assistance programs that primarily benefit individuals living below the poverty line. And on the other hand, it calls for state-regulated family planning to restrict the reproductive choices of Black women. The following subsection details the latter.

The Planned Parenthood Effect

Laced within the welfare queen stereotype is the call for state-regulated family planning for Black women, which provides a direct entry point for Planned Parenthood. The history of Planned Parenthood and African Americans has been very contentious. Coining the term *birth control* in 1910, Margaret Sanger set out to offer women in America education on birth control and outlets for reproductive choices. Although birth control devices were illegal, Sanger opened her first birth control clinic in 1916, now called Planned Parenthood, which forced her to flee the country. Upon her return, Sanger's work was reenergized, and her efforts started to include messages promoting the restriction of reproductive abilities of unfit populations. In a 1921 article, Sanger posed that the most pressing issue facing the country was restricting reproduction among persons with mental and physical disabilities. However, by the early 1930s, her targeting of African Americans for population control became more pronounced than any other aspect of her charge for reproductive rights and regulations. Aligning her birth control efforts with the eugenics movement afforded Sanger a level of public support that was unprecedented.

Sanger's mission of providing reproduction options to women took a back seat to her advocacy for population control for African Americans.

Under both the Eugenics Project and Planned Parenthood, countless numbers of Black women were forced or coerced into being sterilized. State and federal laws permitted the unconsented sterilization of certain groups of Americans, the "undesirable." In 1905, the United States Supreme Court ruled in *Jacobson v. Massachusetts* that states can authorize mandatory vaccinations against any person for the sake of the public's welfare. Further, in 1927, the Supreme Court's ruling in *Buck v. Bell* upheld a Virginia statute that authorized the forced sterilization of individuals under the Eugenics Project who were categorized as unfit for reproduction. Media were used to preach selective breeding across the nation, and countless numbers of Africans were forcibly sterilized and hospitalized in mental institutions under the pretense of being disabled and feeble-minded. Newspaper articles spotlighted heredity as a problem for Americans' health and encouraged careful selection of mates to protect the health of the nation. In addition, articles were designed to validate the placement of undesirable populations (i.e., the feeble-minded) in mental institutions and homes. Over 30 states officially participated in eugenic sterilizations, which affected tens of thousands of Americans. Countless numbers of African American women have reported being sterilized without their knowledge or consent. Fannie Lou Hamer, a noted African American activist, shared her story of being forcibly sterilized in Mississippi. In 1961, Hamer, a 19-year-old, received an unconsented "Mississippi Appendectomy," a medical procedure designed to sterilize women without their consent, during a minor medical surgery. Amidst her experience, Hamer became a civil rights crusader championing the voting rights of African Americans and the rights of women.

Amidst the discrediting of the eugenics movement, Planned Parenthood emphasized its supposed mission of advancing reproductive rights for women and managed to live on. Although eugenics was largely abandoned as a national project, many argue that the mission continues within the walls of Planned Parenthood by targeting Black communities for abortion services. Ironically, Planned Parenthood has created a conflict among the racialized messages about African Americans. First, it frames Black women as most in need of the services by placing the majority of its abortion clinics in Black and Hispanic communities (Enouen, 2017); and second, Black women are then ostracized for utilizing the services of Planned Parenthood.

Many media advertisements have falsely represented African American women as the face of abortion. Consider the Life Always group's anti-abortion billboards plastered across the nation falsely accusing Black women of being the leading cause of death among African Americans. As noted in the introduction to this book, the advertisement reads: "The most dangerous place for an African American is in the womb." The group charged Black women with afflicting abortions on the racial population and thereby resulting in the decline of the African American population growth rate. However, there is insufficient evidence to support such a claim. According to the Centers for Disease Control and Prevention, the majority (55.8%) of women who obtained an abortion between 1997 and 2006 were White (Hispanic and non-Hispanic), while "[B]lack women accounted for 36.4% and women of other racial groups for 7.8%" (Pazol et al., 2009). Despite the easily accessible data, media entities and groups seeking to restrict the reproductive rights of Black women continue to unfairly target Black women.

Racialized targeting of Black women by reproductive corporations has been heavily documented. Protecting Black Life, a branch of Life Issues Institute, reported in its 2012 research that Planned Parenthood systematically targets certain populations of women through clinic placements. The group charged Planned Parenthood with steering its services, including abortions, toward women of color "by placing 79 percent of its surgical abortion facilities within walking distance of minority neighborhoods," and "the abortion giant has accelerated this targeting of minorities near its 25 new abortion mega-centers" (Enouen, 2017). The group further contends:

> Protecting Black Life evaluated the populations within walking distance (2 mile radius) of each of these 25 abortion mega-centers and found that an alarming 88 percent (22 of 25) target women of color. Disturbingly, 80 percent target Black communities, 56 percent target Hispanic/Latino neighborhoods and 80 percent target one or more colleges. In total, 96 percent (24 of 25) of the mega-centers target women of color, college women, or both. (Enouen, 2017)

This systematic targeting continues the reproductive injustice that Black women have experienced since they entered this country under enslavement. Media racism has served to help validate the reproductive ostracism of Black women and the creation of public policies and institutes that strategically target them with race-neutral tactics.

The marginalization of Black women's reproductive rights does not end with systematic targeting for abortions. As legal scholar Dorothy Roberts (1997) points out, legal penalties have been wedged against Black mothers considered unbefitting for motherhood. Roberts argues that law enforcement, including prosecutors and judges, subject Black women to harsh reproductive penalties, such as lengthy prison sentences, because Black women are not considered suitable for motherhood. Aiding these perceptions of Black women are the negative representations of Black women in the media, which help to justify the criminal treatment of Black mothers (M. Gammage, 2015).

CRACK MAMAS AND LEGAL PENALTIES

During the 1980s and 1990s, media representations of African Americans and the "crack epidemic" heightened. Coined in 1971 by President Richard Nixon, the slogan *war on drugs* largely symbolized Nixon's political stance against drug crimes. But, in 1982, President Ronald Reagan officially launched the war on drugs despite the fact that drug crimes were on the decline. The media's linkage between drug violence and Black communities fueled political agendas and helped justify the war on drugs. Racial ideologies paired with media racism against Blacks were used to validate the war on drugs and the harsh legal policies that would follow. Both racially coded and blatantly racist messages about African Americans as the criminal drug offenders of America were highly publicized through various media outlets. Print media, television and film, and music content were engulfed with discourse intersecting race, class, drugs, and violence. As noted by renowned legal scholar Michelle Alexander (2010) in her explosive text *The New Jim Crow: Mass Incarceration in the Age of Colorblindness*, the "crack problem" was attached to the face of African Americans, where Black men were portrayed as dope dealers, Black women were crack mamas, and Black children were crack babies:

> While it is true that the publicity surrounding crack cocaine led to a dramatic increase in funding for the drug war (as well as to sentencing policies that greatly exacerbated racial disparities in incarceration rates), there is no truth to the notion that the War on Drugs was launched in response to crack cocaine. President Ronald Reagan officially announced the current drug war in 1982, before crack became an issue in the media or a crisis in poor black neighborhoods. A few years after the drug war was declared, crack began to spread rapidly in the poor black neighborhoods of Los Angeles and later emerged in cities across the country. The Reagan administration hired staff to publicize the emergence of crack cocaine in 1985 as part of a strategic effort to build public and legislative support for the war. The media campaign was an extraordinary success. Almost overnight, the media was saturated with images of black "crack whores," "crack dealers," and "crack babies"—images that seemed to confirm the worst negative racial stereotypes about impoverished inner-city residents. The media bonanza surrounding the "new demon drug" helped to catapult the War on Drugs from an ambitious federal policy to an actual war. (p. 5)

Researchers have identified the prevailing role of media in constructing images of African Americans as chronically violent drug offenders as well as media's role in creating the fears around the so-called crack plague (Brownstein, 1996; Chermak 1997; Reinarman & Levine, 1989). Jennifer Cobbina (2008) explores in her article "Race and Class

Differences in Print Media Portrayals of Crack Cocaine and Methamphetamine" the role of newspapers in shaping the narrative around crack cocaine usage in America and how the news media framing of race, class, and criminal justice led to a biased overemphasis on African Americans. In her analysis of race depictions of crack in four major newspapers with national news coverage from 1985 to 1987, Cobbina found that news media primarily represented crack cocaine as a problem predominantly affecting economically challenged Black communities, which has resulted in a state of panic over drug usage and violence in America. Cobbina argued that "evidence suggests that race and class influenced both the perception of crack and meth abusers and the response to crack users. It appears that it is not just the depiction of drugs that create moral panics but media representation of crack and meth to particular groups of people are what lead the drug to be viewed as dangerous" (p. 163). Her research also demonstrated the difference in news articles' treatment of the two drugs and their promotion of increased legal penalties for crack cocaine:

> Articles on crack were two times more likely than meth articles to express the need for harsher crime control policies. Journalists reported several calls for "get tough" policies, such as the war on drugs, mandatory prison terms, and three strike laws, in response to the alleged crack epidemic in the mid-1980s. Some researchers suggest that the media manufactured the crack scare to carry out political agendas (Brownstein, 1996; Reinarman and Levine, 1997). Reporters rely quite heavily on public officials to obtain media reports (Young, 1973; Hall et al., 1978; Chermak, 1997). Thus, it is easy to understand how the media's reliance on government officials for information about crime provides political governments the opportunity to advance their own partisan interests through the use of propaganda. (p. 163)

The increased news coverage on African American users and distributors was coupled with a heightened call for harsher policing practices, sentencing laws, and strict legislative policies. Consider the Anti–Drug Abuse Act of 1988 (ADAA). The ADAA was a law passed by the United States Congress for the war on drugs that included funding for the war on drugs and increased penalties for individual users and sellers.

> The new Anti-Drug Abuse Act authorized public housing authorities to evict any tenant who allows any form of drug-related criminal activity to occur on or near public housing premises and eliminated many federal benefits, including student loans, for anyone convicted of a drug offense. The act also expanded use of the death penalty for serious drug-related offenses and imposed new mandatory minimums for drug offenses, including a five-year mandatory minimum for simple possession of

cocaine base—with no evidence of intent to sell. Remarkably, the penalty would apply to first-time offenders. The severity of this punishment was unprecedented in the federal system. Until 1988, one year of imprisonment had been the maximum for possession of any amount of any drug. (Alexander, 2010, pp. 52–53)

The controversial law was highly criticized for its different penalties between cocaine and crack cocaine, especially given that the latter was being publicized as an African American problem. Under the ADAA, possession of 5 grams of crack cocaine carried a five-year minimum prison sentence, while 500 grams of cocaine resulted in a five-year sentence. Chandra Crawford (2005) suggests that the new law "was racially motivated as a result of racial perception linking crack with poor Blacks and deviant behavior" (p. 137). Crawford goes on to argue that the "crack cocaine problem" was constructed and media—news media in particular—played an important role in distributing images of the crack epidemic in Black communities.

Legal scholar Michelle Alexander (2010) goes further to offer a larger political scheme as the underlining rationale for the war on drugs. Alexander argues that the war on drugs was a part of the systematic backlash to the gains of the civil rights movement and offered a race-neutral disguise for targeting African Americans for punitive treatment. She states that "the War on Drugs, cloaked in race-neutral language, offered whites opposed to racial reform a unique opportunity to express their hostility toward blacks and black progress, without being exposed to the charge of racism" (Alexander, 2010, p. 53), and goes on to argue that "conservative politicians found they could mobilize white racial resentment by vowing to crack down on crime" (p. 54). Therefore, in the post–civil rights era, African Americans were the ideal political targets to attack in order to maintain White political control and advance White supremacy.

Against this backdrop, it is not surprising to find *media racism* operating as a political tool to bolster the justification for the war on drugs. In the 1980s and 1990s, the discursive construction of African American women as criminally negligent mothers, due to their addictions to drugs, validated the criminal justice system's harsh punitive treatment of Black mothers and led to increased legal penalties against Black women. Terming Black women as crack mamas became an acceptable norm in the news media and in popular culture expressions such as in print media, rap music, television, and film. Alexander (2010) notes that news media would actively broadcast images of Black women as "crack whores" and their babies as "crack babies" in order to heighten the fear around crack cocaine as dangerous and a deadly drug.

Hip-hop also paralleled the social and political commentary on African Americans and drug distribution and abuse. In 1988, Public Enemy, an

American rap group, debuted their single and music video "Night of the Living Baseheads" on *Yo! MTV Raps* and BET's *Rap City*. Among the first to address the crack epidemic, the lyrics and video chronicled the wide-scale use and impact of cocaine abuse in America from Wall Street to the inner city. The song challenged the narrative of Blacks as the singular group succumbing to crack addictions. But N.W.A.'s "Dope Man" (1987) shifted the narrative to the standpoint of the dealer and also dove into Black women's experiences during the crack epidemic. Some recording artists would represent Black women as drug abusers who were unfit for motherhood in both their rap music lyrics and music videos. One of the most egregious examples of this is the 1991 rap song "Your Mama's on Crack Rock" by The Dogs featuring Disco Rick. The song and supplemental music video represent an African American woman utilizing her body to secure money for drugs, and as a result her daughter is taunted by other children. In the video several African American children tease another African American girl about her mother's substance abuse issues by chanting the song's chorus "Nah-nah-nah-nah, your mama's on crack rock." The young girl attempts to defend her mother, but the other children make claims to the contrary. One child states: "My mama told somebody that your mama's selling her body for money. But I don't know what that means." In the background, The Dogs continue to rap their lyrics as the camera follows the Black mother in the streets as she solicits drugs. At the end of the video, the little girl goes to her mother and pleads with her to stop because she is being tormented by other children.

While some rap artists directly criticized Black mothers using drugs, other rappers took a more critical approach to discussing the social impact of drugs on Black families. In his acclaimed song "Dear Mama" (1995), famed rap artist Tupac Shakur juxtaposed Black mothers and drug dependencies with poverty and hypercriminalization in Black communities. Through his lyrics, Tupac provides a more in-depth perspective on the crack epidemic in Black communities and its link to larger societal issues. Yet, the overwhelming majority of rap music songs and videos that discuss or picture Black women and substance dependency predominantly focus on the negative personal and familial outcomes of drug abuse.

At the same time as the media was oversensationalizing the "crack epidemic" as destructive to American cities, the federal government was simultaneously constructing new laws that would provide incentives to target individuals committing drug crimes, stricter penalties for drug crimes, promotions for felony convictions, and federally sanctioned violence by law enforcement. By 1994, the Violent Crime Control and

Law Enforcement Act was signed into law by Bill Clinton, and the resulting three-strikes rule ushered in thousands of Blacks and Hispanics to the criminal justice system and prison industry permanently with sentences of 25 years to life. Not only did these laws and new rules disproportionately impact Black communities, but they also became a funding stream for the criminal justice system, which has had significant impacts on Black families' wealth holdings and wealth accumulation.

American television and film also supported the criminally dangerous portrayal of African Americans, and Black mothers more specifically. The crack mama stereotype once again showed its face in film dramas on African American families. The American film *Losing Isaiah* (Gyllenhaal, 1995) depicted the assumed social side effects of African American female drug abuse on parenting and child development. The film description on Google reads:

> Khaila Richards (Halle Berry), a crack-addicted single mother, accidentally leaves her baby in a dumpster while high and returns the next day in a panic to find he is missing. In reality, the baby has been adopted by a warm-hearted social worker, Margaret Lewin (Jessica Lange), and her husband, Charles (David Strathairn). Years later, Khaila has gone through rehab and holds a steady job. After learning that her child is still alive, she challenges Margaret for the custody.

The film opens with a close-up on Khaila as she holds her baby, but as the camera pans the room, it is revealed that Khaila is in a dark abandoned building. She twitches and scratches as she walks out of the building looking to get her next drug fix. In a rush, she decides to place the crying baby in a cardboard box and cover him with a cardboard lid. The next morning, sanitation workers arrive to clear the trash in the area. One worker places the box with the baby inside the garbage truck, but just before the box is smashed, the workers realize that a baby is inside the truck. The baby is rushed to a hospital. Margaret Lewin is the social worker on call at the hospital when the baby arrives. The doctors inform her that the baby is suffering from severe side effects from exposure to cocaine, but she encourages them to attempt to save him. Hospital administrators soon discover who the baby is but have not heard from the mother.

Awaking from her drug-induced sleep, Khaila remembers that she stored her baby in a box and runs to retrieve him. However, she is too late; the baby is gone. A nearby male in the alley informs her that the baby is dead and that police were there. Believing that her baby is dead, Khaila runs away in grief. Meanwhile, Margaret becomes attached to baby Isaiah and convinces her family to adopt him. After being arrested for shoplifting, Khaila participates in a drug rehab program and appears to actively work toward improving her life. When she shares with a drug addiction counselor how she lost her baby, she is once again confronted with the ills of her past. After some investigation, the counselor discovers that Khaila's son Isaiah is not dead but instead has been adopted by a White family. Although faced with much criticism and ridicule, Khaila begins a legal case to petition for the return of her son. When the Lewins learn of Khaila's petition, they are dismayed by her audacity to mother Isaiah. Khaila's reputation as a former drug user is weighted against her in the court and by the adoptive family. However, she pushes forward. Her lawyer also raises concern with the Lewins' parenting style and lack of African American cultural influence on the child. In the end, the judge sides with Khaila and orders the return of Isaiah to his birth mother.

After parenting Isaiah for a few days, Khaila decides to contact Margaret in order to return Isaiah to her custody. When Margaret arrives at Isaiah's new school, she is greeted outside by Khaila, who explains to her that she believes that it is in the child's best interest to return him to the Lewins' home. While Khaila does not agree to give up full custody, she does permit her son to return to the care of another family because she does not believe that she can best meet his needs at this time. The movie ends with Isaiah wrapped in Margaret's arms as he plays with blocks on the school floor with the two women. No further information is provided as to illustrate whether Isaiah ever returned to his mother Khaila's home and care. In the film, Khaila is characterized as a stereotypical crack mama who does not possess any maternal instinct. She is initially portrayed as a dangerous mother, later she is represented as a negligent mother given her failure to search for her son beyond the alley, and in the end she is depicted as an unfit and ineffective mother. The representation of Black women as chronic drug abusers who drug their children with crack cocaine has negatively affected the treatment of Black women with drug dependencies in the criminal justice system. Although "research has shown that drug and alcohol abuse rates are higher for pregnant White women than pregnant Black women" (Small 2001, p. 898), "Black women are about 10 times more likely to be reported to authorities under mandatory reporting" (Small, 2001, p. 898). Thus, there are clear racial disparities in the representation of mothers and drug abuse.

In addition to Black women being represented as crack mamas and crack whores, Black women were portrayed as loyal partners and mothers to dope dealers. Media imagery characterized Black women as criminal partners to Black men who sold drugs as well as protective mothers who lied for their sons and covered up their crimes. Legislation aimed at penalizing Black families for the crimes of their family members meant that poor families living in governmental housing would lose their housing vouchers, food stamps, and other governmental aid. Black women were also subject to criminal punishments, were charged as co-conspirators, and served jail time for minor crimes linked to their family members' drug activities or their own drug possessions.

The weight of incarcerated Black mothers brutally affected the welfare of African American children. The collateral consequences of the crack mama and crack whore stereotypes permeated the criminal justice system's family and child welfare policies. In "Prison, Foster Care, and the Systemic Punishment of Black Mothers," legal scholar Dorothy Roberts (2012) investigates the intersection of race and gender, prison, and foster care. Roberts argues that the long-standing stereotypes of the Black woman as criminally and morally unfit for motherhood validate public policies that restrict and limit Black women's right to mother their children:

> Stereotypes about black female criminality and irresponsibility legitimate the massive disruption that both systems inflict on black families and communities. A popular mythology promoted over centuries portrays black women as unfit to bear and raise children. The sexually licentious Jezebel, the family-demolishing Matriarch, the devious Welfare Queen, the depraved pregnant crack addict accompanied by her equally monstrous crack baby— all paint a picture of a dangerous motherhood that must be regulated and punished. Unmarried black women represent the ultimate irresponsible mothers—women who raise their children without the supervision of a man. These stereotypes do not simply percolate in some disembodied white psyche. They are reinforced and recreated by foster care and prison, which leave the impression that black women are naturally prone to commit crimes and abuse their children. Stereotypes of maternal irresponsibility created and enforced by the child welfare system's disproportionate supervision of black children help to sustain mass incarceration, and stereotypes of black female criminality help to sustain foster care. (p. 1492)

The criminal targeting and framing of Black mothers in the war on drugs exacerbated the penalties imposed on Black women and severely hampered their reproductive and parenting rights. According to Roberts (2012), "most incarcerated mothers were convicted of drug-related offenses or property crimes that involve drug use rather than violent felonies. The increased incarceration of nonviolent mothers who are first-time offenders and who have valuable ties to their children, other family members, and neighbors, inflicts incalculable damage to communities" (p. 1481).

Although the majority of media coverage on the crack epidemic focused on African Americans, research demonstrates significant discrepancies between images of Blacks as drug users and dealers and African Americans' actual involvement with drugs. In *The New Jim Crow*, Michelle Alexander (2010) provides mountains of evidence documenting race-based targeting in the war on drugs versus real drug use in America. The *Criminal Justice Fact Sheet* from the National Association for the Advancement of Colored People (NAACP, 2023) highlights drug sentencing disparities in the United States:

- 5% of illicit drug users are African American, yet African Americans represent 29% of those arrested for drug offenses and 33% of those incarcerated for drug offenses.

- In the 2015 National Survey on Drug Use and Health, about 17 million white people and 4 million African Americans reported having used an illicit drug within the last month.

- African Americans and whites use drugs at similar rates, but the imprisonment rate of African Americans for drug charges is almost 6 times that of whites.

Despite this evidence, African Americans have been significantly disproportionately impacted by get-tough policies under the war on drugs. "More African Americans are under correctional control today—in prison or jail, on probation or parole—than were enslaved in 1850, a decade before the Civil War began" (Alexander, 2010, p. 175), and further, "although the majority of illegal drug users and dealers nationwide are white, three-fourths of all people imprisoned for drug offenses have been black and Latino" (Alexander, 2010, p. 97).

Dissimilar legal penalties continue to exist between Black women/mothers and White females. According to The Sentencing Project (2018), in state prisons, the incarceration rates for drug crimes were higher for women than men in 2014. Incarceration rates for Black women are two times the rates for White women (NAACP, 2023; The Sentencing Project, 2018). Although the imprisonment rate is on the decline for Black women yet on the rise for White women (The Sentencing Project, 2018), Black women receive disproportionately harsher penalties (Simmons, 2018; Small, 2001) and are less likely to receive rehabilitation services for drug crimes. According to Deborah Small (2001), "America's enforcement of its punitive drug policy has resulted in a system of apartheid justice. The population of Black and Brown men and women behind bars has caused our prisons to look like Antebellum plantations" (p. 897). Representations of Black women as criminal drug offenders and crack mamas during the height of the war on drugs were part of a systemic racist plan to marginalize African

Americans, by incarcerating them and placing them in a permanent second-class citizenship status (Alexander, 2010) and by removing their entitlement to governmental aid (welfare, public housing, financial aid, etc.).

Media's aggrandizement of the Black crack mama and dope fiend proved to be a form of media racism. Not only were the messages about Black men, women, and children erroneously reported and depicted, but they helped to validate public policies that disenfranchised Black families and communities and significantly impacted the social and economic welfare of African Americans. The lingering effects of this racist stereotype are still felt among Black women across the nation. And unfortunately, the image of the strung-out Black crack mama still appears in modern media representations of Black women. These images continue in the tradition of representing Black women as unfit for motherhood, even in the 21st century. The mythology of the Black criminal mother, along with the violent drug-dealing Black man, reinforces the unsubstantiated criminal targeting of African Americans as the leading drug offenders in America. The correlation between drug policies, media images, and racialized policing demonstrates the power of media to influence public perceptions and legislative agendas, which have crippled the social, cultural, and economic welfare of African Americans.

MASS MEDIA AND THE
BABY MAMA STEREOTYPE

On June 11, 2008, amid the presidential election campaigns, Fox News termed Michelle Obama as "Obama's Baby Mama," which sparked outrage and heavy criticism against the news network. During an interview with Fox News contributor Michelle Malkin where the topic of discussion was whether Michelle Obama was unfairly being targeted and criticized, the graphic "Outraged liberals: Stop picking on Obama's baby mama" was branded across the bottom of the newscast. Right as Malkin argued that there was nothing unfair about criticizing what Michelle Obama said on the campaign trail, but what *would* be unfair and result in backlash would be people taking "cheap shots" at Michelle Obama, the network took a cheap shot at Michelle Obama with the graphic. A term generally reserved for single unwed African American mothers, *baby mama* has been used in the media and politics to criticize Black mothers as illegitimate and incapable of caring for their children. Baby mamas are often represented as uneducated and economically impoverished and are also characterized as very confrontational with the father(s) of their child(ren) as they consistently battle over child support. These women are depicted as self-indulging at the expense of their children, in that they are portrayed as using child support funds, including welfare, to adorn themselves with clothing, hair, and nails.

In 2008, the African American wife of presidential candidate Barack Obama was reduced to this falsified stereotype of Black motherhood. Yet, Michelle Obama does not fit the racist and sexist stereotype. Not only is she married to the father of her children, but she is a highly educated lawyer, is economically wealthy, and does not represent herself as self-indulgent. Yet, this trope of Black womanhood has proven to be universally applied to Black females as they are perceived as unsuitable for motherhood. As Black feminist scholar Patricia Hill Collins (2006) argues, Black women have been grossly miscategorized as unfit for motherhood, yet the same racialized framing of motherhood classifies White mothers as best fit for motherhood in American society:

> In the politicized climate of late 20th century America, the issue of which women are "real" mothers best suited for the tasks of reproducing both the American population and the alleged values of the U.S. nation-state takes on added importance. "Real" has many meanings, such as authentic, genuine, indisputable, and true. "Real" also has physical connotations, meaning concrete, tangible, and material. Another constellation of meanings of "real" refers to sincerity—earnest, honest, truthful, trustworthy, and reliable. Within these intersecting meanings of "real," binary thinking constructs certain groups of women of the right social class, race, and citizenship status as "real" mothers who are worthy and fit for the job. Affluent, married, White, and holding American citizenship, "real" mothers are those who fit cultural criteria for idealized motherhood. Against these idealized "real" mothers, other categories of women of the wrong social class, marital status, race, and citizenship status are judged to be less fit and less worthy to be mothers. Within this intellectual framework, women deemed fit to be "real" mothers encounter state-supported family-planning options that support their contributions as mothers to national well-being. In contrast, those deemed unfit to be "real" mothers experience reproductive policies that are markedly different. (p. 55)

This racially biased representation of motherhood then renders Black women of all economic classes, educational levels, and marital statuses as not suitable for motherhood (Collins, 2006). Thus, the Fox News labeling of Michelle Obama as a baby mama illuminates the embedded racism and sexism against Black women in the media, politics, and American society in general. But how did we transition to this racist label of Black motherhood?

The baby mama caricature was created as an extension of the welfare queen stereotype post–American welfare reform of 1996. As discussed in

Chapter 1, the introduction of the Personal Responsibility and Work Opportunity Reconciliation Act of 1996 signified a departure from supporting families' basic needs to a work-based assistance program that penalized individuals and families for being and remaining in poverty. The new program, called Temporary Assistance to Needy Families (TANF), replaced the Aid to Families with Dependent Children (AFDC) federal assistance program and added new restrictions and work and/or educational advancement requirements. To garner public support for his new initiative, President Bill Clinton's marketing approach modeled that of Ronald Reagan in 1976, where he used the faces of Black women and the unjust welfare dependency stereotype to rationalize the need for restructuring how the federal government provided aid to families. To cement his claim that Black women were in need of federally sanctioned reform, he solicited the participation of Black women in his public announcement. In particular, he used Black mothers who were former aid recipients to speak to the legitimacy and urgent need for the policy reform in order to force Black women to take "personal responsibility" and act independently to meet their and their dependent children's basic needs. Thus, posing Lillie Harden, an African American mother and former welfare aid recipient, center stage at the press release of the TANF program demonstrates the racialized propaganda embedded in American politics and its inherent marriage to mass media.

Paired with this ideology was the promotion of a sexually irresponsible Black woman who had children with men who could not assume financial responsibility for their offspring. The act was supposedly designed to increase family and marriage stability among Americans and decrease the number of children born in single-parent households, which was assumed to be a leading determinant in recipients' need for aid. The act was also designed to reduce dependency on welfare and increase employment while simultaneously reducing child poverty. However, as noted by Robert Hill (2007) in "The Impact of Welfare Reform on Black Families," the welfare reform act of 1996 was not a major contributor in the household dynamics for Black families. Hill observes that although Black families on welfare were on the decline from 1971 to 1991, African American single-parent households increased from 31% to 46%. Thus, the opposite direction of the trends illustrates a faulty correlation between welfare dependency and single parenthood. In fact, according to Hill, in 1991 only a small percentage (18%) of African Americans were on public assistance, despite the looming myth that Black women were the face of welfare. Policy makers' refusal to acknowledge other social and political factors impacting Black families' household composition, such as mass incarceration as discussed earlier, only further bolsters the claim that reducing welfare dependency would increase family stability and childhood poverty.

Coinciding with the shifts in legislative policies were increased images and messages of African American women as single, unwed mothers. These images were overly publicized to validate the unsupported assumption that (1) African American women were dependent on welfare aid, and (2) welfare dependency resulted in single-parent households. Thus, the baby mama was born. In films that focused on Black mothers as well as films that depicted Black family and community dynamics, the image of the illegitimate single Black mother prevailed. For example, *Boyz n the Hood* (1991), written and directed by John Singleton, tells the story of three African American male friends and their experiences growing up in South Central Los Angeles at a time when drugs and gun violence are on the rise. The film provides three depictions of the Black mother: (1) the educated well-to-do Black mother who leaves the child-rearing of her son to his father after their divorce, (2) the low-income single Black mother surrounded by violence and crime, and (3) the teenage Black mother who is left to mother her son alone after the murder of his father. Reva is first introduced as a single mother who is concerned for the welfare of her son, Tre, after he gets into a fight at school. As a result, Reva decides to send Tre to live with his socially conscious father, Jason, in South Central. Once back with his father, who is portrayed as a disciplinarian who seeks to instill responsibility in his son, Tre immediately witnesses the cruel effects of his impoverished neighborhood. Heavy policing, lethal gang violence, drug abuse, and teenage pregnancy all plague the community. Brenda is the single mother to Tre's best friend Ricky, who is the star running back at Crenshaw High School, and his brother Doughboy, who is a member of a local gang and is newly released from prison. Shanice is Ricky's girlfriend and mother to his young son, and they all live with his mother, Brenda.

As the film develops, we watch the deteriorating conditions of their community explode as both Ricky and Doughboy are murdered. Shanice is left to parent without a father to her son, and Brenda now has to help raise her grandson. In all three cases, Black motherhood is represented as compromised, unforgiving, and cloaked in destruction. Shanice's character embodies the stereotype of the irresponsible and hypersexual Black girl who has children she cannot take care of, while Brenda is portrayed as the poor ghetto-stricken mother who cannot protect her children and raises criminals. Although Reva is economically self-sufficient, she is pictured as the sapphire stereotype whose career displaces her parental responsibility. Images such as these were used to advance the idea that Black women were single mothers because of their inability to make healthy mate selection decisions and because of their pathological culture. Yet, the social, political, and economic conditions of America, which drastically devastated the state of Black communities, are rarely underscored in the media. Mass incarceration and economic disinvestment in

Black communities are rarely accounted for when representing Black family dynamics, and collectivism and shared child-rearing practices are most certainly not discussed as cultural models of child care. Instead, Black mothers have been overwhelmingly reduced to the baby mama stereotype.

A barrage of representation of Black single mothers as baby mamas continued to flood the media in the 1990s through the 2000s. Also, the companion to the baby mama, the "baby daddy," was illuminated. Television shows like *Jerry Springer* (Dominick et al., 1991–2018) overwhelmingly cast African Americans as violent, hypersexual, and in frequent disagreement over paternity and parental responsibility. Hundreds of African American cast members would appear on the show to seek paternity and lie detector tests and to confront loved ones about cheating. The popularity of the *Jerry Springer* show validated these representations of African Americans, and the show became known for violent and socially outrageous depictions of Blacks. Other shows such as *Maury* (Faulhaber & Povich, 1991–2022) also disproportionately cast African Americans for segments on paternity and cheating.

Rap artists also started broadcasting the baby mama and baby daddy stereotypes in music lyrics and videos. In 1997, B-Rock and the Bizz released their rap song "My Baby Daddy," which presented a glorified depiction of the stereotypical "ghetto" baby mama. The chorus, "Who that is, my baby daddy," was sung throughout the rap and became a popular slogan to describe Black fathers who were not married to the mother(s) of their children. Krazy's "I Hate My Baby Mama" from his album *My Krazy World* (1998) presents the baby mama and baby daddy caricatures as confrontational, financially selfish, and parentally irresponsible. The chorus—"I hate my baby mama, don't need my baby mama, can't stand my baby mama, dislike my baby mama"—represents the Black family dynamic as dysfunctional and antagonistic. The chorus is followed by lyrics that explain the rationale for their feelings of resentment and anguish. Krazy's lyrics go on to place the baby daddy within the tropes of financial incompetence and sexual recklessness. The second verse of the rap song presents the position of the woman and her assessment of her baby daddy.

The messages found in various rap songs mirror the racist sentiments in American society regarding the Black family. Some hip-hop scholars have argued that this is not by coincidence but instead is a part of the commercial takeover of hip-hop by predominantly White-owned corporations that shifted the audience appeal of rap from a Black audience to a White audience (Bynoe, 2004; Rose, 1994; The Black Dot, 2005). In altering the marketing direction of hip-hop, rap music content began to almost exclusively reflect racial stereotypes of Blackness (Bynoe, 2004; M. Gammage, 2015; The Black Dot, 2005). Thus it is not surprising to find hyperemphasis on Black baby mamas at the same time as public policies were being enacted to reduce single-parent households' dependency on governmental aid.

The baby mama stereotype did not decimate with the turn of the century; instead, the media continued to portray the Black mother as a baby mama. In 2001, *Baby Boy* was released as a film chronicling the life of an African American male, Jody, struggling to sustain employment and healthy relationships with his mother and the mothers of his children. Written and directed by John Singleton, the producer of *Boyz n the Hood*, *Baby Boy* revitalized the baby mama and baby daddy characters. Ten years after *Boyz n the Hood*, African American women were still being represented as chronically unfit baby mamas. Jody's 36-year-old mother, Juanita, is a single African American woman who lost one son and is still housing her adult son Jody. Yvette is portrayed as the on-again, off-again girlfriend of Jody and the mother of his son JoJo. Yvette is employed and largely supporting Jody, who sporadically works. However, she is not satisfied with the state of their relationship and consistently requests that Jody honor his commitment to her and their child. Peanut, whom he frequently engages for sexual pleasure, is the mother of Jody's daughter. After learning of Jody's affairs, Yvette confronts Jody, which erupts into a physical altercation between the two. This causes Yvette to change the locks at her apartment to prevent Jody from returning. The couple argue in front of their young son over the locks, and Jody decides to return to the other women in his life, his mother and his other baby mama. When Yvette's ex-boyfriend, Rodney, forcibly moves into her apartment after he is released from prison, and tries to sexually assault her, Yvette seeks the aid of Jody. But Rodney attempts to kill Jody, though he is unsuccessful. Jody and his friend plan to kill Rodney and are successful. After this situation, Jody officially moves in with Yvette, and the couple becomes pregnant with another child. In the film the characters are represented as lacking sound judgment, moral aptitude, and family stability. Black women are portrayed as irresponsible in their personal and parenting relationships. In general, the Black family is depicted as culturally dysfunctional.

After the "Obama Baby Mama" statement, in 2015 a documentary film titled *72%: A Baby Mama Crisis* was released as an investigative look into the alarming statistic that 72% of African American children are born out of wedlock (Garcia et al., 2015). The film explores the 2013 data of single-mother households in African American communities as an epidemic afflicting the well-being of African American children. Although the documentary explores some sociopolitical factors, such as slavery, mass incarceration, and public assistance reforms, that have been correlated with declines in marriage rates, the documentary places much of the burden on Black women and men for making poor family planning decisions, especially in cases of economic hardship. What is often unexplored are the general declines in marriage rates among all races (M. Gammage, 2015) and the presence of cohabitating parents and stepparents. Also, the discourse around Black women seems to ignore the high value of having children among Black women. As noted by Niara Sudarkasa (1997) in "African American Families and Family Values,"

> First it must be understood that, historically, African American women, like their African ancestors, placed a very high value on having children, and most of them wanted to have their own children even if they adopted or reared others. . . . Second, it has to be understood that because polygamy (or, more accurately, polygyny—the term for plural wives) was not and is not a legal form of marriage in the United States, unequal gender ratios among African Americans living in many areas meant that not all marriageable women would be able to find husbands during their prime childbearing years. (p. 21)

As I argue in *Representations of Black Women in the Media*:

> Lacking an appropriate cultural understanding of the Black family, America's institutions began to criminalize the Black mother and penalize her for her attempt at motherhood. Reinforcing these stereotypes, the media began to over produce programs that displayed Black women as get-over baby mammas or careerists not suitable for motherhood. These types of misrepresentations contributed to negative social attitudes describing Black women as unfit mothers. (M. Gammage, 2015, p. 116)

The film, like many media productions, buys into the assumption that a child born out of wedlock is automatically assumed to live in a single-parent household, which when Black is presumed ineffective in child-rearing.

Ironically, when images of White women as single mothers have been constructed in the media, the conditions of their motherhood status and economic well-being diverge significantly from images of Black single mothers. For instance, in 2008's *Baby Mama*, White single motherhood is represented as a logical and responsible choice (McCullers, 2008). Kate Holbrook, played by Tina Fey, is a highly successful businesswoman who elects to hire a surrogate to carry her child, after she learns that she has a high risk of infertility. However, unbeknownst to Kate, the fertilization process was unsuccessful, but the surrogate deceives Kate until she discovers that she is in fact pregnant with her own child. Later, Kate discovers that she too is pregnant with her boyfriend's child, and the couple becomes engaged. The two women become best friends and support each other while child-rearing. The representation of White single mothers has been markedly different and less damning than the images of Black single mothers. In fact, White single motherhood is represented as a conscious choice and backed by economic security, whereas Black single motherhood is broadcasted as an unintended side effect of hypersexuality and is perceived as financially incompetent. The baby mama character, a stereotype traditionally reserved for African American women, has also been extended to African women. The 2018 film *Baby Mamas* follows the life of four African female professionals who all find themselves living as baby mamas (Zwane, 2018). The men in their lives are portrayed as irresponsible and undependable. Through sisterhood they support each other as they seek love and fulfillment in their lives.

The framing of Black single mothers as illegitimate baby mamas continues to affect the well-being of Black mothers in American society. The media has consistently sensationalized Black single parenthood as pathological. The popularity of the baby mama and baby daddy stereotypes has normalized the terms and made the stereotype commonplace. However, the understanding of single motherhood among Whites, especially economically self-sufficient White women, is treated as more socially acceptable. But the facts speak for themselves: Single-parent households are on the incline in America (Livingston, 2018), and while African American children are disproportionately raised in nonmarried (single-parent) households, White single-parent households outnumber Black ones (Kids Count Data Center, n.d.). Yet Black mothers are almost singularly portrayed as the poster child for single motherhood. This racial categorization of motherhood fits with Patricia Hill Collins's (2006) framework of "fit" mothers, where White working women and White single women are still considered more fit for motherhood than all Black women.

PUBLIC POLICY IN THE FUTURE

In this chapter, I have discussed how public policies and media images have weaponized Black women and characterized Black womanhood/motherhood as criminal acts. The intersection of race, gender, class, and public policy has repeatedly yielded successful political scare tactics designed against Black women, with the intention of advancing anti-Black public policies. Both Republicans and Democrats, along with mass media and Black media productions, have participated in the construction of racialized, sexist, and classist representations of Black women without factual evidence to support the systemic targeting of Black women as the poster child for public reform. This pattern of media racism against Black women to validate public policy reforms is predictive of future policy initiatives. If we pay close attention to the current representations of Black women in the media, particularly as it relates to their health and social behaviors, we may be able to anticipate the next wave of social reforms that endanger the lives of African Americans.

The growing volume of media representing Black women as chronically unhealthy and in need of control presents a new dilemma for Black women and runs the risk of inciting public policy backlash that disproportionately targets Black women for reform. Over the last 10 years, we have experienced a surge in television dramas and reality television shows starring Black women. The next few chapters critically analyze the leading television series featuring Black females in order to assess the representations of Black women in the media and how the current portrayals of Black womanhood impact the lives and well-being of African American females, which may be revealing of the current and next systematic attack against African Americans.

CHAPTER 3

Unhealthy Representations of Black Women in Television Dramas

The rise in health disparities among Black women in the United States has caused much concern surrounding factors contributing to the disproportionate negative health realities experienced by African American females. During the 1990s and early 2000s, many researchers began to compare content of media starring Black women, especially rap music videos, viewership of those videos, and social perceptions of Black women. Given the increase in media starring Black women, it is important that we evaluate contemporary media imagery of Black womanhood in order to determine if the present-day content advances racist ideologies and maintains a negative impact on Black women's overall wellness. Although the music video remains a leading venue through which media imagery of Black women is broadcasted, television dramas starring Black women have recently become one of the highest rated media forms advertising messages about Black womanhood. Therefore, a critical investigation of the content of television dramas starring Black women is necessary to determine if such content negatively contributes to faulty racialized perceptions of Black women and to sociopolitical and economic prejudices.

Television dramas starring Black women have unidimensionally represented Black women as modern-day stereotypes (M. Gammage, 2015). These stereotyped portrayals not only broadcast negative personal character traits as Black values, but also promote unhealthy lifestyles as the singular image of Black womanhood. In television dramas starring Black women, Black women are shown experiencing high levels of stress in their jobs and personal lives, experiencing physical harm or threat, having high alcohol consumption, and exhibiting high-risk sexual behaviors, all of which are presented as self-inflicted. These unhealthy lifestyle portrayals advance a monolithic notion that Black women are unconcerned about their health and the health of others. In leading television dramas starring Black women, the lead Black women have all been involved in sexual affairs with married men, as well as nonmonogamous sexual relationships, and are frequently shown consuming large amounts of alcohol before engaging in intercourse. These are the exact behaviors that researchers are now attributing to increases in sexually transmitted infections and heart and liver disease, among other health concerns. The covertly sensationalized representation of Black women as antihealth represents Black womanhood as pathologically dysfunctional and a risk to the public. Representations such as these validate the public perception that Black women are a public health crisis and need intervention and control. Hikes (2004) theorizes that for non-Blacks, stereotyped imagery promotes faulty representations of Blacks, and this is even more severe "for young Black girls whose self worth and self esteem are frequently being shaped by these unrealistic and harmful images of black womanhood" (p. 40). Thus, the overpromotion of high-risk behaviors among Black women in the media can contribute to misperceptions of Black womanhood, microaggressions against Black women, public policies that aid in the subjugation of Black women and girls, and a whole host of other injustices against Black females.

TELEVISION DRAMAS STARRING BLACK WOMEN

Television dramas are designed as dramatic fictional programs. Each episode is filled with intense scenarios that escalate and come to a head in the series finale. Television dramas starring Black women achieve the exact goal of dramatizing the lives of Black women and successfully portray Black women living unhealthy lifestyles as a personal and social choice. In this chapter, I analyze three popular television dramas starring Black women—*Scandal* (Rhimes et al., 2012–2018), *Being Mary Jane* (Akil et al., 2013–2019), and *How to Get Away With Murder* (Rhimes et al., 2014–2020)—in order to illustrate the extent to which these dramas broadcast antihealth behaviors among Black women. These shows were selected because they were the highest rated television dramas in 2017 and 2018 starring a lead Black female character. Additional criteria included network television shows that were on air for three or more years and that had four or more complete seasons.

First, we examine *Scandal*, a highly acclaimed television drama starring a lead Black woman, created by Shonda Rhimes, which debuted April 5, 2012. *Scandal* details the life of a crisis manager and the high-powered politicians whose challenging circumstances she helps to address. Olivia

Pope (Kerry Washington), the lead female character, is the head of her own crisis management firm and is charged with the task of fixing emergency and potentially career-ending crises for wealthy high-powered clients. Pope is an attractive powerful woman, yet surprisingly she is involved in an extramarital affair with the president of the United States, a White man. Threatened by exposure, Pope and President Fitzgerald engage in a long-term partially secret affair. Searching for stability, Pope turns to her family, but she later finds out that her father is the head of a top-secret governmental organization, B-613, which uses criminal and terroristic actions to control world governments. Her mother, whom she believes is dead, is actually alive and an imprisoned terrorist. Soon Pope finds herself involved in her own scandals and eventually ends up kidnapped and held for ransom. Fearing that she cannot trust anyone, she turns to the arms of Jake, a navy captain and friend of the president, with whom she develops a casual sexual relationship. Realizing that her feelings for the president have not wavered, Pope ends her affair with Jake and turns her focus back to her crisis management firm. In later seasons, Pope devotes her efforts to taking down her father and B-613. Successful to an extent, Pope soon finds herself the head of B-613 and oversees criminal and immoral activities that turn her team against her and result in her being ousted from her crisis management firm and B-613.

The second television drama, *Being Mary Jane*, premiered on Black Entertainment Television (BET) on January 7, 2014, and was created and produced by Mara Brock Akil. The lead character, Mary Jane Paul, played by Gabrielle Union, is a successful news anchor for Satellite News Channel's (SNC) show *TalkBack*. The television drama chronicles Mary Jane's life as an educated single Black woman in search of love, happiness, and family. Although success is growing in her career, Mary Jane discovers that finding a life partner and having children may not come as quickly or easily as she hoped. Even still, Mary Jane remains committed to her immediate family and offers them support and guidance as they navigate their own journeys, which is not always welcomed or well received. Her friendships are often put to the test as they collide with Mary Jane's love affairs. To soothe her sorrows at times, Mary Jane turns to retail therapy and alcohol. In looking for love, Mary Jane finds herself involved, unknowingly, with a married man, Andre. Although she attempts to end the relationship, Mary Jane finds it hard to break things off and willingly carries out a sexual affair with Andre. Confronted with the ills of her relationship, Mary Jane finally puts an end to her affair and quickly attempts to rekindle her relationship with her ex-boyfriend, David. To her surprise, David is in a relationship and is expecting a baby; despite this, Mary Jane wonders if their relationship could work. Realizing that she and David are no longer on the same page, Mary Jane journeys on to find love and career advancement. She moves to New York in the hopes of advancing her career and securing a lifelong partner, but that too proves to be a difficult task as she is portrayed making decisions that derail her goals.

The final television drama starring a lead Black female character under investigation is Shonda Rhimes's second prime-time television drama starring a Black woman, *How to Get Away With Murder*, which debuted on ABC on September 25, 2014. The storyline follows the life of Professor Annalise Keating (Viola Davis), who is a criminal lawyer and professor of defense law. She is married to a fellow professor, a White male with whom she has no children. Professor Keating's unique teaching style changes her students' knowledge of the law by having them practically apply what they learn in class to her real trial cases. As the series develops, Keating and her students end up directly involved in murders that they must cover up to keep from going to prison. Attempting to help her students, Keating uses her sexual affair with Officer Nate Leahy to gain inside information, and she later frames him for the murder of her husband, although she later assists with his exoneration. As her life and work become intertwined and highly stressful, Keating is frequently filmed overconsuming alcohol to the point where she runs the risk of losing it all. Fired from her job at the university and facing disbarment, Keating takes on a class action suit against the state of Pennsylvania for failing to provide adequate legal counsel on the grounds of race to minority low-income defendants. The class action suit proves effective on two fronts: First, she is successful at winning the case for her clients who are then granted the right to retry their cases; and second, Keating is able to restore her reputation as a powerhouse lawyer. The show was one of the highest rated television shows for Thursday and was nominated for and received several awards. According to Nielsen (2017), "Sixty-nine percent of the show's viewership is non-black." In addition, "Sixty-eight percent of viewership is non-black for ABC's 'Scandal,' another 'Shondaland' thriller featuring Kerry Washington as a media consultant to the president," as detailed earlier (Nielsen, 2017). Both shows garnered mainstream appeal that made them the highest rated shows on ABC by 2018.

NORMALIZING HIGH-STRESS LIFESTYLES
FOR BLACK WOMEN IN THE MEDIA

High-stress lifestyles among lead Black female characters in television dramas are a normal occurrence in the 21st-century media. Three shows—*Scandal*, *How to Get Away With Murder*, and *Being Mary Jane*—portray the lead Black female character as overburdened with stress in her job and personal life without any apparent health consequences. In fact, the high frequency of such portrayals connotes a normalcy in this representation; that is, high-stress lifestyles are a regular reality for Black women. However, in portraying Black women's lives as extremely stressful, these television dramas fail to include real-life health consequences for living high-stress lives.

In *Scandal*, high stress appears to come standard with the job. As a crisis manager for high-powered politicians and public figures, Olivia Pope is routinely faced with high levels of stress in the workplace. Whether aiding a client in restaging a murder scene, attempting to destroy a secret spy organization, or helping a political candidate secure office, Pope's job embodies great pressure and stress, which at times has threatened her own safety and freedom. Yet, Pope takes on client after client, and no matter how stressful the case, Pope always shows up ready to work. At the end of each day, she turns to a bottle of wine to relax.

Similar to Pope's job, Professor Annalise Keating's work as a criminal defense lawyer and criminal law professor, in *How to Get Away With Murder*, has afforded her a fair share of highly stressful cases. Keating is frequently shown aiding clients who admit their guilt, which has proven to be extremely stressful. In one case, when the client refuses to take a plea, Keating slaps the client and forces him to take the deal. This incident is captured on courthouse video, after which Keating is suspended and her job is threatened. If that is not enough, Keating has elected to become involved in the criminal actions of her student employees. In two different seasons, her law students murder someone, and she helps to cover it up. This has frequently resulted in Keating becoming a suspect and being placed under criminal investigation. In an attempt to manage the stress of her job, Keating frequently turns to alcohol consumption to help her cope with the stress and fear of being arrested and incarcerated.

Finally, Mary Jane Paul in *Being Mary Jane* has also been portrayed as battling extreme stress in the workplace. Faced with potential unemployment, stereotypical labeling, and negative performance reviews, Mary Jane is consistently shown struggling to maintain professionalism and her sanity. After a car accident that severely injures Mary Jane's face, prior to which she was drinking alcohol, her employer considers replacing Mary Jane as lead anchor permanently (Season 3, Episode 3 [Akil, Goff, et al., 2015]). Instead of healing after several major surgeries, Mary Jane enacts a plan to quickly return to work in order to secure her job. Her health and recovery come second to work, and she runs the risk of permanent scars. Luckily for Mary Jane, she heals *and* keeps her job.

While all three lead female characters frequently encounter extreme levels of stress in their jobs, it should also be noted that the same levels of stress are present in their personal lives. For Mary Jane Paul, family dependency, the suicide of her best friend, and her failed search for love and children all contribute to increased stress in her personal life. The climax of Mary Jane's stressful lifestyle is revealed in Season 2 when she begins to urinate in bed while asleep. During Episode 2 (Akil, Andries, & Akil, 2015), after Mary Jane's home alarm is triggered, she is scared and decides to spend the night at the house of the man she is dating, Sheldon. While asleep, Mary Jane once again urinates in the bed while sleeping next to Sheldon. Embarrassed, Mary Jane attempts to explain what caused this behavior, but Sheldon sees through her excuses about work and challenges her to address the stresses in her personal life.

How to Get Away With Murder's Annalise Keating has also had her fair share of extreme stress in her personal life. During Season 1, Episode 1 (Nowalk & Offer, 2014), Keating discovers that her husband is cheating with a student who ends up dead, and she suspects her husband of murdering the pregnant student. If marital infidelity is not stressful enough, Keating then discovers that her students have accidently killed her husband in her home, and she decides to help her students cover up her husband's murder. Throughout the series, several scenes are dedicated to highlighting Keating's stressful personal life. She is filmed being asked to aid her boyfriend's wife in her suicide, she is stalked by a murder suspect, and later she is shot by one of her students in order to cover up a crime scene. By the premiere of Season 3 (Nowalk & D'Elia, 2016), Keating is harassed at work with flyers posted labeling her a murderer, causing the university to place her on probation during their investigation of these claims. Later in the season, in Episode 4 (Swafford & Sullivan, 2016), Keating is suspended from work due to ethical violations stemming from her slapping a client. Threatened with losing her job, Keating admits to the court that she has a drinking problem, which spirals out of control throughout the season. These illustrations of personal trauma have led to extreme levels of stress for Keating, and high-level consumption of alcohol is presented as a viable means of coping. Instead, her abuse of alcohol only heightens her stress.

For Olivia Pope, of *Scandal* fame, a similar fate is faced. As stated earlier, Pope is involved in a long-term sexual affair with the president of the United States, who is married. The pressure to keep their affair concealed only intensifies her anxiety. In addition, Pope discovers that her only two relatives, with whom she appears to have a connection, are living secret lives. Her mother, whom she believes died when she was a child, is actually alive and in government custody for terrorist activities. Pope's father is in fact the head of a secret spy organization and frequently employs male workers to form false relationships with Pope in order for him to control her. Concerned about both her parents, Pope makes it her mission to destroy the spy organization and capture and imprison her mother. The extraordinary amount of stress Pope experiences is often managed with drinking alcohol and engaging in sexual affairs to mask the pain and betrayal that she is experiencing.

The extreme levels of professional and personal stress faced by lead Black female characters in television dramas connotes an abnormal number of stressors. High levels of stress have been linked to health issues such as heart disease, hypertension, and diabetes and psychological issues such as depression (Boardman & Alexander, 2011). According to the Centers for Disease Control and Prevention (CDC, 2022), heart disease is the leading cause of death for Black women, and life stressors increase this risk. Yet, for Black women in television dramas, they appear to be immune from all stress-related health consequences. This is an unhealthy representation of Black womanhood, and these images misrepresent high-stress lifestyles as habitual and acceptable for Black women. Further evidence of high-stress lifestyles among lead Black female characters is detailed in the next section.

SAFETY CONCERNS AND PHYSICAL VIOLENCE

Physical violence and the potential threat to one's livelihood are additional antihealth issues that can increase health concerns for those affected. Physical violence not only causes bodily harm but may also lead to emotional and psychological distress. Similarly, threats to careers and familihood are linked to physical and psychological health problems. In television dramas starring Black women, the lead Black female characters unfortunately battle with threats to their lives, careers, and families. This has led to anxiety, heavy drinking, emotional instability, and increased stress among the lead Black female characters. The weight of gun violence, stalking, blackmail, and kidnapping has fallen heavily on the lead Black female characters in 21st-century television dramas. These traumatic safety concerns can cause health problems and have resulted in unhealthy behaviors such as alcoholism.

Mary Jane Paul, in *Being Mary Jane*, is frequently displayed as expressing concern for her safety. Several scenes capture Mary Jane pulling out her baseball bat as she walks to her front door. Mary Jane also is shown using her home alarm and calling the police when she feels unsafe. But when Mary Jane is threatened and her job is in jeopardy, she does not exercise the same cautions. At the end of Season 2 of *Being Mary Jane*, Mary Jane discovers, while driving, that her best friend and former boyfriend have secretly been having a long-term sexual affair (Akil & Akil, 2015b). Surprised and hurt by this news, Mary Jane loses control of her car and is in a car accident that causes severe damage to her face. At the start of Season 3, Mary Jane is hospitalized, and it is revealed that she had alcohol in her bloodstream, which threatens her job; and her alcohol usage at work is used to validate reviews of her continued employment. As this occurs, Mary Jane is surprisingly visited by the driver of the other car in the accident who threatens Mary Jane and extorts her for $25,000 (Season 3, Episode 1 [Akil & Akil, 2015c]). The woman, Cece, begins to stalk Mary Jane and threatens to expose her with a lawsuit. Concerned about losing her job, Mary Jane pays Cece, but this does not end the stalking and blackmail. Eventually, Mary Jane gets the police involved when Cece continues to extort her for money and time. Throughout these events, Mary Jane's health appears to not be affected, and she goes on living life without any health consequences.

Scandal's Olivia Pope is another lead Black female character who has experienced constant threats to her safety. Given that Pope is a crisis manager for high-powered political figures, it comes as no surprise that the job frequently requires extra safety precautions. As a security measure, Pope employs a former military agent to work closely with her and to provide protection. However, on several occasions, Pope has required extra security and even armed guards outside of her home. Yet, when threat levels are reduced, Pope can enjoy her home life without security. On one evening, she is shown entertaining her guest Jake with music and alcohol. As Jake steps away to another room, Pope, with wineglass in hand, is suddenly abducted by a terrorist group and held captive. Jake returns to the living room to find wine spilled on the sofa and no sign of Pope (Season 4, Episode 10 [Rhimes & Verica, 2015]). Held in captivity, Pope hopes for rescue and plans her escape. Once she is able to execute her plan, she takes action. In order to escape, she must be willing to kill her abductors, and she is. After killing and injuring some of her abductors, Pope runs to find an exit. Unfortunately, she discovers that additional abductors are in the building and there is no way out. She soon learns of the terrorists' plan to sell her for profit. Pope puts her crisis management skills to work and tricks the men into an open public bid. Her employees and Jake find the auction and attempt to outbid other buyers. However, they are unsuccessful in winning the auction. Pope is sold to an unknown group, and an exchange is arranged. In Episode 13 (Mitchell & Zisk, 2015), Pope is scheduled to be traded for money. At the meet, she realizes that the buyer is a former employee, Stephen Finch, who has come to rescue her with an armed team of men. Enacting her own revenge, Pope takes Finch's gun and shoots her abductor in the leg, and when he falls, she begins to kick him until Finch moves her away. After this, Pope is able to return to her home. Struggling to cope with the reality of her experience, Pope turns to alcohol and forms a casual sexual relationship with a man whom she met at a bar. While her character seems to be exhibiting signs of post-traumatic stress disorder, she does not seek medical support and instead returns to work. The representation connotes a larger stereotype that African Americans do not seek mental health services or therapy and instead can overcome psychological and physical trauma with alcohol and sex, which further advance health risk.

As for Annalise Keating from *How to Get Away With Murder*, she too is routinely shown in high-risk safety scenarios. As a criminal defense attorney, Keating is around criminals on a routine basis. Surprisingly, however, she faces greater threats from her loved ones and her students. For instance, in Season 1, Episode 9 (Foley et al., 2014), during a heated argument with her husband, Sam, she and Sam shout insults at each other, and items are thrown around the house. Soon their argument escalates to physical violence when Sam puts his hands around her neck and proceeds to choke her. Still able to talk, Keating calls Sam out on her suspicion of him killing a student with whom he was having an affair. She believes that Sam enjoyed choking the student to death and dares him to kill her. Instead, Sam lets go of her and returns verbal assaults. She eventually leaves her home alive. This is not her first encounter with physical violence; during a flashback scene, she is threatened by a client and then attacked by the client and injured in a car accident, which results in the death of her unborn child (Season 2, Episode 14 [J. Lee et al., 2016]). During Season 2, Keating and her team are entangled in several murder cases, one of which is committed by her student. In order to cover up the student's murder, Keating devises a plan to frame a murder suspect from a case that she is working on. In order to execute her plan, she asks one of her students to shoot her, as they plan to blame the murder and her shooting on the suspect. Laurel, one of her student employees, does just that. Laurel takes the gun, aims it at Keating, and shoots her in the abdomen. The students all leave her lying on the floor in her own blood. Immediately, Keating realizes that the gunshot wound is much more severe than she anticipated; the plan was to shoot her in the leg (Season 2, Episode 9 [Foley et al., 2015]). She calls 911 for help and then passes out. Fortunately, Keating receives medical attention in enough time to save her life. During Episode 10 (J. Lee & Innes, 2016), we see that she arrives home from the hospital and has a long way to recover. Forced to sleep on her sofa, because she cannot climb stairs, she must take several different prescription drugs to aid her in her recovery. Soon she begins to abuse the drugs and starts to hallucinate. And in typical television drama fashion, the next day she suits up and returns to the courtroom.

The overrepresentation of Black women living unsafe lifestyles in television dramas starring Black women attempts to validate the assumption that Black women live dramatic lives and as a result invite safety risks into their lives. In all three television dramas discussed, the lead Black female characters put their careers before their safety, which results in major threats to their health and security. Although their lives have been threatened, all three characters somehow survive and live to work another day. This leads to another underlying assumption that Black women have superhuman strength and are resilient such that they are fully capable of handling and surviving high-risk attacks on their lives.

However, as noted by several researchers, violence against women calls for public concern and results in both physical and psychological effects. According to Krantz and Garcia-Moreno (2005), "Violence against women is now well recognized as a public health problem and human rights violation of worldwide significance. It is an important risk factor for women's ill health, with far reaching consequences for both their physical and mental health" (p. 818). Black women are not immune to this crisis. In fact, as noted by the United States Department of Justice, "Black and Hispanic females had a higher risk of experiencing a crime of violence than white and non-Hispanic females" (Bachman, 1994, p. 2). Therefore, portraying violence against Black women in television dramas as normal dismisses real-life health consequences of physical threats and violence. If internalized, these representations may not only influence how Black women address violence against themselves but also affect how the public responds to violence against Black women.

ALCOHOL CONSUMPTION AND ALCOHOLISM

High alcohol consumption and alcohol abuse are routinely displayed as normal lifestyle choices among lead Black female characters in television dramas. In fact, shows such as *Scandal, How to Get Away With Murder*, and *Being Mary Jane* represent alcohol consumption as a legitimate coping strategy for Black women. Not only do the lead Black female characters in these shows indulge in alcohol consumption to escape the stress of work and personal life, but these women also all find themselves turning to alcohol to lower their inhibition, which results in them electing to partake in risky sexual behaviors such as sexual affairs with strangers, sex with married men and coworkers, and cheating on their partners. Sales et al. (2012) report that "alcohol use can interfere with cognitive processing of information (e.g., inhibitory control, cognitive escape) and decrease perceptions of risk, which can in turn influence sexual decision making and increase the likelihood of risky sexual behaviors" (p. 2). Similar results are found when examining the drinking habits of lead Black women in television dramas.

In the television drama *How to Get Away With Murder*, the lead Black female character, Professor Annalise Keating, is frequently shown consuming alcohol. However, by Season 3, she must confront her struggles with alcohol and admit to abusing alcohol. After Professor Keating is recorded physically assaulting a client, the court sanctions her and suspends her license. Stressed by the legal consequences of her actions, she turns to heavy drinking and verbal assaults against her boyfriend Nate. She goes as far as physically pushing Nate and asking him to hit her. Recognizing her behavior has been largely influenced by her consumption of alcohol, Nate calls her out on being an alcoholic and tells her to get help (Season 3, Episode 4 [Swafford & Sullivan, 2016]). After this scene, their relationship comes to an end. Faced with being disbarred, Keating decides to admit that she is an alcoholic and agrees to attend a treatment program (Season 3, Episode 4 [Swafford & Sullivan, 2016]). Unbeknownst to the court, she is actually using alcoholism as a ploy to maintain her job after her misconduct; she does not in fact believe that she has a substance abuse issue. The court accepts Keating's admission of an addiction and requires her to seek help along with a mandatory requirement of not consuming alcohol.

Committed to keeping her job, in Episode 5 (J. Lee & Turner, 2016), Keating clears her home of several bottles of alcohol; dozens are hidden throughout the house. This process recalls memories of her dead husband, and she once again turns to consuming alcohol, to the point where she retrieves a bottle of vodka from the trash and begins to drink. Drunk, Keating dances throughout her home with the bottle. Physically burdened by her overconsumption of alcohol, she is shown vomiting and unable to control her own body or emotions as she cries to her student employee, who finds her drunk in her home. Her student helps her into bed, and Keating immediately falls asleep (Season 3, Episode 5 [J. Lee & Turner, 2016]). These instances illustrate her inability to refrain from drinking and thus confirm her addiction.

Running into Keating in an Alcoholics Anonymous meeting, the president of the university where she works urges her to get real help, to no avail. Instead, she turns to binge-eating junk food to cope. Even though Keating attempts to state that she is not really an alcoholic, several scenes show her uncontrollably overconsuming alcoholic beverages to the point where she is irrational and unsafe. As the pressures of work and personal life build, junk food proves to no longer work as a coping agent, and Keating finds herself in a store smelling the alcohol on the shelf. When stared at by a shopper, she feels exposed and ends up purchasing two arms' full of junk food (Season 3, Episode 8 [Balogun & Wilkinson, 2016]).

Concerned with a pending investigation of her ethical conduct, in Season 3, Episode 9 (Foley & D'Elia, 2016), Keating returns home with a bottle of vodka and begins to drink. Once again stressed by work and the mixing of personal with professional life, Keating turns to alcohol to help her cope. Gulping from the bottle, she begins to burn incriminating evidence, and recalls hurtful memories from her past. Drunk, she arrives at her employee Bonnie's house expressing fear of her pending investigation; it is unknown to the viewer how Keating has transitioned to Bonnie's house. Keating pulls out an unopened bottle of alcohol and continues to drink. Bonnie intervenes by feeding her food and escorting her to a bedroom to rest. Once in bed, the drunken Keating attempts to pull Bonnie in intimately and kisses her romantically. Bonnie eventually pulls away and instructs Keating to rest. The cycle of high alcohol consumption and risky behaviors has been proven to be a normal occurrence for character Annalise Keating. Yet, in almost every scene after Keating is displayed as drunk, the next day she is ready to work and prepared for trial. Unfortunately, it appears that although faced with penalties, Keating repeatedly evades all real consequences of her actions, and therefore her heavy alcohol consumption appears to be an effective coping strategy. Misrepresentations such as this further validate the myth that Black women "can withstand any amount of pain and keep on working" (G. McGee et al., 1985, p. 7). Thus, this myth and the representation of this myth "may have significant consequences for African-American women who have substance use disorders—delaying treatment, sacrificing self to care for others, and negating the need for preventive health care and substance abuse treatment" (Substance Abuse and Mental Health Services Administration, 2009).

Scandal's Olivia Pope is another high-powered businesswoman who consistently battles high levels of stress. As a casual coping strategy after each day of work, but especially after a very stressful day at work, Pope routinely consumes alcohol. After surviving a kidnapping from a terrorist group in Season 4, she returns home and tries to busy herself with work. However, the memories of her kidnapping overwhelm her, and she turns to alcohol to help her cope and move forward. Scenes show Pope drinking alcohol directly from the bottle while recalling memories from being held captive. During the day, she pours herself into her work in order to take her mind off her personal drama. However, she eventually must return home, and when she does, she is faced with cleaning her wine-stained couch that was soiled when she was abducted from her home (Season 4, Episode 15 [Fish & Liddi-Brown, 2015]). After cleaning, Pope tries to get back to her normal routine and sits on her couch with a bowl of popcorn and a glass of wine (Season 4, Episode 15 [Fish & Liddi-Brown, 2015]). Concerned for Pope's recovery, her former boyfriend, President Fitzgerald, recruits Jake, another one of her former boyfriends, to spy on Pope and report on her recovery. Jake describes her as "mentally a mess" (Season 4, Episode 16 [Byrne & McCrane, 2015]). He reports that Pope is using alcohol to cope with her traumatizing experience and also holds a gun nearby for protection:

> She is getting out in the world more these days. She picks up a couple of bottles of wine almost every night. (Season 4, Episode 16 [Byrne & McCrane, 2015])

And when feeling lonely, Pope turns to alcohol and nonmonogamous sexual relationships. Pope's reliance on alcohol to help her cope once again promotes an unhealthy response to personal stress and trauma, which only heightens the health risk of individuals who practice and/or adopt this lifestyle.

High alcohol use is also frequently filmed in *Being Mary Jane*, where Mary Jane Paul uses alcohol consumption casually, during times of stress, and as a means to gain encouragement to engage in risky sexual behavior. Throughout the series, Mary Jane's drinking has attracted the attention of her friends and loved ones. During Season 2, Niecy, Mary Jane's niece, accuses her of being an alcoholic after finding several almost empty bottles of alcohol hidden in Mary Jane's bathroom cabinets (Season 2, Episode 3 [Akil, Anderson, & King, 2015]). When Niecy confronts Mary Jane about her alcohol usage, Mary Jane denies that she has a problem, and the women begin to argue.

Mary Jane and Niecy's conversation is brought to an end, but Niecy voices her concern for Mary Jane's drinking to Mary Jane's father. Mary Jane explains that she keeps the alcohol in her private bathroom as a safety precaution for Niecy's children, who are temporarily living with Mary Jane (Episode 4 [Graham & King, 2015]). She also explains that while she drinks after work to help her relax, she does not have a drinking problem:

> Yes, I have a drink after work to relax me. But how is that any different from when you used to have a drink every day after work when you would pour yourself a scotch? Yes, I drink tequila because my mind races at night and I need to turn it off, so I can get some rest to get up early to go to work. (Season 2, Episode 4 [Graham & King, 2015])

Even though Mary Jane rejects Niecy's assertion that she is an alcoholic, signs of dependency are revealed when Mary Jane indulgences in alcohol while undergoing an outpatient reproductive medical procedure to extract her eggs, which requires her not to consume alcohol. By the end of the episode, Mary Jane drinks several glasses of alcohol. It is later revealed that Mary Jane's attempt to preserve her ability to have children was unsuccessful, which leaves the audience wondering if her consumption of alcohol during treatment was a contributing factor. To cope with this news, Mary Jane turns to a bottle of alcohol and casual sex.

Additionally, Mary Jane's alcohol consumption has been linked to aggressive behaviors such as verbal attacks on others. During Season 2, Episode 1 (Akil & Akil, 2015a), Mary Jane is hosting a dinner party, with heavy drinking, and engaging her guest in political debates. Their conversation begins to focus on family as a hindrance to fully enjoying the perks of one's own personal success. When Mary Jane's brother disagrees with her, she verbally insults him in front of her guest and questions his manhood.

> Let me be really really really real. I would have used your ass as an example but you're sitting here. Yeah. You sling your penis to every miff in Virginia Highlands to push off a dime bag. You whack off in your parents' house. (Season 2, Episode 1 [Akil & Akil, 2015a])

Mary Jane's brother and guest are shocked by her actions, and her brother returns insults to Mary Jane. The party is soon brought to an end, and some of her friendships also end.

The common denominator among these three lead Black female characters is that they all use alcohol as a coping mechanism to elevate the stress they experience in their day-to-day lives. A resulting effect of this behavior is that they partake in high-risk behaviors, with seemingly no consequences. Yet, according to the National Institute on Alcohol Abuse and Alcoholism (NIAAA, n.d.), consumption of alcohol over time or consuming large volumes of alcohol in a single use can have major health consequences ranging from brain complications to liver and pancreas diseases and even a variety of cancers. It is noted that the alcohol consumption and abuse can negatively affect the heart:

> Drinking a lot over a long time or too much on a single occasion can damage the heart, causing problems including:
>
> - Cardiomyopathy—Stretching and drooping of heart muscle
> - Arrhythmias—Irregular heart beat
> - Stroke
> - High blood pressure (NIAAA, n.d.)

This is especially concerning for Black women as heart disease is reported as the leading cause of death among African American women (CDC, 2022).

While none of the lead Black female characters in these television dramas have experienced health-related consequences due to their abuse of alcohol, it can be argued that they have in fact experienced social consequences. Annalise Keating, Olivia Pope, and Mary Jane Paul have all experienced relationship problems, strain on their relationships with their families and friends, and threats to their employment. Interestingly, none of these characters have legitimately confronted their usage of alcohol and factors contributing to their abuse of alcohol.

Keating, Pope, and Paul have all consistently had negative relationships with men, worked in Americanized business settings, experienced racism, and largely been separated from their extended families; although Mary Jane is connected to her family, she sees them as a financial and emotional burden. The characters' personal realities have not been addressed as factors contributing to their alcohol usage. Thus, their usage remains a common practice. By representing alcohol abuse as an acceptable social norm among Black women, television dramas promote high-stress lifestyles and risky behaviors as the culture of Black women. Drinking problems have been linked to increased practice of high-risk sexual behaviors causing sexually transmitted infections (Ericksen & Trocki, 1994). According to Ericksen and Trocki (1994), "the second major behavior causing [these infections]—problem drinking—is strongly linked to high-risk sex in both sexes, with a history of multiple partners putting individuals at substantial risk for problem drinking" (p. 262). Therefore, problem drinking is a negative health behavior that should not be promoted as a characteristic of Black womanhood, and when presented in the media, it must be paired with imagery detailing real-life health consequences of heavy alcohol consumption.

HIGH-RISK SEXUAL BEHAVIORS

In television dramas, Black female characters are routinely portrayed as hypersexual. These characters embody the stereotyped notion that Black women's femininity is laced with immoral sexual attitudes and behaviors, despite education level or socioeconomic status. Interestingly enough, these representations are believed to be expressions of sexual liberation. However, given that television dramas represent Black women's sexual practices as high-risk sexual behaviors, we must critically review the lifestyle practices and attitudes being promoted. In all three leading television dramas discussed in this chapter, the lead Black female characters engage in sexual affairs with married men, engage in unsafe sexual practices such as unprotected sex, and engage in sex with multiple partners and/or have a one-night stand, sex with a stranger the first night they meet without any obligations for the future. These repeated high-risk sexual behaviors are represented as normal sexual lifestyles for single and married Black women, yet are frequently portrayed without real-life health consequences.

Sexual Affairs With Married Men

In television dramas, it is not uncommon to find many characters involved in extramarital affairs and concurrent sexual relationships.

However, in television dramas starring Black women, sexual affairs with married men appear to be a characteristic of Black womanhood. In *Being Mary Jane*, *Scandal*, and *How to Get Away With Murder*, all three lead Black female characters are involved in sexual affairs with married men, each one starting in the show's very first season. By engaging in affairs with married men, the lead Black female characters are practicing high-risk sexual behaviors. Sexual affairs with married persons constitute high risk because the married persons' concurrent sexual partners increase in number, which leads to increased health risk (Witte et al., 2010). These facts seem not to deter the lead Black female characters in television dramas starring Black women. In *Being Mary Jane*, throughout Season 1, starting in Episode 1 (Akil & Akil, 2013), Mary Jane Paul is involved in a sexual affair with a married man, and although she does not originally know about his marriage, once she finds out, she fails to immediately put an end to their relationship. When she finally does end that relationship, in the very same season, however, Mary Jane returns to the bed of her former boyfriend, David. When she later finds that David is in a relationship, this does not stop Mary Jane from pursuing him.

In the television dramas *Scandal* and *How to Get Away With Murder*, the storylines each focus on one Black female lead character, and they both are engaged in sexual affairs with married men. In *How to Get Away With Murder*, Professor Annalise Keating is cheating on her husband with a married police officer. During the very first season, Keating is represented as a hypersexual temptress. Season 1, Episode 1 (Nowalk & Offer, 2014) captures her receiving oral sex from her boyfriend, Detective Nate Lahey, in her marital home. Later in the episode, she uses their sexual relationship in the court of law to advance her position on a case and to discredit a witness and the police department he works for. By the end of Season 1, Episode 12 (Harrison & D'Elia, 2015), Keating appears to frame Detective Lahey in the murder of her husband, all while using a night of sex with him as her alibi the night her husband was murdered.

As mentioned earlier, Olivia Pope from *Scandal* carries out a secret sexual affair with the president of the United States. Their sexual affair takes place in the White House, in her home, in church after the christening of her goddaughter, and anywhere else in which they encounter each other. Pope's influence on the president is so powerful that it appears he cannot make a decision without consulting her first; and sure enough, what she says goes. Many grow suspicious of their relationship, including her boyfriend and the president's wife, Mellie Grant. To ward off all suspicions, both Pope and President Fitzgerald maintain concurrent sexual relationships with their partners. When the First Lady's suspicions are confirmed, she confronts Pope about her betrayal, but that does not stop Pope and the president from maintaining their relationship.

In all three television dramas starring Black women discussed in this chapter, the lead Black female character is involved in a concurrent sexual affair, with seemingly no health consequences. To the contrary, engagement in sexual affairs and nonmonogamous relationships has been linked to increased likelihood of contracting sexually transmitted infections (STIs) and is considered risky sexual behavior (Witte et al., 2010). In studies assessing STI risk among couples, evidence illustrates that a partner's nonmonogamous sexual behavior paired with the unawareness of the spouse/partner was linked to an increased risk of having an STI (Boyer et al., 2006; Drumright et al., 2004). Additional studies provide evidence demonstrating that engaging in sequential and concurrent sexual partner relationships presents a significantly greater risk of contracting an STI than engaging in single-partner relationships (Kelley, 2003). Therefore, monolithically representing Black women in television dramas as engaged in high-risk sexual practices, such as concurrent sexual affairs and extramarital affairs, informs the viewing audience that Black women are uncontrollably hypersexual despite the proven health risk associated with sexual affairs. This representation erroneously portrays African American women, dangerously running the risk of real-life health consequences for their concurrent sexual relationships and as a result promotes high-risk sexual behaviors as embedded in the cultural values of Black women.

Unsafe Sexual Practices

In television, it is oftentimes unclear whether a couple uses protection during sex. The camera gaze tends not to focus on safe sex, seemingly as if there is something unsexy about using protection in television dramas. Perhaps the act of securing contraceptives takes away from the intensity of the sexual scene being filmed. Unfortunately, this absence also represents a lack of attention to safe sexual practices and can be interpreted as representing unsafe sexual affairs. In television dramas starring Black women, it is rare to find attention on safe sexual practices and the use of protection. In *Being Mary Jane*, *Scandal*, and *How to Get Away With Murder* there are few illustrations of protective measures among the lead Black female characters. In *Being Mary Jane*, there is a reference to Mary Jane Paul's condom usage in Episode 1 of Season 1 (Akil & Akil, 2013). After a night of sexual encounters with her boyfriend Andre (whom she later discovers is married), Mary Jane steps on what appears to be a used condom with a sticky note attached. Mary Jane's housekeeper discovered the condom on the floor earlier and left a note that read, "Miss Mary me no clean." Mary Jane is left to discard the condom herself. Interestingly, however, it is up to the viewer to interpret the opened condom on the floor as used or unused. There is no explicit display of condom usage between Mary Jane and Andre, or any other men with whom she has sex. Further displaying Mary Jane as using safe sexual practices, in a later season Mary Jane visits a club that allows for secret sexual encounters, and she decides to take a man from the club home (Season 3, Episode 6 [Rivera & Barnette, 2015]). Once in her home, Mary Jane requires that both she and the man take several at-home rapid STI tests. The man agrees, and when the results show negative, the next scene shows Mary Jane and the man having sex. However, even with the use of home testing for STIs, there is still risk of contracting an STI given the concern for false results according to the National Institutes of Health (Peeling, 2006). Once again, no use of protection is present in this scene with Mary Jane. Although Mary Jane states that she requires every man she sleeps with to do this test, this is the first and only scene in all four seasons that captures such precautions, which is not introduced until Season 3. Even with the use of home testing for STIs, risks remain.

Although few references exist in television dramas starring Black women that clearly illustrate the use of contraceptives, there are several references that illustrate lack of protection. For instance, during Season 5, Episode 9, of *Scandal* (Wilding & Verica, 2015), Olivia Pope is back in a relationship with the president of the United States and now lives in the White House. She discovers that she is pregnant and decides to have an abortion, without notifying her boyfriend, the president. This is an indication that either protection was not used, or the protection was ineffective, which exposes individuals to STIs. While Mary Jane Paul, from *Being Mary Jane*, seems to pride herself on safe sex, she does not always uphold her own safety standards. Heartbroken over the fact that David is expecting a baby with another woman, Mary Jane asks David to impregnate her (Season 2, Episode 6 [Giaudrone & Akil, 2015]). The morning after having sex with David, Mary Jane decides that she no longer desires a relationship with him (Season 2, Episode 7 [Akil & King, 2015]). Mary Jane's character displays inconsistent contraceptive usage and inconsistent precautions around her sexual activity. This form of inconsistency increases the risk of individuals' exposure to STIs and HIV/AIDS.

Representing African American women in the media with unsafe sexual practices further validates concerns surrounding increased exposure to STIs among Black women. Therefore, broadcasting high-risk sexual lifestyles among Black women may further contribute to the belief that such behaviors are socially acceptable among Black women despite real-life health consequences and risk; as a result, it threatens the public.

Nonmonogamous Sexual Relationships

In 21st-century television dramas starring Black women, nonmonogamous relationships are normal. Lead Black female characters are frequently portrayed as dating multiple partners and having one-night stands. In all three television dramas discussed in this chapter—*Scandal*, *Being Mary Jane*, and *How to Get Away With Murder*—the lead Black female characters experience noncommittal dating relationships at some point in each show's tenure. For Olivia Pope (*Scandal*) and Mary Jane Paul (*Being Mary Jane*), both Black female characters never experience a monogamous relationship; although for Mary Jane references are made to a previous monogamous relationship with her former boyfriend David, they do not currently have such a relationship. For Annalise Keating (*How to Get Away With Murder*), during Season 1 she is married but not in a monogamous relationship, as both Keating and her husband (Sam) are engaged in extramarital sexual affairs. By the end of Season 1, Sam is murdered, and Keating continues to engage in casual sexual relationships with both men and women. The frequency of these portrayals calls into question the social and health impact of casual dating relationships. Examining the dating habits of the lead Black female characters Olivia Pope, Mary Jane Paul, and Professor Annalise Keating reveals the high-risk sexual behaviors and attitudes that these characters portray and may help us better understand ways to address media promotion of antihealth behaviors.

Mary Jane Paul, a single news anchor, expresses great desire to establish a monogamous relationship that leads to marriage and children. However, the character is portrayed as making a series of life decisions that deter her from the path to marriage and monogamy. Unfortunately, Mary Jane's failed attempts at committed relationships have resulted in her seeking sexual pleasure from men without any obligations or commitments. During Season 2, Episode 10 (Graham et al., 2015), Mary Jane is shown having a sex-only affair with a Black male athlete, Brandon, with whom she does not have a social relationship. Several scenes capture the two meeting at hotels to have sex. The show captures Mary Jane and Brandon discussing the parameters of their engagements where they both agree that they are sexually exclusive with each other but have the liberty to form new relationships as long as they inform the other person, which would result in the end of their sex-only relationship. Soon, Mary Jane develops a strong interest in a new man, Sheldon, and so she temporarily brings an end to her arrangement with Brandon. When her relationship with Sheldon does not work out, Mary Jane once again finds herself turning to casual sexual relationships to fill the voids in her life. During Season 3, Mary Jane explores alternative approaches to dating by visiting a sexual dating club with a friend. At the club, she meets a White male who expresses an attraction toward Mary Jane. Questioning whether she should start a sexual relationship with the gentleman, she turns to Brandon to fulfill her sexual desires, while at the same time engaging in sexual arousal without sex with the man from the club. Concluding that she will not have a serious relationship with Brandon in the future, she then begins a casual sexual relationship with the gentleman from the club (Season 3, Episode 6 [Rivera & Barnette, 2015]). Seeking validation for her actions, Mary Jane invites a girlfriend over to discuss her circumstance. Nichelle and Mary Jane discuss casual dating and sexual freedom with dating multiple partners.

Mary Jane takes the advice of her friend and starts a casual sexual relationship with the man from the club. The relationship does not last long as Mary Jane knows from the beginning that it does not have the potential to develop into a long-term committed relationship.

Starting anew in New York, Mary Jane sets out to embark upon new life journeys with hopes of finding love and marriage. However, in the first episode of the new season (Season 4), Mary Jane starts a similar relationship with a man she meets and engages in sexual intercourse on the first night. Within the first five minutes of Season 4, Episode 1 (Shelton & Van Peebles, 2017), Mary Jane visits a comedy club with her friend and coworker, Kara, and uses this occasion to engage in sexual intercourse with a strange man for one night. Drinking with her friend, Mary Jane informs Kara of her plans to have a one-night stand before she officially starts working with a matchmaking service.

Mary Jane not only follows through with her plans but also encourages Kara to do the same. Alone in the hotel room with the man from the club, Mary Jane goes to the bathroom and calls Kara to alert her of her actions and her safety concerns for such actions. Despite the pending risk, Mary Jane goes forth with her plan and engages in sexual intercourse. Later, Mary Jane learns that the matchmaker will not take her on as a client, and so Mary Jane continues a casual sexual relationship with the man, Lee, and begins to see their sexual encounters as a way to start a monogamous committed relationship. However, later in the series, Mary Jane begins a new romantic and sexual affair with a coworker during her relationship with Lee, which brings their relationship to an end.

Modeling this same behavior, the character Olivia Pope from *Scandal* also engages in a one-night stand that develops into a casual sexual relationship. In Episode 16 of Season 4 (Byrne & McCrane, 2015), Pope is shown drinking at a bar and encounters a male whom she appears to find attractive. Pope is emotionally drained and attempting to recover from a previous sexual relationship and finds herself seeking temporary fulfillment from an emotional and sexual void. Yet, Pope is too nervous to engage in a one-night stand and runs out of the bar. However, Pope returns to the same bar on a different night and once again is drinking, hoping that the man will return. When he does, she pretends to be Alex and takes him home. While kissing, they begin to take off their clothing, and Pope instructs the man, Franklin Russell, to get naked and meet her in the bedroom. He does, and she grabs a bottle of wine and two wine-glasses and follows him into the bedroom. Pope makes these encounters routine and frequently is shown drinking and engaging in nonmonogamous sexual practices. Once again stressed by her work life, Pope turns into her alias, Alex, and requests that Russell visit her for another night of nonmonogamous sex (Season 4, Episode 19 [Rhimes, Mohamed, & Allen, 2015]). When Russell arrives at Pope's house and attempts to end their nonmonogamous relationship, Pope explains that she needs to continue their relationship in order to escape the complications of her life:

> My life is very complicated. And I'm willing to not be complicated. And when I'm with you, when I'm Alex, nothing is complicated. I want that. I need that. Will you please come in? (Season 4, Episode 19 [Rhimes, Mohamed, & Allen, 2015)

Pope's plea convinces Russell to enter her home and have sex with her, as Alex. Their nonmonogamous relationship continues until Pope finds out that Russell was hired to seduce her and sleep with her in order to gain information about matters concerning her work. As this relationship ends, Olivia returns to the bed of Jake, her former lover (Season 4, Episode 21 [Rhimes, Canales, et al., 2015]).

Mass media representations of Black women routinely electing to engage in nonmonogamous and concurrent sexual relationships promote a hypersexual image of Black womanhood. Furthermore, television dramas starring Black women portray casual sexual relationships as sexually liberating and normal but at the same time advance messages of socially destructive and dangerous behaviors among Black women. When examining the dating practices of three lead Black female characters in television dramas, we find that they most frequently engage in nonmonogamous sexual behaviors to temporarily fill an emotional void. This at times develops into an opportunity to segue into new monogamous relationships, yet this approach has never been successful in *Scandal*, *How to Get Away With Murder*, or *Being Mary Jane*. It is also important to note that the women in these dramas rely heavily on alcohol as "liquid courage" to motivate them to engage in nonmonogamous sexual relationships. According to current research, this behavior is unhealthy and leads to increased health risk (Kelley, 2003; Witte et al., 2010).

PROMOTING ANTIHEALTH ETHICS AMONG BLACK WOMEN THROUGH TELEVISION DRAMAS

Leading television dramas starring Black women overly sensationalize the lives of Black women as highly stressed, unsafe, and hypersexual, all of which contribute to the established negative perceptions of Black woman-hood. Within this logic, Black women are portrayed as unwilling to exercise good judgment, which leads to increased health risk. At the same time, professional Black women are represented as excessively concerned with their careers at the expense of their health and the well-being of others. They are often portrayed consuming large amounts of alcohol as a coping mechanism for the excessive stress they experience in their daily lives. In addition, many of these female characters are represented as using nonmo-nogamous sex to fill emotional voids, which is also a high-risk sexual practice. These antihealth behaviors increase concern about the existence of Black women in America and place the Black woman at a disadvantage in life and society. That is, Black womanhood is represented as deliberately unhealthy and a danger to the public. These award-winning representations receive major audience appeal because they reinforce preexisting stereo-types about Black women and help justify the treatment of Black women in the workplace, health care, the legal system, and society as a whole.

The mass media serves as a primary venue through which images and messages are broadcasted. In fact, media have popularized alarmingly unhealthy representations of Black females (M. Gammage, 2015; Kalof, 1999; Pellerin, 2011; Zhang et al., 2008), which have been systematically used to justify public policies that target Black women for marginaliza-tion. The fact that negative, unhealthy, and dangerous behaviors exclusively exist in three leading television dramas starring Black women creates an overexposure to antihealth behaviors among Black women for the viewing audience. As mentioned earlier, *Scandal* and *How to Get Away With Murder* were the two leading shows on ABC in 2018 and received high viewing receptions among both Black and White audiences. Although scripted, the limited representations of Black females as lead characters in television dramas narrow the general public's frame of reference for Black womanhood. Thus, these scripted dramas can inform public perceptions of Black women. Given the negative images, it is only logical to assume that the public view of Black women embodies adverse conclusions about their lifestyles.

Unhealthy images of Black womanhood have become normalized and are assumed to be reflections of Black women's reality, especially given the fact that Black female writers, producers, and production companies are responsible for creating these shows. However, it is faulty to assume this, in the same way that it was erroneous to assume that Black women were "welfare queens" and "crack mamas" in the 1980s and 1990s. Media depictions of Black women, even when created by Black women, must be critically analyzed and informed by Black women's perspectives. Such productions must also be cognizant of the potential impact on Black women, as previous images have been used to further marginalize and oppress them.

CHAPTER 4

Reality Television as a Public Health Crisis for Black Women

For centuries, African Americans' lives have been affected by their status, citizenship, and sociopolitical standing in America. However, much of the discourse around African Americans' lives has been assumed to be a consequence of the inferiority of their race and their inability to assimilate into the American culture. Scholars, politicians, and medical practitioners advanced the racist ideology that Africans and by extension Blacks in America were genetically inferior to Europeans and socially dysfunctional. This racist ideology informed the treatment of Blacks pre- and post-enslavement. In the 1900s, politically charged racist propaganda campaigns were launched against African Americans to justify the denial of full citizenship rights to Blacks. The second-class-citizen status of Blacks included lack of access to quality health care and lack of protection from inhumane research experiments. Therefore, chronic illnesses and mental illness were hypothesized to be innate in inferior racial and ethnic groups, as evident in the eugenics movement. Despite the racist conditioning in America, eugenicists and supporters of the eugenics movement argued that African Americans and other undesirable populations in America required governmental control over their reproductive abilities and social lives in general. Marketing campaigns were used to miseducate the American public about the state of African Americans' health. Even though the theories of the eugenics movement were disproven, the damage had already been done. Countless numbers of African American women were forcibly sterilized and coerced into using dangerous birth controls, both of which have resulted in the death of Black women.

Racist ideologies about African Americans' well-being, and Black women's lifestyles in particular, were once again used in the post–civil rights era, with the labeling of Black women as "crack mamas" and "welfare queens" as discussed in Chapter 2. Accordingly, the political landscape in America around Black women's lives classified them as innately inferior and self-deprecating. Not only were political platforms used to promote this racist categorizing of Black women, but media, news media, motion pictures, and network television programming were also used to validate the stereotypes, and the American public endorsed these ideas about Blackness. However, with the rise in Black political representation and the birth of the discipline of Black Studies coupled with the influx of Black media creators and producers, much of the blatantly racist theories and falsified research about Black health has been consistently disproven. Yet, the racist ideologies still linger on.

The long-standing stereotype of the hypersexual, violent, and unhealthy Black woman has been complemented by 21st-century portrayals of Black women in the media. The picture of unhealthiness among Black women is further advanced through 21st-century media portrayals of "authentic" Black women behaving in the most destructive manner. No longer is faulty science the primary avenue through which racist concepts of Blackness are generated. The past century has ushered in a new wave of systematic assaults on Blacks through media imagery. Media representations of Black women in particular supplement the deeply rooted assumptions about Black women as warranting public concern and in need of social reform and control. Researchers have provided substantial evidence indicating that violent and hypersexual media representations of African Americans generate negative perceptions of Blacks and may directly affect the treatment of African Americans in American society and the world (M. Gammage, 2015; Gan et al., 1997; Hikes, 2004; Kalof, 1999; Rudman & Lee, 2002). Although the blatantly racist discourse around Black women's lives, and reproductive health in particular, has shifted, media representations of Black women's realities are used to reinforce century-old racialized ideologies on Black womanhood.

We must acknowledge the role of reality television in extending the enduring racist stereotypes about Blackness. Reality television is predicated upon the idea that everyday individuals' real lives are being captured on camera, unscripted and uncensored. Thus, this sends the message to the viewing audience that the images are reflections of cast members' genuine lives, attitudes, and behaviors. Situating Blackness as pathologically dysfunctional through the camera lens further subjugates African Americans, but this subjugation is heightened by the concept of authentic representations of real African Americans, and not authors or actors. Removing the authors and the visible script from the racist images created about Blacks opened up a new dimension of racist propaganda in the media. This chapter explores how reality television starring African American women has been designed to further marginalize African Americans by representing them as chronically unhealthy and dysfunctional. It also highlights the economic value placed on portraying Black women as a danger to the American public's health and safety.

INVESTIGATING REALITY TELEVISION SHOWS STARRING BLACK WOMEN

In 2018, six reality television shows primarily starring Black women, each with over five seasons, including seasons airing during 2018, were broadcasted on American television network stations (see Table 4.1). As noted in the introduction to this book, VH1 and Bravo are the current home to most of the "unscripted" reality shows that star Black females, and together the two television networks have majority control over the images of Black females in reality television. To analyze this impact, all six shows' 2018 seasons were examined to determine the messages generated about Black women's health and wellness.

Title	Season	Air Dates	Network	Number of Episodes
Basketball Wives	7	May 14, 2018– September 16, 2018	VH1	17
Love and Hip Hop: Atlanta	7	March 19, 2018– July 2, 2018	VH1	16
Love and Hip Hop: Hollywood	5	July 23, 2018– November 19, 2018	VH1	18
Love and Hip Hop: New York	8	October 30, 2017– March 12, 2018	VH1	18
Married to Medicine	6	September 2, 2018– January 13, 2019	Bravo	18
The Real Housewives of Atlanta	10	November 5, 2017– April 29, 2018	Bravo	22

Table 4.1   Reviewed Reality Television Shows Starring Black Women

VH1 is an American cable network owned by Paramount Global. Paramount Global is a leading international media producer. Paramount prides itself on connecting people from around the world. As noted by Paramount (2022), "Our brands are #1 in key U.S. target demos, including total audience, kids, adults, African-Americans and Hispanics. We have a global reach of more than 4.3 billion subscribers across more than 180 countries." Therefore, media representations of African Americans via Paramount's global brand network have the potential to reach worldwide audiences and influence perspectives globally. In 2018, VH1 produced 17 reality television shows starring or co-starring African Americans, which was the largest cable network production of reality television shows starring African Americans in 2018. Ten of the reality television shows were cited as unscripted reality series that follow the lives of the cast members. Five out of these 10 shows primarily focus on Black female cast members, although Black male cast members are also featured. Four of the series have aired five or more completed seasons since 2011. For the purpose of this research, all four of those series— *Basketball Wives* (O'Neal et al., 2010–present), *Love and Hip Hop: Atlanta* (Abramson et al., 2012–present), *Love and Hip Hop: Hollywood* (Scott-Young et al., 2014–2019), and *Love and Hip Hop: New York* (Scott-Young et al., 2011–2020)—were examined to explore the representation of Black female cast members' health realities and well-being.

Basketball Wives is a VH1-produced American reality television series that focuses on women who are currently or formerly involved in relationships with partners whose careers have been in professional basketball (O'Neal et al., 2010–present). For the show's first seven seasons, the majority of the cast members are Black females. Season 7 (Seliga et al., 2018), over 17 episodes that premiered in 2018, shadows the lives and group interactions of nine females, eight of whom identify as Black. The show has been noted primarily for its dramatized scenes of violence and aggression. As described on VH1, viewers of *Basketball Wives* are invited to "follow the daily lives, drama-filled parties and outrageous fights that unfold between the wives, ex-wives and girlfriends of professional basketball players" (IMDb, 1990–2023; Viacom International, 2023). "With a cast that includes Shaunie O'Neal, Tami Roman, Evelyn Lozada, Jackie Christie, Malaysia Pargo and Jennifer Williams, there's never a dull moment on the home court" (VH1, 2019). The show has reached over 3.5 million viewers per episode and received one of the highest ratings for Monday night (Melton, 2020).

Love and Hip Hop is an American reality television franchise produced by VH1. The franchise in 2018 housed four different installments of the series: *Love and Hip Hop: New York* (Scott-Young et al., 2011–2020), *Love and Hip Hop: Atlanta* (Abramson et al., 2012–present), *Love and Hip Hop: Hollywood* (Scott-Young et al., 2014–2019), and *Love and*

Hip Hop: Miami (Scott-Young et al., 2018–present). This franchise high-lights the intimate details of cast members' lives and careers as they navigate their way through the hip-hop industry in multiple cities across the United States. Over its first eight years on the air, the franchise gained a reputation for broadcasting hyperviolent and hypersexual images of cast members, primarily African Americans (M. Gammage, 2015). This high-drama intensity-filled franchise has raked in over 2 million viewers per episode for each installment (Welch, 2018). In 2018, *Love and Hip Hop* (*Atlanta* and *Hollywood*) ranked number one in Monday cable rat-ings (Welch, 2018). *Love and Hip Hop: New York* is the first installment of the franchise and has completed 10 seasons since Season 1 premiered in March 2011. Season 8 (2017–2018) is comprised of 18 episodes that chronicle the lives of Black women in their personal and professional pursuits, especially as they relate to Black men in the hip-hop industry. The season opener ranked in at number two, second only to a Monday-night regular-season National Football League (NFL) game, and pulled in over 2 million viewers. *Love and Hip Hop: Atlanta*, the second install-ment of the franchise, debuted in June 2012. Season 7 (2018), also over 18 episodes, showcases the lives of African American women and their involvement in the hip-hop industry in Atlanta as artists, producers, and executives. The third installment of the franchise, debuted in September 2014, is *Love and Hip Hop: Hollywood*, which in 2018 launched Season 5 and premiered at number one. The series records the lifestyles and careers of established rap and rhythm and blues (R&B) artists in Hollywood, California. While many well-known Black male rappers and producers are cast members on the show, the series primarily focuses on the female cast members and their involvement in the hip-hop industry. The final installment of the franchise, *Love and Hip Hop: Miami*, completed its freshman year with Season 1 airing on January 1, 2018. Like its predecessors, this highly ranked series focuses on both African American and Afro-Caribbean artists' quests for stardom in hip-hop. Given the short tenure of this series (four seasons, airing through 2022), it was eliminated from this research analysis. The other three installments have been analyzed to provide an in-depth assessment of the representa-tions of Black women's health and wellness in long-standing reality television shows.

Bravo is another network television station that has produced leading reality television shows starring Black women. "Bravo is a program ser-vice of NBC Universal Cable Entertainment, a division of NBC Universal, one of the world's leading media and entertainment companies in the development, production, and marketing of entertainment, news and information to a global audience" (Bravo Media, 2023). NBC Universal was acquired by Comcast. "Comcast is a global media and technology company. From the connectivity and platforms we provide, to the content and experiences we create, we reach hundreds of millions of customers, viewers, and guests worldwide" (Comcast, n.d.). Bravo produces both scripted and unscripted television series. In 2018, the network broadcasted 13 reality television series primarily starring African Americans; four of these are short spin-offs from a larger series such as *Kandi Koated Nights* (Burruss & Tucker, 2018). Bravo produced six "unscripted" reality television shows primarily starring Black women in 2018: *Blood, Sweat and Heels* (Montgomery et al., 2014–2015), *Married to Medicine* (Huq et al., 2013–present), *The Real Housewives of Atlanta* (Hersh et al., 2008–present), *The Real Housewives of Potomac* (Weinstock et al., 2016–present), *To Rome for Love* (Pitman, 2018), and *Xscape: Still Kickin It* (Bauldwin et al., 2017). Since 2008, Bravo has produced one of the leading reality television shows, *The Real Housewives of Atlanta*, and it stars Black women. *The Real Housewives* is an original reality television series produced by Bravo, including 11 different versions of the series in the United States alone. Both *The Real Housewives of Atlanta* and *Married to Medicine* have over five seasons of high viewership ratings. The 2018 season of each show is explored in this chapter.

The Real Housewives of Atlanta (Hersh et al., 2008–present) was the first major reality television show primarily starring multiple Black female cast members. The show is the third installment of the franchise and first premiered in 2008. In 2017–2018, the show broadcasted its 10th season on Bravo. *The Real Housewives of Atlanta* (Hersh et al., 2008–present) spotlights the personal and professional lives of the cast members and their engagement with each other on the show. For years, the show has been the highest rated and most watched series on Bravo, and in general, for Sunday shows airing especially at 8 p.m. (Dougall, 2020; Kissell, 2014; Ng, 2011). The show is rated higher than all other installments of the *Real Housewives* series and has reached over 4 million viewers per episode at its height (Kissell, 2014). The success of the show has resulted in several spin-offs such as *Kandi Koated Nights* (Burruss & Tucker, 2018), *The Kandi Factory* (Burruss et al., 2013), and *I Dream of NeNe: The Wedding* (King et al., 2013).

Married to Medicine (Huq et al., 2013–present) is a Bravo-produced American television series with nine seasons broadcasted since 2013. The show trails the lives of seven African American females whose personal or professional lives are connected to the medical field. The 2018 cast consists of four cast members who are doctors or dentists and three cast members whose spouses are doctors. The show highlights the interactions among the cast members, their professional life, and their family life, with emphasis on their marriages. Bravo has also launched two spin-off series, *Married to Medicine: Houston* (Anderson et al., 2016) and *Married to Medicine: Los Angeles* (Anderson et al., 2019–2020).

REPRESENTING BLACK WOMEN'S HEALTH
CHALLENGES AS SELF-INFLICTED

Twenty-first-century media productions of Black women, and African Americans in general, appear to have retained the racist stereotype that African Americans' health challenges are self-inflicted and a result of cultural inferiority. Several shows, such as *Couples Therapy* (Despres et al., 2019–present), *Celebrity Rehab With Dr. Drew* (Pinsky et al., 2008–2012), *Iyanla: Fix My Life* (Vanzant & Harrison, 2012–2021), and *For My Man* (Smith, 2015–2021), have been created that focus on relationship and personal challenges of guests on the shows. The most explosive scenes have depicted African Americans as consciously making decisions that are detrimental to their health and well-being. For instance, *For My Man* reviews criminal cases of primarily Black females who have been convicted of unthinkable crimes in the name of love. Reality television shows starring Black women concentrate heavily on advertising scenes with Black women electing to undergo dangerous cosmetic procedures, ignoring mental health challenges, abusing alcohol and drugs, and electing to participate in and maintain unhealthy relationships. Evidence of these historic stereotypes about African American women can be observed in all six of the reality television shows analyzed in this chapter. Thus, it appears that the use of political platforms to promote racist ideologies about African Americans has yielded much of its campaigns against Blacks to the media. Reality television, which now occupies the platform to disseminate racist antihealth messages about African Americans, has become a primary branch of the media and a major contributor to the antihealth messages about Blacks. That is, reality television has become an important media branch of racist ideas about African people. No longer is faulty scientific research needed to promote the state of Black health as dangerous to the American public; now media is used to transmit the same message, but with the added pretext that the images broadcasted are factual recordings of African American women's lifestyles.

The VH1 series *Love and Hip Hop* has established a core component of its production around showcasing Black women's life challenges as self-inflicted. In all three of its installments, Black female cast members are represented as making personal life choices that have directly contributed to poor physical and mental health outcomes. In Season 5 of *Love and Hip Hop: Hollywood* (Scott-Young et al. 2018b), several Black female cast members are filmed discussing their current health struggles. In Episode 2 (air date July 30, 2018), Apple Watts and Lyrica Anderson meet to resolve a disagreement. During their discussion, Apple shares with Lyrica that she has been struggling to rebrand herself and move away from stripping, as she is seeking mental wellness. She reveals that she has experienced "drinking, drugs, selling my body; just a whole lot to survive." The discussion is quickly shifted once Lyrica's husband, A1 Bentley, arrives to discuss a cheating allegation against his wife; thus, Apple exits the scene. Later in the season, Apple discloses that part of her emotional well-being has been negatively affected by being abandoned by her parents, which forced her to go into foster care. Although Apple reveals this serious mental health struggle, little attention is given to her health and well-being. Later episodes only show her struggling to establish a relationship with her estranged father, who the show later reveals is only pretending to be Apple's father. The show subsequently portrays Apple as suffering emotionally from this situation, but no indication of Apple receiving emotional support is broadcasted. In fact, whenever cast members have broadcasted their mental health challenges, the production of *Love and Hip Hop*, and other reality television shows starring Black women in general, has not dedicated aired scenes to the resolution of such issues.

Similar treatment has been rendered when Black female cast members have shared their experiences with physical health complications. During Season 5 of *Love and Hip Hop: Hollywood* (Scott-Young et al., 2018b), K. Michelle unleashes a long kept secret that she has silicone injections in her buttocks and that she has been suffering severe side effects as a result of these injections. She explains that the side effects have included chronic pain and paralysis. Episode 6, "Pretty Hurts" (air date August 27, 2018), opens with K. Michelle sharing her current health challenges as a result of silicone injections in her buttocks. K. Michelle is filmed disclosing one-on-one with the camera:

> I enjoyed my fake ass for a long time, and one day I got up out of bed and I could not walk. It gradually got worse. So, I decided to meet with one of the best doctors in Beverly Hills about removing the silicone from my body so that I could really get back to being healthy again. (Scott-Young et al., 2018b)

While awaiting the doctor, K. Michelle and Moniece Slaughter, a fellow cast member, engage in discourse about the confrontations that have exploded between other cast members, which appears to bring a smile to K. Michelle's face. Once the doctor arrives, the tone changes. K. Michelle discloses to the doctor her complications with the five-year-old silicone injections in her buttocks. She shares that for over a year and a half she has been suffering crippling side effects from the injections. The doctor explains what is happening with the silicone medically and discloses that they may not be able to remove all of the particles. However, K. Michelle feels some relief with the expectation of getting her health back. Ironically, as this scene closes, the camera shifts to the logo for a "Secret Pole Dance Studio" as the audience simultaneously hears a female voice stating, "It's called the booty walk." The next scene features two cast members, Apple Watts and Lyrica Anderson, at a pole dancing studio sitting on the floor and scooting forward with their buttocks. Paring these two scenes back-to-back delegitimizes the seriousness of chronic health issues with buttocks injections and turns this medical reality into a comical scene. The production around this health concern appears to be very scripted. All of the advertisements leading up to the airing of the show portrayed K. Michelle's personal choice to inject a foreign substance into her body as self-inflicted pain. The commercials for the episode repeatedly showed a snapshot of a scene with K. Michelle and her doctor as the doctor informs her that her health issues are not completely reversible, and K. Michelle bursts out in tears. When the episode first aired, however, it was revealed that this is not K. Michelle's response to the doctor's statement, but that the scene had been edited to further dramatize the episode in order to build up audience anticipation for the new episode. When the show returns to K. Michelle, she undergoes surgery to remove the silicone from her buttocks. K. Michelle is filmed standing in front of the camera and sharing her fears and expectations for the surgery. She states, "When I wake up from this surgery, I know for a fact that I'm a be in pain. But I also know that it is the beginning and the start of acceptance of me and who I am." This statement marks the end of the scene. When the episode returns to K. Michelle, she is a few days out from her surgery at home with a nurse aiding her. K. Michelle describes her recovery as "hell and pain." Moniece is once again there to support K. Michelle, as K. Michelle shares her struggle with accepting her scarred body after the surgery. Moniece is then shown talking to the camera revealing her own personal struggle with breast augmentation. She reminds K. Michelle of the importance of her surgery being broadcasted. Yet, K. Michelle turns the conversation to a discussion about the lack of support from people who she deemed as friends. The episode ends and never returns to K. Michelle and the resolution of her health complications. Later in the season, K. Michelle shares that she has recovered from her surgery.

Chronic Alcoholism and Drug Abuse

Another way in which reality television shows portray Black women's health challenges as self-inflicted is through the representations of Black women's struggles with alcohol and drugs. Reality television shows capitalize on spotlighting Black female cast members' struggles with alcohol and drug addictions and yet do not broadcast any investment in their recovery and well-being. Throughout the various seasons of reality television shows starring Black women, several cast members have been accused of both alcohol and drug dependencies. Simultaneously, the majority of the scenes aired in the six shows analyzed include moderate to heavy alcohol consumption.

The *Love and Hip Hop* franchise has publicized several cast members' experiences with substance abuse and has largely linked their erratic behavior to their abuse of alcohol and drugs. Cast member Teairra Marí from *Love and Hip Hop: Hollywood* (Scott-Young et al., 2014–2019), for example, is forced to admit her struggles with alcohol abuse and seek help at a rehabilitation center. Her return to the show in 2018 features her attempts to rebuild her career, in which she finds herself in a heavy alcohol-indulgent environment. The filming of the show spotlights highly stressful scenes involving Teairra Marí, including scenes where Teairra has been pressured to consume alcohol despite her expressed desire not to. Although Teairra has repeatedly requested that her current experiences not be linked to her struggles with alcohol, especially since she has chosen not to consume alcohol, the show continuously narrates the dialogue about Teairra around her struggles with alcohol addiction.

In *Love and Hip Hop: Atlanta* (Abramson et al., 2012–present), cast member Tommie Lee is frequently accused of having a substance abuse problem. Other cast members and the show producers have been filmed and advertised discussing Tommie's chronic use of alcohol while working on the show. During Season 7 (Scott-Young et al., 2018a), Episode 5, "Dangerous Liaisons" (air date April 16, 2018), Tommie shares with another cast member, Spice, with whom she is working on a business collaboration, that she uses alcohol to help her cope with the pressures in her life:

> I'm not no alcoholic by any means. But I do drink and it's my outlet. You know, drinking—it allows me to just like be free and open up, and like all of the things I'm like battling with personally—I don't think about it.

Spice is later filmed in a one-on-one with the camera that she hopes that Tommie's drinking does not get in the way of their working relationship. Throughout the season, several scenes are broadcasted emphasizing the amount of alcohol Tommie consumes and the arguments and violence that follow. In Episode 9, "Team Rasheeda" (air date May 14, 2018), Tommie and Spice are scheduled to shoot their music video for their musical collaboration "Imma Get It." Tommie arrives three hours late, and once Spice confronts Tommie, the women begin to argue, and security stands in between the women in order to prevent a physical altercation. Spice calls out Tommie for drinking and discards her drink on set. During Episode 11, "Houston, We Have a Problem" (air date May 28, 2018), the female cast members gather as Rasheeda announces a business venture in Houston and invites the cast to join her. During Rasheeda's announcement, Tommie is portrayed as interrupting in order to inquire about the alcohol available on the table. She then decides to pour herself a glass, which captures the attention of the other women. Although the other women are drinking as well, special emphasis is placed on Tommie and her consumption of alcohol. A part of the scene shows Tommie pouring an entire glass of alcohol down her throat as she holds her head back. She appears to be disoriented. When Spice brings up the issue at their video shoot, this appears to frustrate both the women. Tommie's reactions appear to be irrational and a result of her alcohol consumption. Tommie begins to insult and threaten a producer of the show. As the women attempt to calm Tommie, she continues to drink, and several security guards step into the scene to remove Tommie. A script then appears across the screen with a black backdrop that reads:

> As Tommie was escorted out, she became increasingly agitated. She tried to return to confront Spice, and was stopped by security. (Scott-Young et al., 2018b)

Next, five split screens appear showing short clips of the chaotic and violent recordings. As the audio is played, an additional script reads:

> She then turned her anger on security and a producer who she attacked verbally and physically. The altercation was captured with audio only. (Scott-Young et al., 2018b)

Once the show returns from a commercial break, the production continues with routine scenes from the episode. Later in the episode, a producer shares with the other cast members that the production company has temporarily suspended Tommie from filming after her actions on set. The production company also reports that Tommie's actions on set that day and the events that followed invoked fear in the production crew, who were no longer willing to work with her. Three episodes later, in Episode 14, "Horsing Around" (air date June 18, 2018), Tommie has a meeting with the production company and is invited back to the show under the condition that she agrees to meet with a substance abuse counselor and not to drink on set. In the final episode of the season, the cast members are invited by Tommie to the release of her and Spice's music video. Tommie issues an apology to the cast; then the video plays, and the season ends like it began, with the cast members partying.

The lack of displaying the effects of alcoholism on Black women's health, employment, and personal lives in reality television shows directly negates the real-life consequences of substance abuse. Medical scholars have documented the impact of alcohol consumption among Black women and the physical and psychological health consequences that "include a higher risk for developing alcohol-related disorders, including liver cirrhosis" (Substance Abuse and Mental Health Services Administration [SAMHSA], 2009). "Literature on substance abuse and treatment among African-American women has expanded and environmental stressors have been examined, including psychosocial, sociodemographic, and economic disparities" (SAMHSA, 2009). Yet, little attention has been given to broadcasting the factors that contribute to alcohol abuse among African American women, such as racism in America, and the effects of substance use on Black women's lives. Reality television shows quickly capitalize on the drama among cast members consuming alcohol, yet few protective measures are put in place to safeguard the health and wellness of Black female cast members who are alleged to abuse alcohol and other substances on these shows. Researchers argue that early intervention and support are critical in African American women's recovery from substance abuse (SAMHSA, 2009). However, in the illustrations provided, the African American female cast members are filmed for several seasons before any interventions are rendered. Even still, the interventions offered appear to be superficial and only provided as a response to extreme violence against multiple cast members and the production staff. Overall, the broadcasting of Black women's alleged abuse of alcohol materializes as a self-inflicted disorder that is good for reality television, despite the health impact on Black women.

High-Stress and High-Tension Relationships

Although Black women are filmed expressing that their involvement in reality television is extremely stressful, it appears that network television production around reality television shows starring Black women requires cast members' cooperation and participation even if it is not good for their well-being. During the Season 7 "Reunion" episode of *Basketball Wives* (air date September 16, 2018 [Seliga et al., 2018]), the host and the cast members admit that the topics discussed and the relationships among the cast members are very stressful. Topics such as conflicts among cast members, infertility, police brutality, natural disasters, and the death of family members are all jammed into a one-hour-long reunion show. Cast member Malaysia Pargo verbally states that she is stressed by the conflicts they are forced to discuss. Throughout the tenure of the reality television show, decade-long friendships are repeatedly strained by secrecy and lies, which has resulted in both verbal and physical altercations. After the explosive scenes of violence from Episode 16 (air date September 9, 2018), Jennifer Williams elects not to attend the reunion show because of her concern for her safety and well-being. Her concern is dismissed by the host and the cast members as illegitimate. Yet, another cast member, Tami Roman, decides to leave the reunion show after an intense discussion with Evelyn Lozada that resulted in verbal attacks and threats. Despite this, executive producer and cast member Shaunie O'Neal ties the ladies' presence at the reunion show and attendance throughout the show to their employment on the reality television series, regardless of the stressful dialogue and health risk.

Similarly, the *Real Housewives of Atlanta* series (Hersh et al., 2008–present) has been marketed around the contentious relationships of the Black female cast members. For 15 seasons, the show's promotional advertisements have highlighted scenes of verbal and physical altercations among the cast members. "Shade," a phrase used to describe antagonistic statements about another person that may not be truthful, was popularized on the show, as the women were filmed repeatedly commenting negatively about the other cast members. Those same scenes have been replayed during reunion shows, which are used to enflame the disputes among the cast. As a result, past reunion shows have led to physical violence among the cast members. Throughout Season 10 (Weinstock et al., 2017–2018), face-to-face "shady" comments also result in both physical and verbal altercations. Ironically, despite these quarrelsome relationships, the women are recurrently filmed accompanying each other to events, on domestic and international trips, and to reunion shows, all of which seem to center on the hostility among the women.

In all installments of the *Love and Hip Hop* franchise series (Abramson et al., 2012–present; Scott-Young et al., 2014–2019; Scott-Young et al., 2011–2020; Scott-Young et al., 2018–present), African American personal and romantic relationships are portrayed as unhealthy and dysfunctional. From marital infidelity to unethical business ventures, Black women and men are represented as unable to establish and/or maintain stable nonvolatile relationships with family, friends, and partners. Marital stress and conflict among female cast members appear to provide the most frequently displayed images of self-inflicted stress. In *Love and Hip Hop: Atlanta*, Season 7 (Scott-Young et al., 2018a), several of the cast members' romantic relationships are strained by marital infidelity. Rasheeda and Kirk Frost are a long-standing lead couple in the series; however, their relationship has been overly advertised as habitually perfidious. During Season 7, it is revealed that Kirk fathered a child outside of the couple's marriage. Although divorce is alluded to, the couple decides to reside in the same household in order to co-parent their children. Later in the season, Kirk experiences the loss of his mother, and Rasheeda's support for Kirk seems to restore the couple's relationship. Similar problems are broadcast involving the other couples on the show. Stevie J and Estelita Quintero are involved in a personal and business relationship. Although Stevie J has been exposed for having multiple romantic relationships that have caused strife for Estelita, she is portrayed as willing to endure the stress of the relationship for other personal gains. In Season 7, Episode 7 (air date April 30, 2018), she states:

I know my friends are going to judge me for getting back with Stevie, but when we reconnected at the Penthouse photo shoot I remembered everything I liked about Stevie in the first place. This is huge. Penthouse, come on. I'm not forgetting all the bad things he has done to me, but there is something about him that is impossible to resist.

While some may argue that these instances can be interpreted as a reflection of the resilience and commitment of Black romantic couples, it must be noted that the majority of the Black couples presented in these reality television shows have been portrayed as constantly violating the terms of their unions, the great majority of which end in separation and divorce.

Involvement in very stressful relationships is displayed even in prayer in *Love and Hip Hop: Atlanta* (Abramson et al., 2012–present). During Season 7, Episode 6 (air date April 23, 2018 [Scott-Young et al., 2018a]), cast member Tommie returns from her suspension from filming by hosting an event with several cast members. While riding in a vehicle to the event, Tommie begins to pray:

God, I beg you that today go as smoothly and as peacefully as possible. I have nothing but love for all of those women in there, except for a couple of bitches. God please. Thank you. I love you. Amen. (Scott-Young et al., 2018a)

Advertisement of scenes such as these misrepresents the Black woman as a willing participant in her own destruction. By showcasing Black women as willingly engaging in increasing their stress levels and inciting frustration and anger amongst themselves, these images validate the negative assumptions about Black culture.

Love and Hip Hop: New York (Scott-Young et al., 2011–2020) has consistently portrayed Black romantic couples, friends, and business partners as hyperdysfunctional. The bulk of the controversial relationships center on dishonesty and disrespect. Several cast members' personal relationships over the show's 10 seasons have been broadcasted within the realm of chronic infidelity and violence. From male cast members getting multiple female cast members pregnant at the same time to repeated physical confrontations, the cast of this *Love and Hip Hop* installment is publicized as socially disorderly. In addition, when cast members and their spouses have experienced criminal punishment and imprisonment, the franchise has chosen to advertise it all. Remy Ma and Papoose have been filmed throughout their time on the show dealing with Remy Ma's eight-year incarceration. In Season 8 (Scott-Young et al., 2017–2018), cast member Yandy Smith-Harris is striving to keep her family afloat while supporting her husband Mendeecees Harris, who is currently in prison. Yandy has struggled with confrontations with Mendeecees's other children's mothers, and this season Mendeecees's own mother is portrayed as stalking Yandy to ensure that she remains faithful to her husband. When the couples of *Love and Hip Hop: New York* are not dealing with incarceration, they are often portrayed as struggling with marital infidelity. During Season 8, Episode 5, "Streets Are Talking" (air date November 27, 2017), Lil' Mo reveals the results of her husband's lie detector test, which was used to assess whether or not Karl Dargan, her husband, has in fact been unfaithful. After Lil' Mo's son questions his mother about whether the information on the internet about his father cheating on his mother are true, Lil' Mo is represented as losing trust in her husband. She therefore requests that he take a lie detector test. In Episode 5, the results indicate that Karl was not being truthful during the lie detector examination. The couple does seek marital counseling and agree to work on establishing a healthy marriage. However, as the season unfolds, the show focuses on the couple's challenges with trust. New cast member Anaís is introduced as a sensual artist and woman. She has been married for 14 years with children; however, she represents her marriage as unsupportive and unfulfilling. On camera, Anaís is showcased as starting a sexual affair with fellow cast member Rich Dollaz. Anaís's husband is unaware of their affair, and when he surprises his wife at her artist meet-and-greet event, during Season 8, Episode 11 (air date January 8, 2018), he discovers that Rich and Anaís are having an affair. This results in a verbal and physical altercation between the men. Anaís's husband throws his ring on the floor and notifies Anaís that he will file for divorce. Anaís realizes the impact of her actions and expresses remorse. Later in the episode, Anaís's husband schedules a meeting with Anaís's management company to dissolve their business agreement since he has been financially backing her career. Ironically, Anaís's friends are shown earlier in the season discouraging her personal relationship with Rich, especially since Rich has been portrayed as a sexual deviant in previous seasons. During the meet and greet, Rich is shown on camera securing the contact information of another woman at the event. Thus, Rich is represented as willingly engaging in an affair with a married woman without commitment, and Anaís is portrayed as placing her faith in establishing a committed relationship with Rich. When Anaís and Rich meet to discuss the fallout, Anaís comes to the conclusion that she made a major mistake in assuming that she would be able to establish a committed relationship with Rich. Throughout the entire eighth season of *Love and Hip Hop: New York*, the production focuses on Black romantic couples' struggles in their relationships and their breakups. The majority of the couples broadcasted during Season 8 end their relationships on the show. While new relationships are often quickly formed, they also rapidly come to an end amidst the drama and violence.

In *Love and Hip Hop: Hollywood* (Scott-Young et al., 2014–2019), multiple couples are portrayed as having extremely stressful and contentious relationships. Season 5 (Scott-Young et al., 2018b) demonstrates the overemphasis on Black couples' relationships as unhealthy and dysfunctional. In particular, Black couples are represented as naturally combative and violent with their partners, families, and friends. The relationship of one of the main couples on the show, Ray J and Princess, has almost exclusively been publicized as exhibiting all the warning signs of an unsafe and unhealthy relationship. Whether making cheating allegations or starting fights with former romantic partners, this couple has been represented as toxic to each other's lives. Despite this representation, the couple gets engaged and then married. In Season 5, the couple is expecting their first child. Although both Ray J and Princess express a commitment to Princess's health during her pregnancy, several scenes throughout the season display the couple engrossed in high-tension arguments and confrontations with each other, other cast members, and even their in-laws.

Another couple that is portrayed as dysfunctional is A1 Bentley and Lyrica Anderson. A1 and Lyrica are married, and both are involved in the music industry. Beginning with their introduction on the show, their relationship is portrayed as poisonous and volatile. When the couple first gets engaged, both sides of their family—their mothers in particular— disagree with their union, and multiple filmed scenes show violent quarrels between both families (M. Gammage, 2018). Several arguments between the couple have also been filmed. During Season 5 (Scott-Young et al., 2018b), the couple finds out that they are expecting their first child. However, their excitement is met with much controversy as Lyrica is accused of having a sexual affair with another cast member, Safaree Samuels. At their pregnancy announcement dinner, verbal and physical fights erupt among their family and friends. RoccStar, another Black male cast member, also insinuates that he has been sexually engaging Lyrica. Later, in Episode 8 (air date September 10, 2018), A1's friends host a sit-down with A1 to offer information and advice about the cheating allegations against his wife and other male cast members. Unsurprisingly, the gatherings turn hostile, and security escorts A1 out of the public restaurant. The remainder of the season, the couple is faced with rumors and attacks from their family and friends. Upon request from her husband, Lyrica agrees to take a paternity test. During Episode 17, "Reunion: Part 1" (air date November 12, 2018), the couple reveals that A1 is the father of Lyrica's unborn child. Both Safaree and RoccStar admit that they were not sexually involved with Lyrica.

A final couple that is represented as unhealthy is Teairra Marí and Akbar Abdul-Ahad, who are in a dating relationship that Teairra Marí believes to be exclusive. Her friends, however, share with Teairra that Akbar is married and also has another girlfriend. When Teairra confronts Akbar, the other two women in Akbar's life engage in both verbal and physical disputes with Teairra and her friend. In the next episode, Episode 8 (air date September 10, 2018), the production company airs a scene from a news broadcast revealing that a pornographic video of Teairra Marí was leaked on her social media page. The scene then changes to a filmed scene of Akbar talking to an executive producer on the show about his car windows being broken. Teairra Marí is brought in by the production company, and she admits that she vandalized his vehicle. Teairra explains that she responded this way because she believes Akbar was responsible for leaking the tape. After she accuses Akbar of releasing the pornographic videotape of her, Akbar asks her if she still loves him, and she responds:

Teairra Marí:	"Not no more."
Akbar:	"You don't love me anymore? In my mind you're still my woman."
Teairra Marí:	"Naw."
Akbar:	"We gonna get over this."
Teairra Marí:	"This shit is crazy." (Scott-Young et al., 2018b)

Teairra then walks away. Ironically, Akbar's other girlfriend is standing next to him the entire time. Later in the episode, it is revealed that Teairra posted comments stating that she still loves Akbar. When the episode returns back to Teairra, she admits that this experience is negatively affecting her and may cause her to relapse on her sobriety. Teairra decides to seek legal counsel against Akbar for the release of the videotape without her consent. During the meeting with her lawyer, Teairra expresses concern for her safety given that Akbar has access to her personal residence. Her lawyer educates her that revenge porn is a form of "sexual assault designed to humiliate and embarrass" the other person. Teairra Marí decides to take legal action and share her story at a press conference. The other cast members are broadcasted dismissing the seriousness of the crime and instead making comic relief at the expense of Teairra. Her own friends are represented as unsupportive and distrustful of Teairra. Not only is Teairra's relationship with Akbar characterized as unhealthy, but her relationship with her friends is cast in the same light. Her same friends are filmed earlier in the season investigating Akbar, and his other relationships, under the pretense that they are looking out for Teairra's best interest. However, when Teairra is faced with personal challenges, the production around her relationships with her friends focuses on their unwillingness to support Teairra in her legal actions against Akbar. The women are advertised as not trusting that Tierra has ended her relationship with Akbar, and therefore reluctant to offer support to her. Thus, the women are publicized as eager to disrupt Teairra's career and relationship but disinclined to help her repair her life. Later in the season, in Episodes 12 and 13 (air dates October 8 and 15, 2018), evidence is presented by cast members, including Akbar, revealing that Teairra has maintained a relationship with Akbar. These scenes are used to justify the women's lack of support and trust in Teairra.

The portrayal of Black romantic relationships as socially and criminally dysfunctional is not new in the media (M. Gammage, 2015). For centuries, Black couples in America have been demonized and ostracized in both politics and research. Media has adopted this treatment of Black romance, and as a consequence, media representations of Black females' romantic and communal relationships are situated in this historical false narrative. In reality television shows starring Black women, emphasis is placed on romantic couples with conflicts and struggles within their marriage. Consequently, de-emphasis is placed on those romantic couples who have not been filmed with scandals attached to their marriages. Prominence is given by the production company to scenes displaying adultery, dishonesty, infidelity resulting in children outside of legitimate relationships, violence, and financial challenges. In general, Black romantic relationships are represented as highly stressful and very dysfunctional. Experts show that involvement in high-stress, and abusive, relationships leads to increased mental and physical health risk (Boardman & Alexander, 2011; West, 2008). From heart disease to depression, high levels of stress can result in a whole host of health challenges that negatively affect African American women's well-being. Yet reality television shows, and media more generally, overemphasize the contentious encounters of Black women with their partners and friends and fail to adequately represent the health effects of such high-stress lifestyles. And, when health challenges are presented among Black female cast members, the storyline depicts the women as inflicting those health struggles on themselves.

DENIGRATING PERSONAL
HEALTH AND WELLNESS

The denigration of African Americans' health is connected to a long legacy of dehumanizing African people around the world. The stereotypical assumption that African Americans' health challenges are simply a result of their cultural practices, resulting in poor diets and lack of exercise, has invaded the American psyche and has affected the treatment of African Americans. Media productions of African Americans' "reality" have mirrored these stereotypes and have in fact portrayed African Americans as adopting this approach to their health and participating in their own condemnation.

Throughout all six reality television shows examined in this chapter, scenes of African American female cast members have been broadcasted highlighting their attempts to maintain their overall health. From exercises to psychological counseling, Black female reality stars are repeatedly shown engaging in health-conscious choices. However, the majority of these scenes are paired with discussions of contentious relationships and verbal and physical altercations. In addition, several scenes are dedicated to spotlighting other cast members' dismissal of Black women's health challenges. With the overabundance of scenes delegitimizing Black women's health and well-being, it appears that production companies are promoting a stereotyped image of Black women's health.

Reality television shows are marketed as broadcasting the everyday lived experiences of cast members. Therefore, it is not surprising to find scenes with Black women engaged in health-enrichment activities. However, the camera's emphasis has been less on cast members' personal health and instead has focused more on controversial interactions among cast members. For example, during *Basketball Wives*, Season 7, Episode 14 (air date August 26, 2018 [Seliga et al., 2018]), Jackie Christie invites two of the other cast members, CeCe Gutierrez and Ogom "OG" Chijindu, to join her at a sea salt spa as part of her routine for relaxing before traveling internationally. Jackie describes this experience as a way to pamper themselves and "get in the right head space" before the cast group trip to Amsterdam, Netherlands. The ladies immediately begin to make light of the experience and make sexual references to the salt. OG states "I want to lick the salt" as she sticks her tongue out, and Jackie responds with "you know I'm a salt licker. Honey, I will lick it all." The women encourage each other to taste the salt, and Jackie states, "Isn't that sexy." CeCe states, "So this is detoxing us, and all our toxins, and all the evil is coming out?" Soon, the women begin to discuss the confrontational relationships among themselves and the other cast members. The women do not appear to relax and rejuvenate but instead engage in stressful conversations about the antagonistic relationships between CeCe and other cast members. Once the women arrive in Amsterdam, it is not long before combative conversations start and arguments escalate. Cast member group vacations in reality television shows foster an atmosphere of aggression and violence. "These planned and filmed getaways create a setting where tensions often are heightened and violence ensues despite attempts to problem solve" (M. Gammage, 2015, p. 84). Even cast member Tami Roman admits this side effect of cast trips and thus decides not to join the group on this trip. Tami states:

> I don't want to go to Amsterdam because every time we go on vacation there is always an elevated amount of drama. And, I feel like I'm experiencing that here. I have never had fun on one single vacation. (Season 7, Episode 14 [Seliga et al., 2018])

Thus, as anticipated, the women's scheduled gatherings on the trip, such as planned dinners, open the door for personal assaults and arguments. At the cast's first dinner, CeCe and Evelyn Lozada get into a heated discussion that results in verbal attacks and name-calling. It appears that the women's attempt to de-stress and mentally prepare for the trip was unsuccessful. Also, their discussion at the spa about the tensions seems to have only increased cast members' sensitivity to each other as opposed to reducing the tensions.

Another method in which Black women's health is denigrated is by linking their wellness to employment and economic gain, and their wellness is often delegitimized. African American women's health has historically been impacted by their labor and employment. From the system of slavery through Jim Crow, Black women were denied quality health care, and their well-being was marginalized for their labor (M. Gammage, 2015). Under enslavement, Black women's free labor superseded their health, and as a result, Black women were forced to work despite illnesses. In fact, many diseases and illnesses that Blacks suffered from during enslavement were a byproduct of the inhumane treatment they experienced as enslaved beings. Infections from whippings and amputations and diseases like smallpox, malnutrition, sexually transmitted infections, miscarriages, and infant mortality, to name a few, were all directly tied to the conditions of enslavement. The end of enslavement did not result in quality health care options for Blacks in America. Instead, in the early 1900s, the system of Jim Crow ushered in a new wave of calculated injustices on Blacks' health and overall well-being. From the denial of access to quality health care facilities, to sexually and physically abusive employers as in the case of Black domestic workers, to deadly experimental treatments, health of Blacks in America has been largely affected by their social and political treatment. Despite all this, African Americans have been forced to continue to work even when battling chronic illnesses or violent employment. African Americans have worked diligently to combat this treatment in American society, which has taken the form of social movements and the creation of Black-owned businesses (J. Gammage, 2017). Yet media entities have repeatedly tied the health of Blacks, and Black women in particular, to their labor. Stereotypes were created to control the narrative around Black women in the workforce. The sapphire stereotype in particular positioned the Black woman as an aggressive laborer who compromises herself in order to advance in the workplace. Both early and modern cinematic productions represented the Black woman in this fashion, eager to work and never yielding to her personal health or family's well-being. Current popular reality television shows have adopted this portrayal of the Black woman but have also added a layer of delegitimizing Black women when they experience health challenges. For instance, during Season 5, Episode 9, of *Love and*

Hip Hop: Hollywood (air date September 17, 2018 [Scott-Young et al., 2018b]), Moniece Slaughter is filmed working with producers in a studio on a song. She steps out to review the track and greet a friend. When Moniece returns to the recording, she begins to experience some health complications that result in her breathing heavily and sitting on the floor. The other cast members and production company seek medical attention for Moniece. As Moniece waits for medical attention, the producer RoccStar and cast member Brooke Valentine dismiss Moniece's current health challenges. They suggest that Moniece is falsifying a health scare to get out of singing since her recordings have not been going well. Although Moniece has been transported to the emergency room, RoccStar and Brooke disregard this health crisis and proceed with working on the track with Brooke replacing Moniece. Ironically, Brooke is only at the studio as a supportive friend and guest of Moniece. The episode ends with no follow-up on the state of Moniece's health. Instead, the production around this health crisis focuses primarily on invalidating Moniece's health challenges.

The dismissal of African Americans' health and wellness on reality television shows does not end with berating and belittling the health of immediate cast members but extends to cast members' families. An illustration of this can be noted in Season 6, Episode 2 (air date September 9, 2018) of *Married to Medicine* (Huq et al., 2013–present), when Toya Bush-Harris criticizes Dr. Contessa Metcalfe for electing to care for her sick father instead of attending Toya's party. Toya goes to the extent of accusing Contessa of not being a genuine friend for not attending her event, which ironically was a medical-themed party. In Episode 3 (air date September 16, 2018), the severity of Contessa's father's sickness is revealed—her father has cancer—and she shares with the group at a cast gathering. Yet, Toya is portrayed as completely unconcerned with the welfare of her friend Contessa's family. Later in the season when Contessa undergoes a surgery to lower her risk for breast cancer given her family's history, Toya is once again portrayed as lacking genuine concern for her well-being. At a housewarming party, the female cast members inquire about the status of Contessa's recovery. Toya is depicted as focused more on her lack of communication with Contessa about her surgery than her actual health. The other cast members are represented as not agreeing with Toya's response, and one-on-one camera scenes are played demonstrating their disagreement. Portrayals such as these contradict the collective nature of African Americans and are counterproductive to the well-being of African Americans.

Although Black female cast members' health concerns have largely been depreciated in these shows, cast members have nonetheless still elected to disclose their personal health complications on air. The discussion of cast members' health challenges has increased over the years in reality television; however, the representation of their health struggles is often vilified and represented with violence. For instance, during Season 5 of *Love and Hip Hop: Hollywood* (Scott-Young et al., 2018b), K. Michelle opens the season with a revelation about her enlarged buttocks and the health complications she has been experiencing as a result of her body enhancements. While rehearsing for an upcoming show, K. Michelle and Lyrica Anderson sit down and discuss their performance collaboration, but their discussion quickly turns verbally aggressive and leads to verbal insults. Lyrica decides to leave the venue, and as she walks out, she is surrounded by representatives of the production company. The camera returns to K. Michelle as a medical practitioner administers an IV to her. K. Michelle explains that she needs the IV to increase her energy because "these hoes are draining." As the medical practitioner sets up the IV, K. Michelle continues to angrily express her frustration for Lyrica. Lyrica returns, and the women once again shout verbal insults at each other. K. Michelle, while connected to the IV, jumps off the stage and appears to attempt to physically assault Lyrica. Security immediately steps in; however, K. Michelle is able to successfully push a barstool at Lyrica. Security then escorts Lyrica out of the venue. Moreover, this episode demonstrates a complete neglect for the health and well-being of cast members.

Broadcasting a cast member receiving medical attention while simultaneously engaging in verbal and physical violence transmits the message that Blacks' behavior is animalistic. Animals violently attack when they feel threatened, when they are hunting, and when they engage in surplus killings. Animals lack the level of intelligence of humans and therefore attack even without a real threat. When humans have attempted to provide medical care to injured wild animals, animals have reportedly attacked humans (Thornton, 2022; USDA Forest Service, n.d.). Their limited intelligence causes them to fight over saving their own lives. This behavior is considered animal nature and is often attributed to wild animals that are not suitable for human engagement (Thornton, 2022; USDA Forest Service, n.d.). Thus, representing Black women as electing to fight instead of receiving medical care characterizes Black women as animalistic in nature and unable to coexist in society without major control and restrictions. Moreover, these portrayals signify to the public that Black women's health and wellness are not valued, and their health challenges are a result of their degenerative culture and lifestyles.

CATEGORIZING BLACK WOMEN
AS A DANGER TO THE PUBLIC

Unfortunately, the treatment of social isolation and restriction is not a new experience for Blacks in America. For instance, during the Jim Crow era, Blacks were denied access to public spaces such as schools, hospitals, hotels, and restaurants. This racialized treatment was predicated on the idea that Blacks were socially inferior to Whites and could not exist in the same spaces. The civil rights movement challenged these racist policies in American society and made this type of treatment illegal. However, the backlash to the gains of the civil rights era shifted the tactics used to restrict Blacks from "White" spaces. Thus, "White Only" came to apply to private clubs, venues, and housing communities. And media was once again used to reinforce the racist ideology that Blacks were social degenerates in need of social control. Today, the majority of media representations of Blacks, and Black women in particular, reflect century-old stereotypes of Blackness as racially and culturally dysfunctional. When Black men and women are repeatedly shown in the media and on reality television unleashing acts of violence in public spaces such as restaurants, charity events, and other public venues, these images transmit the message that Blacks are naturally aggressive and volatile even in public and should therefore be approached with caution and unwelcomed. This stereotype of Blackness has increasingly been captured and reported in 21st-century America.

As if the denigration of Black women's lives coupled with the false portrayal of Black women's health challenges as self-inflicted was not enough, reality television shows starring Black women go a step further to portray Black women as not only dangerous to themselves but also a danger to the public. Research demonstrates that routine exposure to aggression and violence can result in increases of destructive and violent behaviors among viewers (Chen et al., 2006; Wingood et al., 2003). Yet, despite these findings, reality television shows have not altered their approach to representing Black women as antagonistic and violent. Instead, reality television shows broadcast Black female reality as naturally vicious and hostile. This representation reflects the 19th-century stereotype of the Black professional woman as an aggressive sapphire (M. Gammage, 2015). The sapphire was a caricature based in stereotypes of the Black woman in the workforce. She was represented as untrustworthy, aggressive, and sexually deviant. Reality television shows have advanced this stereotyped portrayal of Black womanhood and have been rewarded with over a decade of success. Yet, these shows fail to include the real-life health effects of living high-stress and dangerous lifestyles. Reality television shows instead opt to capitalize on the misrepresentation of Black women as extremely aggressive and violent.

Acts of physical violence and confrontations are routinely filmed among Black female reality stars. In fact, many of the media advertisements for reality television shows starring Black women center on broadcasting violent scenes for the upcoming or current season. Not only are the advertisements used to set the tone for extreme violence in these shows, but the first episode of each season is also used to create a hyperviolent context for the season. In all six of the reality television shows examined in this chapter, scenes with verbal altercations and/or violence are broadcasted in the first episode of their 2017–2018 seasons. During Season 6, Episode 1 (air date September 2, 2018) of *Married to Medicine* (Huq et al., 2013–present), the women gather together for their first all-female cast event of the season. Dr. Simone Whitmore hosts a party designed to help the women, including herself, embrace their sexuality and strengthen their relationships with their husbands. The event is soon side-tracked by a verbal altercation between Dr. Heavenly Kimes and Mariah Huq. The women hurl insults at each other, which escalates into malicious assaults on each other's husbands, including allegations of infidelity. As the women physically move closer to each other, the other cast members step in to intervene so as to prevent a physical altercation.

In Season 8 of *Love and Hip Hop: New York* (Scott-Young et al., 2017–2018), Episode 1 (air date October 30, 2017) is titled "Unity." Ironically, the majority of the episode is dedicated to scenes of the female cast members discussing their antagonistic relationships. The primary focus on cast members Brittney Taylor and Bianca Bonnie is the drama and violence that exist between the two aspiring hip-hop artists. The first time that the women interact in the episode, they engage in a physical altercation at an industry party at a nightclub. Interestingly, both women are at the event to build networks within the music industry, yet the women are represented as violent and out of control. Another example can be observed during Season 5, Episode 1, of *Love and Hip Hop: Hollywood* (air date July 23, 2018 [Scott-Young et al., 2018b]), where five scenes are dedicated to verbal and physical altercations. In fact, over 10 minutes (25%) of the 41-minute episode, not including commercials, are exclusively dedicated to showcasing Black women engaged in verbally and physically violent confrontations. This percentage does not include the amount of Episode 1 broadcasting time (2.43 minutes) used to advertise previous scenes or promote upcoming scenes that include violence and aggression. Still another set of minutes is used to broadcast one-on-one discussions of these verbal altercations with the cast member in front the camera. Finally, another 2.5 minutes are used at the end of the episode to highlight violent scenes from the upcoming season. Combined, almost half of the episode is focused on violence. By showcasing the start of each reality television show starring Black women with hyperviolence and hyperaggression, not only does the message of extreme violence among Black women get transmitted, but the expectation of ongoing violence is also developed. These shows utilize advertisements within and outside of the episodes to promote scenes of anger and rage among Black women. But they do not stop there; an increased level of violence is broadcasted in each episode that results in chaos.

With the established anticipation of hyperviolence in reality television shows starring Black women, production companies readily meet the expectation by delivering a full season of vicious verbal and physical alter-cations. For example, acts of violence are present in every single episode of *Love and Hip Hop: Hollywood*, Season 5 (Scott-Young et al., 2018b). Acts of violence include altercations between Black female cast members, between Black male cast members, and between Black female and Black male cast members. Verbal altercations and verbal attacks on others are inclusive of violent language, profanity, and threats. Acts of violence also include attempts at physical violence and physical altercations. Physical violence among cast members includes throwing tables, chairs, and other objects at another cast member, as well as kicking, hitting, spitting, and pushing. In every single episode, multiple acts of violence are broadcasted as noted in Table 4.2. It must be observed that additional scenes with vio-lence from past episodes and upcoming episodes are also frequently linked into current episodes as side clips that are played on screen as a double scene when these altercations are referenced.

The overpromotion of extreme violence in reality television shows star-ring Black women has escalated in recent years. In 2015, I reported the alarming rate of violence in reality television shows focused on the lives of Black women in my text *Representations of Black Women in the Media: The Damnation of Black Womanhood* (M. Gammage, 2015). Since then, the rate of violence has increased in these shows and includes not only the Black female cast members but the male and older cast members as well. The type of violence has also shifted. In earlier seasons of these shows, networks broadcasted verbal and physical altercations; however, they now repeatedly broadcast the same scenes with violent attacks and verbal assaults. Scenes portraying Black women as aggressive and hostile are edited into multiple scenes and episodes in order to extend the length of exposure and heighten filmed violence. For instance, in *The Real Housewives of Atlanta*, Season 10, Episode 4, "All White Never Forget Showdown" (air date November 26, 2017 [Weinstock et al., 2017–2018]), NeNe Leaks, a veteran cast member on the show, hosts an all-white party and invites several of the other Black female cast members. Shereé Whitfield decides to invite a former cast member, Kim Zolciak, to the gathering. Kim is a White American reality star and star of her own reality television show, *Don't Be Tardy* (Weinstock et al., 2012–2020). Once Kim arrives at the event, she immediately starts criti-cizing NeNe's home and soon starts to antagonize Kenya Moore, a current Black female cast member. Soon the women begin shouting insults and verbal profanities at each other. The insults escalate to verbal attacks on Kim's parenting style and her daughter. The episode ends, and the start of the next episode, 5 (air date December 3, 2017), returns to the verbal altercation. Just seconds into the new episode, Kim attempts to engage Kenya physically. Security and cast members restrain the women in order to prevent a physical altercation. The production company representatives follow Shereé and Kim to the home of another

Episode Number	Episode Title	Verbal Altercations: Total	Verbal Altercations: Women With Women	Verbal Altercations: Men With Women	Verbal Altercations: Men With Men	Physical Violence	Violence Among Black Female Cast Members	Violence Among Black Male Cast Members
1	Clutch Your Pearls	3	2	1	0	2	3	0
2	The Bro Code	5	3	1	1	2	3	1
3	Separation Anxiety	4	0	2	2	3	1	2
4	Three Years	3	1	2	0	2	2	0
5	School of Rocc	5	3	1	1	3	3	1
6	Pretty Hurts	3	1	1	1	1	2	1
7	Shaking the Table	5	0	4	1	3	3	1
8	Sex, Lies and Videotape	4	1	2	1	2	0	2
9	True Hollywood Story	2	1	1	0	1	0	0
10	Mind the Gap	3	3	0	0	0	0	0
11	Bad Grandmas	4	4	0	0	1	1	0
12	Last Tango With Paris	4	2	1	1	1	1	0
13	Keep That Same Energy	6	2	3	1	0	0	0
14	Oops She Did It Again	6	3	2	1	2	0	1
15	When Wigs Fly	3	2	1	0	1	1	0
16	Wedding Crashers	5	2	2	1	2	1	1
17	Reunion: Part 1	15	8	7	0	1	1	0
18	Reunion: Part 2	9	6	3	0	1	1	0
1–18	Total	89	44	34	11	28	23	10

Table 4.2 Acts of Violence in *Love and Hip Hop: Hollywood*, Season 5, by Episode

cast member, Porsha Williams, as the women share their perspective on the confrontation at NeNe's house. The production around the scene was split into two episodes in order to extend the drama. Later in the season, additional episodes (e.g., Episode 9, air date January 14, 2018) recap the scenes from this altercation and show the women engaging in dialogue about the confrontation. This disagreement is also advertised as igniting additional conflicts among the cast members. Thus, the broadcasting of the original altercation was publicized and expanded into a season-long quarrel among the women.

African Americans are made even more frightening by scenes capturing calculated attacks against each other in public spaces. Several scenes in multiple shows portray Black female and male cast members plotting and planning verbal and physical altercations. The production companies not only film and broadcast these scenes, but they also assist cast members in setting up the showdowns. Production companies schedule meetings for cast members with conflicts such as reunion shows and planned sit-downs at the expense of cast members' health and safety. An illustration of this can be observed in *Basketball Wives*, Season 7, Episode 16 (air date September 9, 2018 [Seliga et al., 2018]), when Jennifer Williams encounters the women in Amsterdam. The episode description reads as follows:

> Bringing Jen to Amsterdam backfires in spite of Evelyn's good intentions; Jen's presence ignites a firestorm that no one could have expected; Malaysia reaches her breaking point; Evelyn hears rumors about her family that Jen has been spreading. (Seliga et al., 2018)

Jennifer, who was not invited by Shaunie O'Neal, the trip host, was convinced by Evelyn Lozada to fly to Amsterdam, despite the fact that she was not invited, to discuss and resolve her issues with the other ladies. When the women first encounter Jennifer, they are shocked and confused. Soon Malaysia Pargo and Jennifer get into a verbal altercation that turns violent. Several of the other female cast members attempt to restrain Malaysia to prevent a physical altercation between the women. Malaysia throws a table at Jennifer. Capitalizing on this moment, the production company chose to play this part of the scene in slow motion, four times in a row, from different angles. Only one security guard steps into the camera's view, as he attempts to stop the table from hitting Jennifer. This, however, does not stop the feud, arguments continue, and other cast members begin to argue with Jennifer. In the end, Jennifer is left standing alone in front of the restaurant in Amsterdam. Several European locals are filmed watching this entire ordeal. All of the other women return to their hotel, without Jennifer, and decide to smoke marijuana to relieve stress from the day. Malaysia shares with the camera:

We had a very bizarre day. I feel awful, because I blacked out. And I threw a table. And I just really hated that I had to go there. And I just wanna get high. (Seliga et al., 2018)

The scene closes with the women blowing smoke from the marijuana into the air. Scenes such as these portray Black women as reckless and callous. Throughout the scene, several of the women, including Malaysia, discuss the potential of criminal action taken against them; however, the women are represented as not being concerned about the consequences of their actions.

Another illustration is provided in *Love and Hip Hop: Atlanta*, Season 7, Episode 15 (air date June 25, 2018 [Scott-Young et al., 2018a]), where multiple cast members are represented as planning attacks and orchestrating contentious encounters with others. First, Erica Mena is shown sharing with the camera that she purposely sent a combative message to Stevie J in order to warn him that she has a conflict with him. Steve J shares his awareness of this message with the camera as a group of cast members are celebrating another cast member's performance. Arguments are heard in the background. It is soon revealed that Erica and Stevie J's daughter is engaged in an altercation over Erica's message. Security and Stevie J remove his daughter from the venue. Erica is then filmed sharing with the camera:

Stevie being the little bitch that he is, I set up the perfect trap. I decided to send Stevie a little DM and let him know that he is officially going to be my bitch since he wants to talk about me around town. Stevie showed everyone this DM including his daughter. (Scott-Young et al., 2018a)

Stevie J addresses the situation with Erica, and the situation becomes hostile. As they argue, Just Brittany arrives, which is ironic because she was removed from the artist showcase and has noted conflicts with the performers and other cast members at the event. Just Brittany reveals to the camera that she intentionally attended the event to cause trouble and strife. As planned, as soon as she walks in, the other cast members stop arguing over the situation with Stevie J and Erica and instead turn their attention and verbal assaults to Just Brittany. And Just Brittany returns insults back at them. Within seconds, several of the women attempt to physically assault Just Brittany, but she is removed by security. Just Brittany states to the camera:

And that right here is exactly why I came tonight. [She motions a smile on her face.] The Taco Tuesday twins wanna come to Houston, start drama at my performance, and I'm just returning the favor. Have a good night, ladies. (Scott-Young et al., 2018b)

These images misrepresent Black women as calculated violent offenders who require physical restraint and control.

Similarly, in *Love and Hip Hop: Hollywood*, Season 5 (Scott-Young et al., 2018b), several scenes showcase African American female cast members engaging in verbal and physical altercations at home in the United States and abroad. During Episode 12 (air date October 8, 2018), the women are filmed at a restaurant in London, England, to celebrate their final night abroad. The women discuss some of the contentious relationships among the female cast members, and within seconds of the scene starting, Teairra and Moniece begin to discuss challenges in their friendship, which leads to a verbal altercation and a decision to end their friendship. When the ladies return to the United States, they continue to discuss the conflict. K. Michelle, who has been a central part of the discussion although she was not in London, is brought into the fold and asked to meet with Paris Phillips. The women meet in a public restaurant to discuss the parameters of their friendship and former working relationship given the allegations that Paris stole money from K. Michelle. Once again, within seconds of the scene's start, K. Michelle and Paris verbally argue, which quickly turns into a physical altercation when Paris throws a drink at K. Michelle. Throughout the scene, the camera shifts focus onto the other customers in the restaurant as they are disrupted by the altercation. Security is then shown removing Paris, but the women continue to shout insults at each other. Whether domestic or international, representations of Black women in reality television shows, and the media in general, overemphasize extreme violence and aggression. Although each of these shows seems to be equipped with security, they nevertheless allow high levels of violence among cast members, and the companies that produce these shows choose to replay, emphasize, and promote images of Black women as disorderly, disruptive, and dangerous to the public.

Another illustration of extreme violence promoted as the face of Black Americans is displayed in reality television shows' representation of Black men. Black male cast members have increasingly been shown unleashing violence in public spaces, most frequently over the Black female cast members. Cheating allegations, sexual affairs, and work conflicts often result in filmed scenes of Black males engaging in verbal and physical altercations. Violence among Black males in reality television has become so perverse that death threats and even physical confrontations with family members are filmed and broadcasted. In Season 5, Episode 3, of *Love and Hip Hop: Hollywood* (air date August 6, 2018 [Scott-Young et al., 2018b]), A1 Bentley and his older brother attempt to physically fight each other at a restaurant, and A1 jumps over the table attempting to strike his brother, but security intervenes. During this same season, in Episode 5 (air date August 20, 2018), A1 is filmed attempting to jump over a parked car to fight another Black male cast member, Safaree Samuels; however, security intervenes. During Episode 8 of Season 5 (air date September 10, 2018), A1 and Lyrica confront Safaree about the rumors that Safaree and Lyrica have been having a sexual affair. The confrontation immediately turns verbally hostile, and attempted violence is filmed. A1 jumps over the table at the restaurant, and several security guards restrain A1. Altercations involving Black men are also broadcasted between Black men and Black women. During Season 5, Episode 2, of *Love and Hip Hop: Hollywood* (air date July 30, 2018 [Scott-Young et al., 2018b]), for example, A1 arrives at a restaurant to confront his wife about cheating allegations. Their conversation becomes verbally aggressive, and Lyrica walks out and attempts to leave the restaurant. However, the production company follows Lyrica outside and requires her to return to the restaurant to continue her discussion with her husband, A1. Lyrica reluctantly returns only for the argument to escalate.

Throughout reality television shows starring Black women, extreme violence is represented as a perverse "normality," where reality television production appears to provoke and support altercations among cast members. General attempts to regulate Blacks' presence in the public domain have been reported in the criminal justice system, corporate America, health care facilities, and higher education, to name a few. In 2018, *The Chronicle of Higher Education* reported several incidents of racial profiling of Blacks by students on college campuses. In the article "A White Student Called the Police on a Black Student Who Was Napping. Yale Says It's 'Deeply Troubled,'" Katherine Mangan (2018) outlines the circumstances leading up to a Black graduate student, Lolade Siyonbola, being questioned by three police officers after a White student called the police on the student for resting in her dormitory. Siyonbola was reported as refusing to be forced to justify her existence in a dorm and on a campus where she paid tuition. Like many Blacks across the nation, Black college students experience harassment and racial treatment despite their academic achievements and contributions to their universities. A similar incident caught national attention when a major restaurant/coffeehouse chain was cited for racial discrimination of Black men. In 2018, two Black men, Rashon Nelson and Donte Robinson, were arrested and forcibly removed from a Starbucks in Philadelphia (Stevens, 2018). The restaurant manager called the police to have the men removed for allegedly not patronizing the company. The men were reportedly awaiting a third party to begin a business meeting. Ironically, Starbucks is known for customers and noncustomers gathering to conduct business, read a book, or simply enjoy the space. Yet, the racist discrimination of Blacks in public spaces overrides common public practices because Blacks are perceived as unfit to exist in public. Twenty-first-century media representations of Blacks as a danger to the public further exacerbate these problems of racism and discrimination and make mistreatment and marginalization of Blacks in this country seem justified.

BUILDING A CULTURE OF
UNHEALTHY LIFESTYLES

In the 21st century, media racism has become a substitute for and complement to the racist science and mythology of past centuries that were designed to "prove" that Blacks were inherently inferior to Whites, socially dysfunctional, and in need of social control. Today, media productions such as reality television shows transmit the same message by showcasing everyday Blacks—noncelebrity and celebrity, wealthy and economically challenged, educated and uneducated—as fulfilling the long-standing stereotype of racial deficiency. This new system of White supremacist racist propaganda, cleverly disguised as reality television, is then used to rationalize public policies that target Black women, men, and children as criminally unhealthy and unfit for existence in American society. Therefore, it is not surprising to see public health and law enforcement policies coupled together to unleash a host of punishments against Blacks as they are labeled mentally and physically dangerous to the American public. Health data and criminal arrest records are used to supplement the racial labeling and targeting of Black Americans as unfit for full citizenship, and reality television and media in general only further validate these racist assumptions.

Manufactured Blackness in the media serves as the pretext for the American public's current understanding of African Americans' realities. The image of self-imposed physical illnesses abounds in reality television shows and promotes the message that the African American community is innately inferior, unhealthy, and dangerous. Representing the Black woman as a public health crisis in reality television shows, then, is a way of subjugating all Black women. These images damage the Black woman by representing her reality through the lens of century-old racist and sexist stereotypes of Black womanhood. Although reality television shows may argue that they do not directly require or ask the women to engage in physical and verbal altercations, they do create the context for such altercations and foster an environment for chronic disputes among the cast members. Over the years, several cast members have made it clear that they have not had contact with other cast members, especially those with whom they have had conflicts, outside of the show. The women are also given a major monetary promotion to behave in these violent and unhealthy ways. From six figures to multiple millions of dollars, Black women in reality television shows have been paid very handsomely to behave in a stereotypical manner.

The image of unrestrained violence, hypersexuality, and substance abuse among Black women has proven to be commercially valuable to media producers. Yet, it ignores the real-life consequences of such high-risk health behaviors. As the viewership and ratings increase, the picture of chronically unhealthy Blackness becomes even more valuable. But to say that economics is the singular driving force behind this treatment of Black womanhood would be grossly erroneous. Instead, we must recognize the dual purpose of racially commodified Black womanhood in reality television and the media in general. The first is to advance the racial subjugation of Blacks, and the second is to secure commercial profit from such racist productions.

Casting the Black woman as a chronically unhealthy being, and thus a threat to public safety, transmits the message that her right to freedom and liberty does not matter and thus her life does not matter. Media and reality television shows in particular foster and advance the notion that Black females' lifestyles are a public health crisis by allowing and encouraging Black female cast members to perform or act out uncontrolled violence, engage in substance abuse and high-risk sexual behaviors, and maintain unhealthy relationships for the shows' production. The conflict between sustaining an environment of high-risk behaviors and addressing chronic antihealth behaviors has been yielded to production companies' own economic interest. For VH1, the *Love and Hip Hop* franchise is the highest rated series on the network and has raised its overall network ratings (Andreeva, 2022). Comparably, not only is *The Real Housewives of Atlanta* the best performing installment in the *Real Housewives* franchise for Bravo, but it is also the highest rated reality television series on Bravo (Taylor, 2020). Thus, normalizing unhealthy lifestyles among Black women in reality television shows has been the trend for several years. Ever since the start of reality television shows starring Black women, such as *I Love New York*, which first aired in 2007 on VH1 (Abrego et al., 2007–2008), Black female cast members have been systematically targeted and groomed to perform as uncontrolled, sex-crazed sapphires. In fact, VH1 is notorious for producing reality television shows starring Black women that represent Black womanhood as habitually unhealthy and dangerous. From *Love and Hip Hop: New York* (Scott-Young et al., 2011–2020) to *Basketball Wives* (O'Neal et al., 2010–present), Black female cast members in reality television shows on VH1 are consistently shown exhibiting alarming self-destructive behaviors. Yet, reality television shows' profit margins leave little doubt that the picture of chronically unhealthy Black womanhood will change. Also, the increase in the number of reality television shows starring Black women is a testament to the widescale commitment to promote a singular image of Black womanhood as a public health crisis.

The chief danger of these shows is that they divert attention away from the historical, social, political, and economic factors that have shaped and still impact Black women's lives. When Black womanhood is showcased as chronically unhealthy, Black women's health realities are summed up as a product of culturally informed self-inflicted antihealth behaviors. As a result, the link between health disparities and social degeneracy is being marketed to the American public as the face of Black womanhood. This is also seen in the images of Black grandmothers and mothers-in-law on reality television shows (M. Gammage, 2018). Moreover, through media, chronic unhealthiness is broadcasted as a Black cultural trait, inheritable and passed on from generation to generation, which is a form of media racism.

It is clear that reality television has mastered the art of commodifying Blackness as racially inferior and chronically unhealthy. The desire for Black women to showcase their lives to a national audience has been superseded/overshadowed by racist and economic tactics designed to further oppress Blacks. Although reality television shows are exploiting Black women, Black female cast members are also participating in their own exploitation. The end result of both is the larger subjugation of all Black women and the larger Black community in general. Perhaps the most tragic aspect of Black women's portrayal in reality television shows is their unconscious participation in their own damnation. While some Black female cast members and producers have experienced career growth and economic success, these shows are designed to stifle Black women's collective advancement, citizenship rights, and freedom. That is, the intended long-term effect of Black women's misportrayal in the media is to convert Black women's citizenship into a marginalized existence, similar to enslavement, Jim Crow, and mass incarceration. Therefore, the media and reality television have become a tool to further the notion that Black women exist within the confines of social degeneracy. What is to follow is a demand for social regulations and control over Black women's existence. These representations not only shape our understanding of Black womanhood, but they also permeate the demand for policies that will determine Black women's lives and social rights in America.

CHAPTER 5

Black Lives Matter? Devaluing the Health and Safety of Blacks in the Media

The health and safety of African American men, women, and children have existed under hostile circumstances in the United States and globally. From forced enslavement and sexual exploitation to medical injustices and environmental terrorism, African people's health has endured a legacy of devaluation, oppression, and abuse. Black lives have also been undervalued and attacked by domestic terrorists, such as the Ku Klux Klan and extreme White supremacists, and by American law enforcement, which was created in the 17th century and formally established in the 1830s to maintain order and protect the property of Whites, including enslaved Africans (Berry, 1995). For centuries, Blacks in America have been subject to punitive policing and brutality that has resulted in countless deaths and has left a permanent scar on the face of African Americans (Blackmon, 2009). The horrors of anti-Black policing, while started during enslavement and continued through the civil rights era, still exist today and have severely negatively impacted the health and wellness of African Americans for generations.

Public health scholars have recently begun to study the connections between police brutality and low quality of health among African Americans (Alang et al., 2017; Krieger et al., 2015; Sewell & Jefferson, 2016). Alang et al. (2017), in their article "Police Brutality and Black Health: Setting the Agenda for Public Health Scholars," argue that African Americans' direct and indirect experiences with police brutality influence poor health outcomes such as increases in mortality rates, morbidity, stress and strain, and systematic disempowerment. The researchers argue that "police brutality is a social determinant of health" and can result in major health complications (Alang et al., 2017, p. 2). According to the authors, the consistent threat and legitimate fear of police brutality cause an individual's body to shift to survival mode, which can become dangerous and deadly as a result of rapid deterioration of bodily organs. "Deterioration of organs and systems caused by increased allostatic load occurs more frequently in Black populations and can lead to conditions such as diabetes, stroke, ulcers, cognitive impairment, autoimmune disorders, accelerated aging, and death" (Alang et al., 2017, p. 3). Health complications can be further exacerbated by racist public reactions (Alang et al., 2017) and failed pursuits of justice. The endemic problem of extreme police violence against African Americans is not only traumatizing but is also detrimental to the well-being of African Americans.

The negative effects of lethal force by law enforcement on the overall health and wellness of African Americans have not gone uncontested. African Americans continue to work collectively to address institutional racism in law enforcement and the American criminal justice system. In 2013, Alicia Garza, Patrisse Cullors, and Opal (Ayọ) Tometi created #BlackLivesMatter as a practical Black-oriented movement of political and social empowerment. As reported in Chapter 1, "Black Lives Matter is an ideological and political intervention in a world where Black lives are systematically and intentionally targeted for demise. It is an affirmation of Black folks' humanity, our contributions to this society, and our resilience in the face of deadly oppression" (Black Lives Matter Global Network Foundation, 2018). The global movement has over 40 chapters nationally and billions of supporters globally. The momentum of the movement has led to local and national protests and legislative reform agendas. News media have captured snapshots of the movement, primarily focused on protest and police disruption of protest, and recently, scripted and unscripted television shows have attempted to engage aspects of the Black experience with police brutality and the Black Lives Matter movement. For example, the single-season series *Seven Seconds* (Sud, 2018) and *Shots Fired* (Blythewood & Prince-Blythewood, 2017) provide a scripted enactment of the killing of Black youth and the legal proceedings that follow. Similar to hundreds of real legal cases, in both shows the police officers are acquitted, and no justice is rendered for the families of the victims. Television dramas and reality television shows have also incorporated content revolving around the value of Black lives and the Black Lives Matter movement. Ironically, much of the discourse presented appears to validate the harsh policing against Blacks by representing African Americans as hostile, aggressive, and lacking genuine value for their own lives.

BROADCASTING A DEPRAVED NEGLECT
FOR BLACK MOTHERHOOD

The historic mistreatment of Black motherhood has been well documented (Collins, 2005; Du Bois, 1999; M. Gammage, 2015; Roberts, 1997). Scholars have also drawn connections between the racist and sexist devaluing of Black women and their motherhood (Collins, 1999; M. Gammage, 2015; hooks, 1992). The discourse on Black womanhood has been expanded to include media representations of Black motherhood, and scholars argue that methodical undervaluing of Black motherhood is rooted in the pursuit for economic and social control over Black women's reproduction. Accordingly, media outlets have been used to disseminate racist messages about Black motherhood that correlate with political ideologies used to marginalize Black mothers. In *Representations of Black Women in the Media*, I argue that

> in the 21st century the marginalization of Black motherhood has been adopted in the media and has advanced to the point of damnation. Black women's right to motherhood has been regulated to a unidimensional existence that renders them unsuitable for motherhood. Television dramas, reality television shows, and news outlets have all viciously attacked and misrepresented Black women as jezebels and sapphires who require intervention. The acceptance and use of these manufactured images have rationalized and validated the systematic assault on Black womanhood. (M. Gammage, 2015, p. 134)

These media entities promote an inferior valuing of Black motherhood and can be noted in current media representations. Reality television shows in particular frequently broadcast scenes illustrating a lack of value for Black women's lives. From aggression and confrontations at celebrations of Black motherhood to violence against pregnant Black women, reality television shows have presented a depraved neglect for Black motherhood.

Media has produced shows that highlight violence against "real" Black women even while pregnant. The network television station VH1 has chosen to broadcast several scenes with violence against and around pregnant Black women. For instance, in the very first episode of Season 5 of *Love and Hip Hop: Hollywood* (air date July 23, 2018 [Scott-Young et al., 2018b]), Princess, who is in her third trimester of pregnancy, is filmed undergoing physical violence. In the scene, Princess arrives at a fashion show to confront Moniece Slaughter, another cast member, about her false allegations about Princess's pregnancy. Moniece is physically frustrated to the point that she grabs a chair and rushes toward Princess. Several cast members intervene, and a couple of security guards stand near Princess. Broadcasting this type of violence demonstrates a depraved neglect for the health and lives of all Black women, and it appears to be intentional given that it is aired in the very first episode. Simultaneously, these shows represent the Black female cast members as lacking concern about their baby's health and safety, as well as their own, because they put themselves in danger. Princess is shown planning to confront Moniece despite the fact that she is pregnant and has a history of violence with Moniece. Although Princess is encouraged by her husband, Ray J, not to engage Moniece while pregnant, she enlists the help of her friends, who notify her of Moniece's whereabouts. With this information, the show portrays Princess as willingly verbally attacking Moniece and inciting the violence against her. When confronted by Ray J in Episode 3 (air date August 6, 2018 [Scott-Young et al., 2018b]), Moniece admits her actions and does not express any remorse, and the production company does not advertise any penalty for this type of behavior.

In both *Love and Hip Hop: Hollywood* (Scott-Young et al., 2014–2019) and *Love and Hip Hop: Atlanta* (Abramson et al., 2012–present), verbal confrontations have turned into physical assaults at celebrations of Black motherhood. In Season 5, Episode 2, of *Love and Hip Hop: Hollywood* (air date July 30, 2018 [Scott-Young et al., 2018b]), Ray J and Princess host a gender reveal party at a public venue, which soon turns confrontational as Princess and her mother-in-law and sister-in-law argue over conflicts in Princess's marriage. But the aggression doesn't end there. Soon, Lyrica Anderson arrives and immediately confronts Brooke Valentine, a fellow cast member and friend, about her spreading rumors about Lyrica flirting with a man who is not her husband. When Brooke confirms that she believes this is truthful, Lyrica is visibly frustrated and pushes the table coverings and the table over toward Brooke. The camera quickly shows Princess watching the altercation, yet no security is nearby. Security then escorts Lyrica out of the venue. Similarly, in Season 7, Episode 16, of *Love and Hip Hop: Atlanta*, titled "Peace and Blessings" (air date July 2, 2018 [Scott-Young et al., 2018a]), the cast members are celebrating at a baby shower that quickly turns into an altercation. A baby shower is being hosted for Jessica Dime and Shawne Williams. The cast first all appear to be very excited for the couple; however, within two minutes of the scene beginning, two male cast members, Stevie J and Sean Garrett, engage in a verbal altercation that turns physical. While the camera quickly shows Jessica Dime away from the confrontation, the violence was still filmed with her and older Black women in the space. The repeated broadcast of violence against and around Black women, even when pregnant, represents African Americans as lacking respect and value for Black women's lives. These images also portray the Black community as chronically violent and lacking control. Moreover, there appears to be a lack of concern for the health and safety of pregnant

Black females and Black female cast members in general. Instead, it appears that Black women's health and safety are sidelined for an alternative agenda that seeks to represent Blacks as in need of social regulation and control.

This is troubling given the historic abuse against Black women in America and globally. From sexual terrorism to domestic exploitation, Black women have endured centuries of physical and psychological violence. "During the system of enslavement, African women exercised limited to no control over their pregnancy and birthing experience" (M. Gammage, 2015, p. 22). Pregnant Black women were forced to work physically strenuous jobs for the economic benefit of Whites, were beaten and raped, and were denied quality nutrition and medical care. Yet, despite these racially oppressive conditions, Black women resisted. They maintained their humanity and fought to preserve their dignity. Black women's club movements and suffrage movements were formed in America as early as the 19th century to address racial and sexist marginalization and to restore dignity to their womanhood. Yet, American society has proven itself to be calculated in its attempts to devalue the Black woman. As noted by bell hooks in *Ain't I a Woman* (1981), the "systematic devaluation of black womanhood was not simply a direct consequence of race hatred, it was a calculated method of social control" (pp. 59–60). Similar to the racist and sexist propaganda campaigns used against Black women in the early 1900s with the eugenics movement and later in the 1970s, 1980s, and 1990s with the "welfare queen" and "crack mama" labels, media broadcasting of Black women as lacking value and in need of social control is used to socialize the American public into accepting that Black women's lives do not have value and do not matter. If Black women's lives do not matter, what does this say about their children?

DELEGITIMIZING BLACK PARENTS' PROTECTION OF BLACK YOUTH

African American parents have had the unfortunate burden of protecting their children from violence and death since the enslavement era. For decades, Black families were subjected to domestic terrorism that resulted in lynchings, burnings, rapes, beatings, mutilations, and castrations. Black families and communities have fought collectively against such violence through the 21st century. As homicide rates in Black communities rose, Black families continued to fight to preserve the humanity of their youth. In the 21st century, the Black community formed a new resistance movement, the Black Lives Matter movement, to address the racial injustices in the criminal justice system faced by African Americans. The unarmed shooting of Black men, women, and children on camera sent shock waves across the nation. African Americans are still fighting for justice and safety. In several reality television shows starring African Americans, cast members have discussed how this racial reality has impacted their lives and their families. *Basketball Wives* cast member Malaysia Pargo, for example, chose to share her family's experience with police violence. In Season 7 (Seliga et al., 2018), Malaysia shares that her brother was unjustly killed by a police officer, which has resulted in much pain and fear. Malaysia reveals that she has developed a phobia of police officers as a result of her family's experience. However, Malaysia hopes to find healing and understanding as she is now charged with the task of raising her young male son. The show films Malaysia discussing the racial realities of being a Black male in America with her son. The production company does not broadcast video footage covering the legitimate rationale for why Malaysia must racially socialize her son. Instead, Malaysia's phobia is portrayed as illogical and unwarranted, in scenes showing a White male officer active in a Black community. When Malaysia encounters the officer, she immediately bursts out in tears and runs away. With some encouragement from a friend, Malaysia has a conversation with the officer, which is portrayed as alleviating her fears. This scene only further increases the idea that Malaysia's fear was unjustified and irrational.

Not only is African Americans' legitimate concern for the safety of their children portrayed as unnecessary, but reality television shows also portray African Americans as lacking real concern. In fact, African American mothers are routinely represented in the media as lacking maternal instinct, neglectful, and hostile toward their children. Reality television shows produce similar depictions of African American women, and their motherhood has largely been encapsulated in misrepresentations of them as criminally unfit (M. Gammage, 2015). For instance, during Season 5 (Scott-Young et al., 2018b) of *Love and Hip Hop: Hollywood*, Black female cast member Moniece discusses with her son's father the impact of his representation of her on the show as a "deadbeat mom." Scenes in Episode 13 (air date October 15, 2018) showcase Lil' Fizz and Moniece meeting to discuss their co-parenting relationship. While talking, Moniece discloses that she has been stigmatized as an unfit mother on the show, which has resulted in the general public characterizing her as an incompetent parent. The show production then splits to a past-season scene of Fizz describing Moniece's relationship with her son as neglectful. Although Moniece states that she is a good mother and Fizz apologies for the impact of his actions, the production company has not broadcasted any scenes to support the idea that Moniece is a loving and caring parent. Instead, throughout the seasons, including Season 5 (Scott-Young et al., 2018b), discussion of Moniece's parenting has centered on her past actions and claims of her being negligent. Unfortunately, Moniece is not the only Black female reality star who has been publicized as not suitable for motherhood. *Basketball Wives* cast member Jackie Christie has frequently been represented as an aggressive and hostile mother. The entire Season 6 (Emmerson et al., 2017) broadcast of Jackie's motherhood focuses on portraying Jackie as combative and aggressive with her children. Although the show does not have actual scenes demonstrating these relationships, the show airs scenes of other cast members spreading rumors about Jackie's relationship with her children. This results in many verbal and physical altercations among cast members Jackie and Evelyn Lozada; because Evelyn is represented as the primary person spreading the rumors, Jackie begins to attack Evelyn's motherhood. The start of Season 7 (Seliga et al., 2018) returns to the women's contentious relationship, but a tentative cease-fire is agreed upon, and Jackie has tried to reconfigure the image of her motherhood on the show. Co-star Evelyn is also represented as a criminally neglectful mother on *Basketball Wives*. In Season 7, Episode 16 (air date June 25, 2018), the other cast members share with Evelyn that her friend, fellow cast member Jennifer Williams, has rumored that Evelyn abandoned her children to pursue romantic relationships with professional athletes and therefore left her daughter to attend to the affairs of their home. No evidence is broadcasted on the show to support these claims, yet continued discussion persists around Evelyn's parenting. The season ends without any reconciliation on the matter.

Another instance in which African Americans are represented in reality television shows as lacking concern for Black youth's well-being can be observed in negative portrayals of Black parents' advocacy initiatives for Black children. In the seventh season of *Love and Hip Hop: Atlanta* (Scott-Young et al., 2018a), cast member Rod "Shooter" Gates shares on camera his loss of his young son due to gun violence. Taking advantage of his celebrity on the show, Shooter allows the production company to film the Stop the Violence rally that he hosts in honor of his son. In Season 7, Episode 6 (air date April 3, 2018), a rally planning meeting is held with Shooter and a few close friends and family. As the scene opens, cast member Sierra Gates, stepmother to Shooter's son, walks into the meeting and is immediately hit by a marker thrown by another Black female cast member, Keely Hill. The women are physically separated from each other, but the camera switches to a one-on-one with Keely admitting that she willingly tried to attack Sierra because of their personal conflicts. The scene returns to the meeting, and the women are verbally shooting profane insults at each other. The male cast members call out this behavior as unacceptable. At the rally, the camera focus quickly shifts to discussions of verbal conflicts among cast members. Not long after, two Black male cast members, Stevie J and Rich Dollaz (a cast member on *Love and Hip Hop: New York* [Scott-Young et al., 2011–2020]), and a Black female cast member, Erica Mena, are filmed in a verbal altercation. Erica is shown attempting to leave the event but is followed by Rich Dollaz, and the verbal altercation escalates. Interestingly, an early scene in the episode shows the men planning to confront Erica at the Stop the Violence rally. The Black female and male cast members are portrayed as completely disrespectful of the purpose of the rally and ill concerned for the well-being of Black youth. This could not be further from the truth. African Americans have sacrificed their lives so that their children and grandchildren could have freedom and justice. Black mothers and fathers have marched thousands of miles protesting oppression and discrimination. Therefore, representing Blacks in antiviolence settings as irrational and uncontrolled contradicts the legacy of freedom fighting that African Americans still practice today.

MISREPRESENTING BLACK WOMEN AND THE BLACK LIVES MATTER MOVEMENT

African Americans' well-being in America has historically and contemporarily been tied to their agency and thus their ability to advocate for their humanity, cultural independence, equality, and freedom. Historically, Black women and men have started political, social, cultural, and legal movements to address the systematic injustices faced by African people. These movements have altered the state of America, yet contemporary activism has proven necessary amidst the continued injustices that persist in American society. Today, we operate in the era of the Black Lives Matter movement where African Americans and ally communities are advocating for the justice and humane treatment of Black men, women, and children by law enforcement. Recognizing the impact of this movement, scripted television dramas have included discussions, scenes, and entire docudramas to detail the complexities of Black experiences with law enforcement and the criminal justice system. Television dramas starring African American women have placed the Black woman at the center of this fight for justice and equality. However, these series have yet to abandon the stereotypical portrayals of Black womanhood, and thus the representations of the Black Lives Matter movement have been swallowed up by selfishness, corruption, and criminality. In the television dramas *Scandal* (Rhimes et al., 2012–2018), *How to Get Away With Murder* (Rhimes et al., 2014–2020), and *Being Mary Jane* (Akil et al., 2013–2019), for example, the lead Black female characters are portrayed as the poison killing the movement instead of the vital contributors.

False Possession of Power Over Justice

Framing of the Black Lives Matter movement and the pursuit for racial justice in scripted television series have allowed for a fantasy approach to be taken to the retelling of African Americans' stories. In television dramas starring African American women, they have become the face of the movement and voice of the Black community. These symbolic representations position the Black woman in an idealistic position of power and control, which is dangerous given the stereotypic portrayal of Black womanhood in the media. For instance, in *Scandal* (Rhimes et al., 2012–2018), a false possession of power over justice is rendered to the lead Black female character. *Scandal* is an American television drama series that chronicles the professional and personal life of high-powered Washington, DC, fixer Olivia Pope, an African American woman. Pope is portrayed as a political mastermind who has been able to resolve the problems of the wealthy and influential people of Washington. In 2015, for the first time in the history of the series, the show explored an issue directly impacting African Americans in the District of Columbia: police brutality. Season 4, Episode 14, "The Lawn Chair" (air date March 5, 2015 [Z. McGee & Verica, 2015]), presents an enactment of the Black Lives Matter movement and African Americans' pursuit for justice. The scene opens with Pope in a car and on the phone as she arrives to a place where a crowd has gathered and police are present. She walks up to the police to inquire about the status of the incident. She is informed that a 17-year-old African American boy, Brandon Parker, has been shot by a White police officer. The camera zooms in on the boy's body lying in the street. Pope immediately urges the chief of police to quickly remove the child's body. Seconds later, a gunshot is fired by the boy's father, Clarence Parker, as he calls out for the officer responsible for killing his son. Pope strongly recommends that the chief call the officers off the shooter. He agrees and gives authority to Pope, a civilian, who begins to negotiate with Mr. Parker. Pope, hired to help with the media on this case, is represented as being in control of the investigation and the police proceedings. Here, an African American woman is being portrayed as possessing the power to control the route to which justice is achieved or not achieved. Not only does she express power with the police, but she is also shown extending her power to the attorney general and the White House. Representations such as these become problematic because they falsely place the weight of achieving justice in the hands of one individual. That individual, who is not a lawyer or a judge or even the president, Olivia Pope, becomes justice.

The scene continues with a neighborhood activist, Marcus Walker, who brings Mr. Parker a folding chair, and they begin to discuss the situation with Olivia Pope. Mr. Parker accepts the chair, places it over his son, and sits with his gun in his hand. The crowd, comprised of local neighbors, rallies in support of Mr. Parker and justice for his son. Pope then goes to the police station to discuss the incident with the shooting officer, Newton, and backup officers. The typical tale is told that the officer feared for his life after the child raised a knife at him. Pope returns to the scene and confronts Marcus, accusing him of being interested not in justice but in retribution. He agrees and challenges Pope to desire the same. Marcus goes further to allege that Pope lacks a true investment in their Black community and instead is being used to advance White supremacy. Other scenes continue as usual with discussion of White House matters. Not only does the show falsely represent a civilian with power to control the police department and the search for justice, but it also erroneously portrays local activists as inciting violence and rage in Black communities. The depictions are used to delegitimize and criminalize activists in the Black Lives Matter movement. Black activists have risked their lives and freedom to move the needle forward on justice and equality. Countless numbers of African American activists have been incarcerated, exiled, and killed in the quest for racial freedom and justice. Yet, this representation ignores this legacy of sacrifice and instead portrays Black activists as self-serving at the risk of their own communities.

Next, as the crowd increases, the police grow impatient and prepare to force the crowd to disperse. Recognizing the pending actions of the police and her potential loss of control over the situation, Olivia Pope joins the crowd and begins to protest. Pope convinces the attorney general to subpoena the surveillance footage, after her team uncovers that the police department is holding the footage. The footage shows Brandon taking something out of his pocket. After viewing the footage, the father agrees to remove himself from the chair over his child in order to check for the alleged knife. When the boy's body is lifted by Mr. Parker and Marcus as approved by Pope, a knife is shown underneath the child's body. Mr. Parker in disbelief shouts out that his son does not carry a knife and points his gun at the police. Pope convinces the police not to shoot Mr. Parker, and for him to lower his gun. Pope's team examines the footage and finds that another person was in the back of the officer's car and may have witnessed the shooting. Pope confronts the officer and accuses him of covering up the murder and planting the knife. When Officer Newton is confronted with charges by the chief of police and the attorney general, he verbally attacks Pope with racist ideas about African Americans lacking respect for police officers' authority. The officers are arrested, and an independent federal investigation is launched, all in 24 hours. Pope then shares with Mr. Parker the truth about his son's murder, and Mr. Parker surrenders. But Pope informs him that he is not going to be arrested. Mr. Parker is then escorted by Pope to meet the president at the White House. The episode ends with Mr. Parker crying and being embraced by the president. The show inaccurately portrays justice as swift and fair, and also controlled by a Black woman. Yet, Black women have historically and contemporarily fought to bring about justice, and with each blow we have moved closer; however, justice and racial justice have not been actualized in this country. In addition, the inauthentic representation of Mr. Parker not being criminally prosecuted for his actions, including discharging a firearm in public, transmit a dangerous message that if adopted can place Black fathers and mothers in an unsafe and even deadly position. The truth of the matter is that African American parents who have been terrorized by the murder of their children by law enforcement have not been given a pass; instead, they have been forced to be poised and polished in their grief because one sign of their hurt can be and has been used against them to further terrorize them and destroy the name of their children and their struggle for justice. Yet, Mr. Parker is given more than a pass—he is rendered justice.

Later in the season, the show returns to this case with the discussion of creating a bill to institute ways of reforming the criminal justice system. Episode 19, "I'm Just a Bill" (air date April 16, 2015 [Mohamed & Allen, 2015]), details an attempt to pass a bill named in honor of Brandon Parker, the Brandon Bill, designed to provide a national standard of accountability in the justice system in order to address police brutality and police abuse of power. The president attempts to pass this legislation as part of his presidential legacy. Thus, his team works hard to get the bill passed. Ironically, the second storyline unfolding in this episode focuses on Marcus, the local activist who is now running for mayor, and the scandal he is tied up in. Marcus is having an affair with his opponent's White wife. While with the mayor's wife at the mayor's home, Marcus is forced to hide in the closet as the couple believes that the mayor, her husband, has returned home. But the men who have entered the home are not with her husband and are there to murder her. Marcus witnesses the entire ordeal while standing in the closet and calls Olivia Pope for help. Pope and her associates clean up the crime scene and discard the body. They use the evidence pointing to the mayor as the person responsible for his wife's death to leverage Marcus's candidacy for mayor. The current mayor agrees to step down and support Marcus. However, Marcus does not go through with the plan and instead outs the mayor for murdering his wife, which ultimately eliminates his run for mayor. Meanwhile, on Capitol Hill, when the votes become tied and the vice president is required to break the tie, the bill undergoes major scrutiny by the vice president. Upon discussion, the president agrees that the Brandon Bill requires restructuring in order to ensure that it is an enforceable and realistic bill to address racial injustice in the criminal justice system at the legislative level. The bill is then pulled from the Senate floor. In Season 4, Episode 22 (air date May 14, 2015 [Rhimes et al., 2015]), during a phone call between Pope and the president, the president acknowledges that the bill is being signed into law in the very spot where Brandon Parker was murdered. The show does not, however, actually show the bill being signed into law. The bill is once again wrapped up in scandal when the bill returns to the show in Season 5, Episode 4, "Dog-Whistle Politics" (air date October 15, 2015 [Fish & Fuentes, 2015]), when several male Republican senators attempt to leverage the president to remove the Brandon Bill in order to avoid impeachment. With the president facing scrutiny and attack should he be outed for his long-term affair with Pope, the senators threaten to start impeachment procedures against him unless he agrees to drop the Brandon Bill, which the senators believe has caused much strain on their relationship with law enforcement. Under pressure, the president choses to flaunt his affair with Pope to eliminate the leverage of the senators. Interestingly, the president is still married, and his wife, Mellie Grant, is a senator and a member of an all-female senator group. After seeing the president's actions, Mellie and the female senators agree to work to impeach the president. With several senators on board, the impeachment procedures begin but are quickly ended after Pope's power of influence is used on the now former First Lady, who agreed to illegally aid in the release of Pope's father from prison in exchange for Pope's father blackmailing the senators and forcing the Senate to dismiss the impeachment charges against the president. The corruption around the Brandon Bill undermines the legitimacy and necessity of the bill, and it ultimately dismisses the usefulness of this type of legislation by portraying criminality as unphased by law when orchestrated by the wealthy and powerful. Thus, those in the position of power to evade the law and/ or who have the power to control those in position of enforcing the law are above laws and are not subject to the penalties of laws. Overall, the representation of justice is tied to criminal and illegal actions with Olivia Pope at the center of it all.

On one hand, this representation presents a fantasy portrayal of the Black Lives Matter movement, and on the other hand, a grotesque treatment of Black womanhood is imagined. Olivia Pope's character is dreamed up as having the complete possession of power in politics, law, and government. Pope, an African American woman, is described as earning her power and influence though her political and legal connections. With this enormous power, she has dictated what justice looks like and how it operates in American society. In these episodes, Pope has willed her power to grant justice for Brandon Parker with the prosecution of the officers and the freedom of Mr. Parker. This fairy-tale depiction of Pope ultimately places racial justice in the hands of one single African American woman, who simultaneously is portrayed as wrapped up in her own self-inflicted scandals because of her sapphire behaviors. First, the error in this portrayal is the complete elimination of White supremacy, power, and privilege. Ignoring White power in American society is equivalent to disregarding African Americans' oppression. White power is the complete and absolute control of American and global institutions and governance for the benefit of Whites. African Americans have actively resisted this institutional racism and have not controlled the source of their oppression. Instead, African Americans have fought against injustices and challenged America to transform into a society rooted in equality and respect for all humans. Converting White power into a tool used by a Black woman to determine justice is a gross misrepresentation of African Americans' struggles and fight for their humanity. The problem of justice is not the sole responsibility of a single African American woman; nor do Black women possess the singular power to render justice or allow injustice to exist. Placing this burden on the Black woman makes her responsible for the lack of justice that has persisted in America for centuries, which could not be further from the truth. Also, this narrative is historically inaccurate in that it is inconsistent with African Americans' historical fight for justice, which has been rooted in their collective movements such as direct-action protest (J. Gammage, 2017). Second, and maybe more outrageous, is the representation of Olivia Pope's conditions of justice being smothered in her own hypersexual, violent, and criminal scandals. In each episode in which Brandon Parker's case and the Brandon Bill are addressed, Pope is concurrently engulfed in criminal, illegal, and immoral actions. Housing the power of justice within a vessel that lacks control and morality, and placing a Black woman as the face of that vessel, delegitimizes Black women's involvement in the pursuit of racial justice and renders her the problem. That is, if not for the hypersexual, hyperviolent, aggressive, and self-serving ways of Olivia Pope, true justice could be established. This is the definition of the sapphire, a stereotype of Black women in the workforce created by White men to control the narrative around Black women in order to restrict their economic, political, and social power. Thus, Pope's possession of White power is nothing more than a nightmare fantasy used to blame African Americans for their own oppression and marginalization. This representation ultimately transmits the message that African Americans' inability to receive justice and equality in America is a result of the Black woman's criminally degenerative behavior and the inferiority of the African American culture. Thus, portrayals such as these conclude that African Americans' wellness of being cannot be fully established.

Dismissal of the Movement

Being Mary Jane (Akil et al., 2013–2019) is an American television drama series that follows the life of a successful African American female news anchor, Mary Jane Paul. While the show has primarily focused on the personal and professional life of Mary Jane, Season 3 expanded its scope to include critical topics such as race-based beauty standards, suicide, and drug abuse. Police brutality is an off-camera topic discussed at Mary Jane's news station; however, the journalist has not directly reported on the subject matter. In the Season 3 finale, Episode 10 (air date December 15, 2015 [Akil & Scott, 2015]), the topic of police brutality hits close to home for Mary Jane when she learns that a recent videoed incident of police brutality against a young African American woman was inflicted against her niece, Niecy.

In the thick of the Black Lives Matter movement, show producers incorporated a scripted enactment of the violence experienced by millions of African Americans at the hands of police officers. In the final minutes of the season finale, Niecy is shown driving a car, with her two young children in the back seat, when she is signaled to pull over by a police car. Two police officers exit the car, and one officer approaches Niecy's driver's side window. Niecy is asked for her license, registration, and insurance. Niecy questions the officer about why she was pulled over, and the officer replies that they will get to that. Niecy continues to question the rationale for pulling her over. The officer than notifies Niecy that her music was too loud. Physically aggravated, Niecy responds by questioning whether playing music too loud is a crime. The officer then adds that Niecy was also pulled over because she did not have any tags on her car. Niecy responds by stating, "It's a new car, duh!" Niecy then notifies the officer that she is about to leave. The officer reaches to open her car door, but Niecy objects and requests that the officer not touch her car. The officer proceeds with opening the door and forcing Niecy out of the car. Niecy is shocked by the officer's actions and pleads with the officer to take his hands off of her. As the situation escalates, Niecy struggles to release herself from the officer's grip. As she pulls away, the officer pulls out his Taser gun and shouts "Taser!" as he hits Niecy with the Taser. Niecy is tased and falls on the ground as she is shocked. Niecy's son Treyvion witnesses the entire assault and shouts out for his mother. The episode returns to Mary Jane's workplace where a couple of coworkers are discussing the recent incident, which was videotaped and posted on social media. One of the coworkers calls Mary Jane over and shows her the video. Mary Jane immediately realizes that the young woman in the video is her niece. The episode ends with Mary Jane tuning out her coworker as she stands in shock viewing the video.

Season 4 opens with a black screen and the words "One year later" (Shelton & Van Peebles, 2017). The opening scene follows Mary Jane's footsteps as she walks in red high heels and escorts a man into her hotel room. The episode then shifts to two hours earlier, and we discover that the man in Mary Jane's hotel room is a man she met earlier that night at a New York City club. Both Mary Jane and her friend and coworker Kara have moved to New York for new career opportunities with a larger national news station. Before the start of Mary Jane's first workday, the friends decide to go to a club to meet men with whom they both plan on having one-night stands. The episode does not mention the incident with

Niecy until Mary Jane arrives at work the next morning and shares with Kara her fears about going back to the news camera. Mary Jane informs Kara that while Satellite News Channel, her former employer, allowed her to resign, she was actually fired from the job. Kara questions whether her firing was "because of the Niecy stuff," and Mary Jane responds: "I knew when I was defending her it was ruffling feathers. But then I started really reeling about police brutality and racial profiling."

Mary Jane then takes her microphone, puts on a smile, and walks out to start her first segment. Ironically, while the show's producers chose to display the violent attack on Niecy, they do not highlight the criminal and social proceedings that followed. What makes the representation worse is the simple summary of the aftermath in a two-minute clip, which is overshadowed by the overemphasis on Mary Jane's new job and search for a romantic partner. In addition, faulting involvement in the Black Lives Matter movement for losing her job dismisses the necessity of journalists and news anchors in critically engaging and reporting systematic racism and its impact on the nation. In fact, journalists and news stations have played a primary role in broadcasting the narratives around social movements. Historically, while much of the reporting around African American social movements has been analyzed from a Eurocentric perspective, which largely attempted to delegitimatize these movements, journalists with critical race consciousness have pushed the boundaries in order to more accurately report from a Black perspective. Therefore, stifling Mary Jane's career as a result of her critical consciousness is an unhealthy and dangerous representation.

Next the episode turns to Mary Jane's family, who at first seem to have moved on with their lives, as the family are shown watching Mary Jane on television. As Mr. and Mrs. Paul call for their oldest son, Patrick, to join them, he notifies them that he is preparing a statement to respond to the officer who tasered Niecy, returning back to work. Patrick attempts to discuss the statement with Niecy, but she is portrayed as being disinterested. Later, Niecy is shown discussing how the attack, news coverage, and protest have been negatively affecting her and her children, and this is why she does not want to continue to address her assault. She "just wants this to be over," and she does not want to "keep reliving being tased." We then learn that Niecy is scheduled to receive a settlement check, in the amount of $150,000, as a result of the brutality she experienced. When Niecy receives her payment, she is shown as being blinded by the possibility of love and spending her money on a $45,000 car for her daughter's father. Later, in Episode 5 (air date February 14, 2017 [Fisher et al., 2017]), the show returns to Niecy as she decides to treat her girlfriends to a girls' night out, which soon erupts into a verbal and physical altercation with another woman at the club. This altercation is also videoed by the crowd and posted on social media with the title, "Why the bitch got tased." Soon a media storm of insults is rained down on Niecy, and she decides to defend herself. However, her comments violate the terms of her settlement agreement, which forces Niecy to return the settlement money. Yet, Niecy has already spent most of the money, and when her family learns that she bought a car for someone else, they force her to repossess the car.

Representing Black women as criminally hostile, violent, and reckless and therefore responsible for provoking attacks by police officers is a gross misrepresentation of Black womanhood. The show goes even further to cement the idea that immaturity is a predictor of injustice when Niecy's grandmother confronts Niecy about her recent actions and cites that she hopes that this experience will be "a wakeup call" for Niecy. Unjust use of force against, beating, and murdering unarmed and even restrained African Americans is never justified, especially not because of their personality or past. American youth consistently make mistakes, yet White privilege allows for White American youth to escape the burden of their faults. However, redemption is hard to come by for Black youth, especially when they end up in jail or the cemetery. Thus, the portrayal of Niecy as "ratchet," a contemporary term used to describe someone or something that is of lesser value and is socially unacceptable, categorizes Black youth as a public nuisance that should be approached with caution and concern. African American youth culture and social behaviors are not the real issue; the underlying issue is racist assumptions about Blackness that compartmentalize Black youth into a criminal box. Therefore, any representation of Black youth experiences with the criminal justice system must be certain to include the presence of institutional racism. The mere portrayal of violent attacks is not sufficient or healthy, and it completely underscores the issues.

Even more threatening is the inaccurate representation of Black women refusing to engage in resistance movements and support for family and community victims of racial injustices, under the gauze of preserving their health and careers. When Mary Jane is informed about the current situation with Niecy, she responds by stating that she "needs to keep a healthy distance from all of this." Broadcasting Black women's involvement in the Black Lives Matter movement as unhealthy is contradictory to the real-life health effects of racial injustice on the lives of African Americans. African Americans have had to consistently fight against racism to maintain the very breath of life.

Not resisting deadly, violent, and psychological terrorism is unhealthy. African American resistance movements have been the heartbeat for Blacks in order to maintain their sanity and lives. Thus, representing personal health as a scapegoat for activism could not be more insulting to Black activists around the world. This narrative is similar to the rationale given by Mary Jane when she moves to New York and decides not to continue to use her platform as a news reporter to address police brutality. Portraying Mary Jane as abandoning the fight for racial justice because it is unhealthy, and it damaged her career, is like killing Black activism twice. The truth of the matter is African Americans would not have access to careers in America if it were not for their resistance against racially oppressive systems such as enslavement, Jim Crow, and discriminatory hiring and educational policies (J. Gammage, 2017). And while unemployment is a real issue, African Americans have historically and contemporarily sacrificed their jobs to stand up against injustice. In the 21st century, African Americans' collective resistance and activism have still proven necessary, including in the area of employment. African Americans have the highest rate of underemployment despite their educational attainment (Allen & Anderson, 2014; Jones & Schmitt, 2014). In addition, an economic wage gap has continued to persist for the Black woman (National Partnership for Women and Families, 2022). Black women have started social media movements such as #BlackWomenAtWork to socially document their struggles as Black women in the American workforce, and they continue to work collectively to address institutional racism. Moreover, Black women are vital to African American social movements and willingly make personal sacrifices in the pursuit of justice, and their stories are important enough to be told.

While Mary Jane is portrayed as attempting to separate herself from the legacy of Black social activism, her brother Patrick is represented as rising to the task of defending his daughter and family and becoming an advocate for others. Early in Season 4 (Shelton & Van Peebles, 2017), the show introduces Patrick as developing an interest in advocacy work, but it is not until Episode 14, "Feeling Friendless" (air date August 8, 2017 [Fisher & Green, 2017]), that the show explores Patrick's work as a local activist. This is also the first time that the show displays the name *Black Lives Matter*, although the term is mentioned briefly in a few other episodes. Interestingly, Episode 14, is the only episode in the 20-episode season to detail Patrick's involvement; however, the majority of the episode is focused on the fallout of Mary Jane's "unprofessional" rant toward a White female colleague who is portrayed as a racist White supremacist. Yet, Mary Jane's experiences with racism at work are never fully explored, nor are they linked to the larger social and institutional racism experienced by African Americans every day. The scenes that do focus on Patrick's work are diverted by an emphasis on homophobia among Black activists. While this is also an important topic to discuss, the problem is that neither subject is adequately addressed. Overloading discussions of Black Lives Matter with issues within Black communities in a few minute-long scenes directly dismisses the significance of the movement and the importance of addressing internal issues. While Patrick is a supporting character on the show, in past seasons and in Season 4 multiple episodes are focused on Patrick's life, especially when he has struggled with drug and alcohol addiction. Ironically, now that Patrick is involved in community uplift-ment, his presence on the show is minimized. In fact, later in the season, in Episode 18 (air date September 15, 2017 [Akil et al., 2017]), Patrick discovers that his dad is not his biological father and that his biological father abandoned his mother while struggling with his own addictions. The show then regains interest in Patrick as he struggles to remain drug free. Thus, the show has represented those who remove themselves from Black social movements as worthy of highlighting, and those who are involved in these movements as undeserving of camera time. Discussing the Black Lives Matter movement and Black social activ-ism in scripted television is a difficult task but must be addressed if media are to accurately represent Black humanity. Adequate focus and time must be given to fully flesh out the multiple dimensions of such realities and cannot be summed up in one convoluted episode.

Selfish Misuse of the Movement

Another fashion in which Black women's involvement in the Black Lives Matter movement has been erroneously represented is in the por-trayal of Black women selectively using aspects of the movement to foster their own personal and business interests. An example of this can be noted in ABC's television drama *How to Get Away With Murder* (Rhimes et al., 2014–2020). *How to Get Away With Murder* is a highly ranked and nationally awarded drama series focused on the life of law professor and criminal lawyer Annalise Keating. Professor Keating is an African American woman who has established herself as a brilliant law professor and undefeatable attorney. Yet, Keating's questionable law tactics and instructional style frequently get her tangled in criminal activity. During Season 3, Keating undergoes legal evaluation and receives court-ordered rehabilitation for alcoholism. In addition, Keating loses her position as a faculty member amidst her suspension from practicing law. During the season, Keating is arrested and incar-cerated for arson and is being investigated for murder. By the end of the season, Keating is acquitted of the charges of murder and arson, but her reputation is damaged, and she must fight to keep her law license. Facing disbarment in Season 4, Keating searches for a new focus and purpose in order to rebrand herself and keep her law license. Unable to secure work in her previous practice and living in an economy hotel, Keating begins to offer free legal services to incarcerated individuals under the pretense that they "need" her.

Attorney Annalise Keating's first client is an African American woman, Jasmine, whom Keating met while she herself was incarcerated (Season 4, Episode 2, air date October 5, 2017 [Goldsmith & Barclay, 2017]). Jasmine has been charged with possession of a firearm. During her first court hearing, Keating attempts to have a motion to suppress the evidence against her client under an unjustified stop and frisk. Keating argues that "being Black is not adequate grounds for suspicion." However, her motion is denied, and the case against Jasmine proceeds. When video evidence reveals that Jasmine may have also been soliciting and battering an officer, Keating brings this to the attention of her client. While talking, Jasmine begins to question Keating's motives for taking her on as a client.

Jasmine: "I should've known you can't get nothing good for free."

Keating: "I'm trying to help you here."

Jasmine: "You tryna help yourself. I knew it the minute you rolled up in here feeling all proud that you about to help your poor Black sister."

Keating: "And what's wrong with that?" (Goldsmith & Barclay, 2017)

Jasmine further explains that Keating does not possess the power to save her, because she has been victimized since she was a 13-year-old child. While Keating does not deny her own motives for taking the case, the women agree to proceed with Keating's free representation. In the next scene, Keating discusses the situation with her therapist, who also questions the rationale for Keating selecting Jasmine as her first client, noting that although Keating suggested that Jasmine needed her, Keating in fact went to Jasmine. Keating responds by stating that Jasmine helped protect her while she was in prison, and that this is the only reason. She then asks whether her therapist believes her, and surprisingly to Keating he responds no. He implies that Keating is deceiving herself if she believes that the only reason she is helping Jasmine is because Jasmine helped her. Keating does not change her answer, however.

Proceeding with preparation for the case, Keating discovers that Jasmine has decades of arrests for prostitution that have primarily resulted in plea deals. Finding indication that Jasmine was mistreated in the criminal justice system as a minor, Keating argues that her client may have been railroaded in the criminal justice system because of her race. During her court arguments, Keating interrogates the judge who originally sentenced Jasmine for solicitation when she was 13 years old. Keating highlights the fact that the judge rendered a different judgment for three other young women, all White, who were charged with the same crime but were offered rehabilitation services and no criminal record. In her arguments, Keating begins to use the language of the Black Lives Matter movement, arguing that "if Jasmine was treated like a White girl," she would have been given a chance to have a different outcome in life, but because she is Black, "we tell them that their lives don't matter, but they do matter. Jasmine Bromelle matters." Keating successfully argues for the release of her client and the sealing of her prior convictions. The judge apologizes to Jasmine for the mistreatment that she has experienced and offers Jasmine a semi–"fresh start," the ability to apply for jobs without having to report previous convictions. Interestingly, while the courtroom proceeding is happening, a second script is also unfolding, which centers on Annalise Keating and her therapist, who continues to question why Keating chose this case. Her therapist then suggests that Keating sees herself in Jasmine given their shared experience with childhood sexual abuse. Keating responds by stating, "I'm not her," which is the title of the episode. After the verdict is delivered, Keating returns to her therapist to report the outcome and wedge a bet against Jasmine, whom Keating believes will end up back in jail within three months. At the end of the episode (Goldsmith & Barclay, 2017), Keating learns that Jasmine has died of a drug overdose.

Despite Keating's previous argument that she only worked with Jasmine because Jasmine helped her, Keating decides to request clients from the public defender's office in Episode 4 (air date October 19, 2017 [Russo & Smith, 2017]). Keating signs up to work on the Philadelphia Right to Counsel program run out of the public defender's office. But once again, Keating is questioned about her motives for taking on this type of free work. The head of the program questions whether Keating is there to help their clients or "her reputation," but Keating changes the conversation to focus on the need for more lawyers to service the large number of defendants. Keating is given an appeal case where a young father has been convicted of murdering his fiancée. During the course of the case, Keating receives video evidence proving that the young mother committed suicide. Keating uses this information to get her client released but also uses it to highlight the deficiencies in the public defender's office. Keating purposely gets the chief public defender to reveal on court record that she has had access to this videotape the entire time but did not disclose it due to insufficient time to prepare for each case. When confronted about her actions that damaged the career of another colleague, Keating states, "It was for the greater good," which is the title of Season 4, Episode 3 (air date October 12, 2017 [Harrison & Rubio, 2017]). Keating links these issues to a larger systematic inability to adequately provide quality legal counsel for individuals in need of a free public defender. These cases become the foundation for Keating developing a class action lawsuit against the state of Pennsylvania and the entire justice system for unjustly providing ineffective legal counsel to vulnerable populations. However, Keating once again turns to her court-ordered therapist to discuss the outcome of her case, and he once again questions her rationale.

Keating: "This is an opportunity to help people who are desperate."

Therapist: "People or yourself?"

Keating: "Both. Because I want to feel better and this idea makes me feel better." (Harrison & Rubio, 2017)

Here, Keating once again admits that her pursuit of justice for others is also rooted in her personal needs. This revelation, however, does not deter her, and she moves forward with her case. While met with much contention, Keating proceeds with her class action lawsuit but soon finds herself, and her character in particular, on trial during her class action case. However, in typical Keating style, she is able to evade all judgment and is granted approval, and the class action is successfully certified. In Episode 13, "*Lahey v. Commonwealth of Pennsylvania*" (air date March 1, 2018 [Balogun et al., 2018]), the class action case is heard before the Supreme Court, and the verdict is returned in her favor. All of her plaintiffs are granted the right for an appeal.

In Season 5 (which aired from September 27, 2018, to February 28, 2019), Keating uses her success from the class action case to leverage her return to teaching at her former university and to a prestigious law practice. She is successful at both, and the new season starts with Keating portrayed as lucratively reestablishing her reputation. Returning to the university, students overcrowd Keating's classroom, hoping to get a seat, which allows her to handpick her students; and the students who previously distanced themselves from her now want nothing more than to be chosen. Not only is Keating's classroom overenrolled, but Keating also secures a high-paid job with funding for her legal clinic, research, and a more than $64,000 student scholarship. With the change in her economic status, Keating quickly moves out of her low-income hotel rental and into a luxury high-rise condo.

In this illustration, Keating is broadcasted as using momentum from the Black Lives Matter movement to advance her own agenda but does not display any real investment in the movement. Outside of the brief references in her case, no other mention of Black Lives Matter exists in the show. Although the show is set in Philadelphia, a city known for its high population of African Americans, there is no representation of the local Black community and their local activism. Thus, the fate of her clients, and the larger pursuit for justice, rests in the hands of Keating.

In addition, the show repeatedly highlights instances where Keating's rationale for taking on these cases is questioned. The show chooses to characterize Keating as knowingly and selfishly developing her class action case in order to return herself to a grander level of prestige in the field of law. Thus, if she can win an unwinnable case of justice in an unjust system, then Keating will be crowned a national legal powerhouse. In Season 5, we observe Keating rise as she is recruited by multiple law firms.

Similar to the representation of Black women and the Black Lives Matter movement in *Scandal*, justice is once again strapped to the back of one Black woman whose character is consistently questioned and portrayed as morally corrupt. Annalise Keating has directly participated in covering up murders, has been labeled an adulterer, has blackmailed several individuals, has defended clients whom she knew committed heinous crimes, and has used her legal knowledge to illegally advance her personal agendas and bolster her business interests. Over the show's six seasons (Rhimes et al., 2014–2020), Keating is also portrayed as abusing drugs and alcohol, which negatively impacts her life and career. When faced with the opportunity to make righteous decisions, Keating routinely errs on the side of corruption. Thus, it is not surprising that Keating's motives for developing the class action lawsuit are repeatedly questioned by friends, colleagues, and professionals. Despite these challenges, Keating perseveres in order to reach her lifelong goal of arguing a case before the Supreme Court and winning. In Season 4, Episode 13 (Balogun et al., 2018), Olivia Pope from *Scandal* is brought in to aid Keating. Yet, the fate of criminal justice reform will now be determined by Keating, and when her personal life interferes with her preparation for the case, she is tempted to use alcohol to cope with the stress, which could cause her to be disbarred. Pope uses her powers of persuasion to encourage Keating to get up off the floor and wipe her face. With less than one minute remaining, Keating walks in to start the hearing before the Supreme Court.

The treatment of Black Lives Matter in *How to Get Away With Murder* is comparable to the approach in *Being Mary Jane* and *Scandal*. While the majority of the season does not primarily focus on Keating's case, despite the fact that she is the lead character, the show instead develops the script to include other heavy storylines centered on criminal actions, murder, and corruption. Scenes detailing her former students' illegal pursuit for justice for their deceased classmate and the consequences that arise from their actions take center stage. It is not until the students' action backfires and a classmate is shot that Keating's law students begin to help her on the class action case, which appears to be in exchange for Keating helping them clean up their own mess. As for Keating, the storyline highlights her struggles with alcoholism and her strained personal relationships. The de-emphasis on the importance of the case is informative and points to a lack of authentic investment in using this media platform to shed light on the impact of racial injustice in the American criminal justice system.

Narrating the storyline around one Black woman eliminates the collective activism of African Americans and the American people. Even more unhealthy is layering the historic task of reconstructing the American justice system in one case and with one woman who is portrayed as morally degenerative. Thus, in the same way Olivia Pope from *Scandal* becomes the mistress of justice, so too does Analise Keating. On the one hand, maybe justice can be determined by Black women given that they have borne an enormously heavy burden of injustices in America; however, on the other hand, characterizing Black women as untrustworthy and even criminal and immoral strips them of their dignity and ability to be fair and honest. Therefore, these portrayals suggest that Black women cannot be the face of justice, nor should they have a voice in the debate over justice. The show *How to Get Away With Murder* appears to recognize this dilemma and sums it up in a conversation between Olivia Pope and Annalise Keating's mother. Keating's mother states:

> People needed me. People needed me. That's for sure. Sometimes I think this whole country would just fall apart if we weren't around to clean up all the mess. Only this time, I made the mess. (Balogun et al., 2018)

Captured in this statement is the complex representation of Black womanhood in the media. Trapped in her bosom is both liberty and justice, and criminality and corruption. These dueling positions are not mutually exclusive, nor can they be separated. Instead, the burden of injustice is blamed on the Black woman because of her morally corrupt state of being. These are inauthentic and unhealthy representations of Blackness and Black womanhood, and they are rooted in century-old stereotypes of African people.

It is unacceptable to blame victims of injustices and abuse for their mistreatment. Yet, Black women and African people in general have consistently been blamed for the inhumane conditions that have been forced upon them. Dr. Michael Tillotson (2011) calls this the victim-blame ideology, where African Americans are excoriated for their political, social, and economic challenges. Victim blaming is a political tool that is being used in media representations of Black womanhood to validate the idea that the Black woman is chronically unhealthy and cannot use her own agency to liberate her community. These images do not correlate with African American women's agency historically or contemporarily. From Harriet Tubman, Sojourner Truth, and Shirley Chisholm to Alicia Garza, Patrisse Cullors, and Opal Tometi, the three Black female creators of the Black Lives Matter movement, Black women have chosen to exercise their agency for the liberation of African people throughout the world, and they have done this in conjunction with the Black community and its allies. Thus, their media representations, even in scripted dramas, must include healthy realistic portrayals of their womanhood.

BLACK WOMEN'S WELLNESS
IN THE MEDIA

The current media representation of Black humanity and the Black Lives Matter movement is a form of media injustice. Media injustice is a systematic structuring of representations of a particular group to reflect and endorse standing stereotypes of that group despite their inaccuracy. Media injustice against Blacks is birthed from racist ideologies of Blackness and African humanity and created to justify the systematic oppression and assaults against Blacks. Thus, the portrayal of African Americans undervaluing their own lives and the misrepresentation of Black women's involvement in the Black Lives Matter movement in scripted media promote a racist narrative that is used to govern our understanding of the real-life health and safety concerns of African Americans. This is injustice because media propaganda, whether intentional or unintentional, is used to advance the idea that Black lives do not have value and do not matter. And these images are creating a media climate to not respect or support Black lives. To the contrary, the lives of African American women, men, and children matter, and media must reflect a healthy investment in representing Black lives with human value and not simply monetary value rooted in stereotypes. According to Hardeman et al. (2016), "Disparate health outcomes and systematic decrements in the well-being and livelihoods of black Americans in the United States must be seen as an extension of a historical context where non-white—and specifically black—lives have been devalued" (p. 2). Therefore, media, including Black-oriented media, have the opportunity to be just and responsible in their representation of Black women, and African lives in general, and their experiences with injustice by law enforcement. As noted by Alang et al. (2017), "Experiencing or witnessing police brutality, hearing stories of friends who have experienced brutality, and having to worry about becoming a victim are all stressors" and increase health risk (p. 663). Media representations of Black experiences with law enforcement have ignored these important health consequences and instead have chosen to stereotypically portray African Americans as warranting these mistreatments and injustices, and this is a byproduct of media racism. Advocacy efforts must be made within the media industry to produce more affirming and liberatory images of African Americans. In order to do this, media must recognize that police brutality is a public health concern (Krieger et al., 2015) and a legal, political, and social crisis. Failure to address this means that media are endorsing racism and discrimination against Blacks by providing images to support their subjugation. In addition, media must go beyond the surface-level review of Black humanity and begin to interrogate and acknowledge racism as a contentious determinant of Black reality. Therefore, media producers must be conscious in their story and scene selections so as not to singularly focus on narratives that undermine the value of Blacks. Simply showcasing issues impacting African Americans' health and wellness, laced inside of racist and sexist images, is not an adequate proxy for the struggles of African humanity. The media industry has a creative and broadcast responsibility to showcase the various mechanisms that impact human lives; omitting this jeopardizes the lives of African Americans and questions whether Black lives matter.

CHAPTER 6

Black Women's Lives Versus Black Women's Representations

Throughout this text, I have explored both the historic and contemporary framing of Black women in the media as pathologically unhealthy and how their public portrayals have influenced legislative policies, general public perceptions, and their overall treatment in American society. A common misperception about Black women is that they lack any real investment in their health, and their distrust in the health care industry only further hinders their ability to live and sustain quality lives. This erroneous assumption stems from racialized ideologies that frame African Americans as culturally degenerative and self-defeating. Media representations of Black women have adopted this belief about Black women and have methodically portrayed them as chronically harmful and socially reckless. However, limited research exists assessing Black women's perceptions and attitudes, and even fewer studies are disruptive to the stereotypes that Black women are ill concerned about their overall wellness and pathologically place themselves at increased health and life risk. At this point, it is imperative that we directly engage Black women's lives and life work and their perceptions of media images of Black womanhood.

Employing the Africana Womanism theoretical framework, this research engaged African American females as definers of their own lives and realities. The Africana Womanism theory is an Afrocentric framework that is based in the cultural perspectives of women of African descent (Hudson-Weems, 1997). Self-definition is an essential component of Africana Womanism and calls for researchers to engage Black women's thoughts and perceptions about their experiences. This chapter provides a historical and contemporary analysis of Black women's lives through their social, cultural, and political advocacy and work to improve their lives and the lives of their families, communities, and larger society. Quantitatively exploring the relationship between media representations of Black women and Black women's lives, this research surveys 97 Black women and compares their attitudes with images of Black women in the media. Using the African American Women's Health Survey (AAWHS), created for this study, African American women were surveyed to determine their overall attitudes about their lives and health behaviors. In addition, participants were asked to evaluate the representations of Black women in reality television shows and television dramas starring Black women, in order to determine Black women's perceptions of media portrayals of Black women's lives.

BLACK WOMEN AS AGENTS OF SOCIAL CHANGE

Black women such as Harriet Tubman, Anna Julia Cooper, Rosa Parks, Shirley Chisholm, Ella Baker, and Fannie Lou Hamer have been hailed for their heroic advocacy and unrelenting commitment to social change. Their work and activism have helped to transform the lives of African Americans, Black women, women in general, and society in general (Conway, 2021). The Black women's suffrage movement and Black work as antislavery advocates propelled their campaigns for human and civil rights and serve as the foundation for many Black-women-created movements today. Black women proved instrumental in the civil rights movement of the 1950s and '60s; the Black Power movement of the 1960s, '70s, and '80s; and the student and campus movements of the 1960s and '70s (Alameen-Shavers, 2016b; Gyant, 1996; Kendi, 2012). Their contributions demonstrate their responsibility to the well-being of African Americans and humanity.

Today, Black women have birthed social and political movements that center justice and human rights. The creation of the hashtag #BlackLivesMatter in 2013 by Alicia Garza, Patrisse Cullors, and Opal (Ayọ) Tometi was a call to action for African Americans to work collectively toward the dismantling of anti-Black racism and violence against Black lives (Garza, 2014). Their work to move the hashtag to a global movement was intentional, centering the humanization of Black bodies, Black children, and Black lives. According to Garza (2014),

> Black Lives Matter is an ideological and political intervention in a world where Black lives are systematically and intentionally targeted for demise. It is an affirmation of Black folks' contributions to this society, our humanity, and our resilience in the face of deadly oppression. (p. 23)

Black-justice-centered social advocacy continues to affirm Black people's cultures and lives. The recognition of Black women's lives and experiences has also given way to new social justice movements that center women's rights and freedom from sexual exploitation. Activist Tarana Burke created the Me Too movement in 2006 to address the marginalization of women of color in racial justice and sexual justice discourse (Burke, 2021). Underscoring the intersection of sexual violence and racial injustice, Burke worked to establish spaces for women who were survivors of sexual violence to seek justice and heal. More specially, the movement highlights how Black women experience targeted violence, gendered racism, and sexual violence (Gill, 2020). The Me Too movement as a practice has faced criticism regarding the continuation of racial marginalization for women of color and Black women in particular as White women's voices and experiences were elevated as they co-opted the hashtag and movement (Onwuachi-Willig, 2018). However, Burke argues that while the hashtag became popular when Alyssa Milano and others shared it on Twitter, the media played a major role in centering White women's experiences and demand for justice (Gill, 2020).

The media continues to play a significant role in the representations and marginalization of Black women and Black lives, as demonstrated in the previous chapters. The portrayal of Black women's advocacy departs from the historic and contemporary legacy of Black women activists and justice movements. When surveyed about media representations of Black women in television dramas and reality television shows, Black women expressed limited connection with the portrayal of womanhood. For the AAWHS, as detailed in "A Methodological Approach to Understanding Black Women," participants' evaluations of media representations of Black women reveal a rejection of the depictions as accurate images of Black womanhood. The mean score on the *Media Representations Scale*, for example, was low at 36.1 with a standard deviation of 8.4. Low scores on the *Media Representations Scale* are reflective of negative ratings of media portrayals of Black women.

A METHODOLOGICAL APPROACH TO UNDERSTANDING BLACK WOMEN

Population

Using convenience sampling, African American adult females were recruited using flyers, email announcements, and social media. Participants who gave their consent were directed through an online tool to participate in the study. Participants then completed a survey assessing the extent to which media representations reflect African American females' attitudes about their health.

(Continued)

(Continued)

Ninety-seven African American females completed the online survey. The mean age was 30, with participants' ages ranging from 18 to 61. Of the participants, 29.8% ($n = 29$) ranged in age from 18 to 21, 16.4% ($n = 16$) ranged in age from 22 to 25, 11.3% ($n = 11$) ranged in age from 26 to 30, 22.6% ($n = 22$) ranged in age from 31 to 40, and 19.5% ($n = 19$) ranged in age from 41 to 61. The majority of participants resided in the state of California (51.5%, $n = 50$) and were single and never married (66%, $n = 64$). Another 16.5% ($n = 16$) were married, 7.2% ($n = 7$) were divorced, 8.2% ($n = 8$) were cohabitating, and 2.1% ($n = 2$) were widowed. Almost 80% of participants reported some type of employment; 43.3% ($n = 43$) were employed, and 36.1% ($n = 35$) were employed students. Another 16.5% ($n = 16$) of participants were students, and only 4.1% ($n = 4$) of nonstudents reported being unemployed. Type of employment was not collected. The majority (89.6%, $n = 87$) of respondents reported pursuing higher education at various levels. Forty-five participants (46.4%) reported completing some college, 16.5% ($n = 16$) reported having completed college, 5.2% ($n = 5$) reported completing some graduate school, and 21.6% ($n = 21$) reported having completed graduate school. The average household income reported among participants ($n = 80$) was $51,124 (standard deviation $48,645). Among the participants, 17.5% ($n = 14$) reported income ranging from $1 to $10,000, 16.25% ($n = 13$) reported income ranging from $10,001 to $30,000, 16.25% ($n = 13$) reported income ranging from $30,001 to $50,000, and 40% ($n = 32$) reported income over $50,000 (with 8 participants reporting income over $100,000). On average, participants watched 2.8 hours of television dramas starring Black women, and 2.9 hours of reality television shows starring Black women, per week. Although this sample cannot be generalized to the larger African American female population, the data are an important starting point to understanding Black women's value for their health and wellness and their assessment of the images of Black womanhood in the media.

Measures

The African American Women's Health Survey (AAWHS) is a 51-item questionnaire made up of three components. The first component gathers basic demographic information from participants. Eight items are in the demographic section and ask questions regarding race, gender, residence, marital and employment status, education attainment, and annual household income.

The second component of the AAWHS is the *Health Attitudes Scale* and contains 20 items divided into three subscales: (1) *Personal Worth*, (2) *Physical Health Investment*, and (3) *Relationship Risk*. Scores range from 100 to 0 on the *Health Attitudes Scale*. High scores of 70–100 represent positive health attitudes of low risk, scores of 30–69 demonstrate moderate health risk attitudes, and low scores of 1–29 denote negative high-risk health attitudes. The *Personal Worth* subscale contains nine questions assessing participants' evaluation of their personal worth. Each of the questions in this section uses a five-point Likert-type response scale ranging from *strongly disagree* to *strongly agree*. *Personal Worth* statements include "I think I am beautiful"; "I am smart"; "I deserve to be respected"; and "I do not like it when people mistreat me." The *Personal Worth* scores range from 45 to 0. A high score of 45–34 on the subscale is reflective of high self-esteem, a score of 22–33 demonstrates moderate self-esteem, and a low score of 21–10 represents lower self-esteem. A score of 9 or below illustrates that the respondent was unable to make a judgment on the scale.

The second subscale is the *Physical Health Investment*, which solicits responses regarding participants' preventative care beliefs and attitudes about social health behaviors. Five items make up the subscale, and the response format is a five-point Likert-type response scale ranging from *strongly disagree* to *strongly agree*. Statements include "It is important to get physical check-ups"; "It is important to protect yourself when having sex"; and "It is acceptable to use street drugs." Scores on the *Physical Health Investment* subscale range from 25 to 0. High scores range from 20 to 25 and represent a positive health care attitude. Scores from 13 to 19 indicate moderate health care attitudes, and scores from 12 to 6 reflect poor health care attitudes. A score of 5 or below illustrates that the respondent was unable to make a judgment on the scale.

Assessing attitudes about romantic relationships, the third subscale of the *Health Attitudes Scale* is *Relationship Risk*. The *Relationship Risk* subscale includes six statements on a five-point Likert-type response scale ranging from *strongly disagree* to *strongly agree*, evaluating respondents' perceptions of appropriate dating behaviors. Statements

(Continued)

(Continued)

in this section include "I prefer to be in a committed relationship"; "It is acceptable to date a married man"; and "It is acceptable to have a one-night stand." Higher scores (30–25) on this subsection indicate low health-risk romantic partner beliefs, while lower scores (14–7) indicate higher health-risk beliefs. Scores between 24 and 17 are representative of moderate health risk, and scores of 6 or below illustrate that respondents were unable to determine their position on the statements.

The third component of the AAWHS measures attitudes about media representations of Black women. This section, the *Media Representations Scale*, contains 25 items divided into two subscales: (1) *Reality Television Assessment* and (2) *Television Dramas Assessment*. The *Reality Television Assessment* subscale contains 12 items divided into three categories. The first set of questions gauges viewership of reality television shows starring Black women. The second set contains four statements that assess participants' views on the portrayal of Black women in reality television shows. Statements include "Reality television shows accurately represent Black women"; and "Black women in reality television shows have good jobs." All of the statements are on a five-point Likert-type response scale. Four of the statements' responses range from *strongly disagree* to *strongly agree*, and one statement response format assesses frequency from *never* to *always*. Scores on this subsection range from 20 to 0. High scores (20–16) reflect a positive reception of the portrayals, moderate scores (15–11) represent a modest reception of the portrayals, and low scores (10–5) demonstrate negative receptions of the portrayals. A score of 4 or below indicates that the respondent had no opinion on the subject. Some participants bypassed this section because they do not watch reality television shows starring Black women. The third category of questions measures participants' willingness to adopt the lifestyles of Black women in reality television shows. This section contains five statements; all are on a five-point Likert-type response scale. Four of the statements' responses range from *strongly disagree* to *strongly agree*, and one statement response format assesses frequency from *never* to *always*. Statements include "I can identify with the women in reality television shows"; "Acting like the women in reality television shows will not impact my health"; and "I ____ act like the women in reality television shows." A high score (25–20) on the subsection represents a rejection of the behaviors represented, a moderate score (19–13) illustrates a neutral assessment of the behaviors presented, and a low score (12–6) indicates an adoption of the behaviors. A score of 5 or below indicates that the respondent had no opinion on the subject. Some participants bypassed this section because they do not watch reality television shows starring Black women.

The subscale *Television Dramas Assessment* includes 11 items divided into three categories. The first category's three questions gauge viewership of television dramas starring Black women. Participants who did not watch any television dramas starring Black women were permitted to skip this section. The second category contains six statements that assess reception of Black women's portrayals in television dramas. Statements include "Television dramas accurately represent Black women"; "Black women in television dramas have healthy dating relationships"; and "Black women in television dramas have good jobs." All of the statements are on a five-point Likert-type response scale. Five of the statements' responses range from *strongly disagree* to *strongly agree*, one statement response format assesses frequency from *never* to *always*, and the final statement is also on a frequency scale and range from *overly* to *not at all*. A high score (40–30) reflects a positive reception of the portrayals, a moderate score (29–20) represents a modest reception of the portrayals, and a low score (19–9) demonstrates negative receptions of the portrayals. A score of 8 or below indicates the respondent had no opinion on the subject. The third category of questions includes two statements that assess respondents' identification with the lead Black female characters in television dramas. Each statement uses a five-point Likert-type response scale. One statement response ranges from *strongly disagree* to *strongly agree*, and the other statement response format assesses frequency from *never* to *always*.

Assessing the reliability of the survey, a Cronbach's alpha was tested for internal consistency. The Cronbach's alpha calculated for the AAWHS was .715. High reliability for the instrument was produced based on the Cronbach's alpha score. A principal component factor analysis with

(Continued)

(Continued)

varimax rotation was conducted on the AAWHS questionnaire. The scree plot method was used to determine the factor solution. The factor solution included 39 items grouped into five factors. In the initial test, all five factors accounted for 100% of the variance; however, after rotation, only two factors accounted for 65% of the total variance. Factor 1, *Personal Worth Subscale* (eigenvalue = 2.072), accounted for 34.35% of the variance. Factor 2, *Physical Health Investment Subscale* (eigenvalue = 1.218), accounted for 31.434% of the variance. All of the factors were accepted for analysis in this study.

Procedures

The AAWHS was administered online through SurveyMonkey. The site was reserved for one year to invite participants to the study. When potential participants entered the site, they were informed of the purpose of the study and asked about their interest in participating. For those who were interested, they were linked to the statement of informed consent to review. Once consent was secured, participants were asked to complete a 55-item survey that assessed the extent to which media representations reflect African American females' attitudes about their health. The survey took approximately 20 to 25 minutes to complete, and there was no compensation for participation in this study. After completion of the study, participants were thanked for their time and released from the study.

Assessments of television dramas starring Black women demonstrate inconsistencies in the media representations of Black women and Black women's lives. Sixty-eight percent of responding participants ($N = 91$) stated that they never ($n = 34$) or rarely ($n = 28$) act like the lead Black women in television dramas. Only 30% ($n = 29$) of participants stated that they can identify with the lead Black female characters in television dramas. The mean score on the *Television Dramas Assessment* subscale was 17.5 with a standard deviation of 5.4. This score denotes a negative reception of the portrayals of Black women in television dramas and lies within the low range. The majority (55%, $n = 53$) of participants disagreed that "Television dramas accurately represent Black women," while another

30% of participants ($n = 29$) were undecided (see Figure 6.1). As discussed in Chapter 5, television dramas have erroneously represented Black women's involvement in social advocacy as self-motivated and self-serving. To the contrary, Black women have sacrificed their lives for justice and liberation and continue to work to challenge injustice, racism, and sexism.

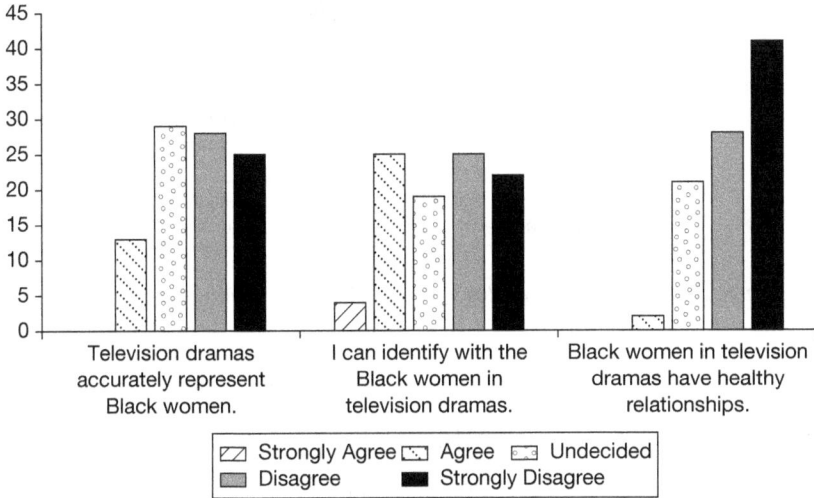

Figure 6.1   Black Women's Perceptions of Television Dramas

Even more revealing was Black women's assessment of reality television shows. On the subscale *Reality Television Assessment*, participants' mean score was 18.4 with a standard deviation of 4.1. The mean score is in the low range and signifies a negative response to the representations of Black women in reality television shows. Ninety-one percent of participants ($n = 71$; $N = 78$) disagreed that "Reality television shows accurately represent Black women" (see Figure 6.2). It appears that media images of Black women do not parallel Black women's lives and advocacy. Respondents in this study find the portrayals of Black women in both television dramas and reality television shows fail to accurately represent Black women and instead depict Black women as living unhealthy lifestyles. Black women creatives work to recenter Black women's lives and to give voice to their authentic realities, which is discussed in the final chapter of this book.

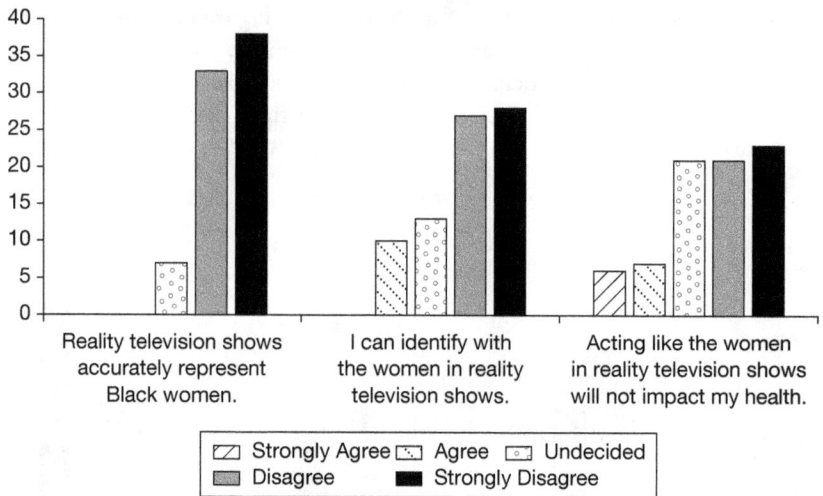

Figure 6.2 Black Women's Perceptions of Reality Television Shows

HEALTH ADVOCACY AND THE FIGHT FOR
REPRODUCTIVE JUSTICE

Health inequities continue to persist for Black women and Black families; however, Black women have played a significant role in shedding light on the disproportionate health care outcomes and medical injustices. Black women health advocates have produced groundbreaking research, led movements, and started national and local initiatives that champion and advance quality and culturally conscious health care. For the past five decades, the Black Women's Health Imperative (BWHI, 2023), a national health organization founded and led by Black women, has focused on "eliminating barriers to wellness for Black women and girls." The first of its kind, this nonprofit promotes health equity and justice by "leading health policy, education, research, knowledge and leadership development and communications designed to improve the healthy outcomes of Black women" (BWHI, 2023). From data-driven policy reform that centers Black women to self-care and health improvement programs, the BWHI continues to provide transformational change to the lives of Black women, increasing health outcomes and dismantling systemic barriers.

At the local level, organizations such as Black Women for Wellness (2022) in Los Angeles, California, champion culturally informed wellness for Black women and girls. Three central pillars govern the organization: (1) education, (2) empowerment, and (3) advocacy. Establishing a commitment to reproductive and maternal health in 1994, the nonprofit focused on policy change in California in 1997.

Black Women for Wellness believes in the strength and wisdom of our community and allies. We believe that we have the solutions, resources and responsibility to create the shifts and change needed to impact our health status. Each of us must develop our personal power, hold accountable and support acknowledged leadership, and most importantly, contribute to our survival and growth as a community. (Black Women for Wellness, 2022)

For over 20 years, Black Women for Wellness has worked to empower Black women and their communities to disrupt health care disparities and injustices. Many other Black-women-created and -led health initiatives and organizations exist across the nation and globally that center health justice for Black women. From breast cancer prevention and adequate diagnostics to heart disease prevention and reproductive justice, Black women seek wellness through community-based approaches and policy advocacy.

While Black women have a long history of culturally informed healing and restorative justice health care, from midwifery to national campaigns, media routinely does not align with the work of Black women health advocates. Instead, many media representations broadcast Black women living chronically unhealthy lifestyles, as discussed in Chapter 4.

Assessing Black women's thoughts about their health, we find that Black women in this study demonstrated positive attitudes about healthy lifestyles and low-risk health behaviors. The mean score on the *Health Attitudes Scale* was 97.9 with a standard deviation of 8.8. The mean score falls within the high rating category, which reflects positive attitudes about health-conscious behaviors, preventative care, and healthy lifestyle choices. When asked whether "It is important to get physical checkups," 97.9% of participants strongly agreed (n = 74) or agreed (n = 21). Also, when analyzing sexual and reproductive health, the majority of participants agreed (n = 11) or strongly agreed (n = 84) that "It is important to protect yourself when having sex."

Investigating the impact of media viewership of Black women in reality television shows and television dramas on Black women's health attitudes, a Pearson correlation coefficient was calculated for the relationship between participants' health attitudes and viewership of reality television shows starring Black women. A weak negative correlation that was not significant was found ($r(71)$ = –.110, p > .05). Health attitudes were not related to reality television viewership. A second Pearson correlation coefficient was calculated for the relationship between participants' health attitudes and viewership of television dramas starring Black women. A weak correlation that was not significant was found ($r(87)$ = .076, p > .05). Health attitudes were not related to television drama viewership.

Exploring the relationship between participants' reception of media representations of Black women in reality television shows and television dramas and their health attitudes, a Pearson correlation coefficient was calculated for the relationship between participants' health attitudes and ratings of reality television shows starring Black women. A weak negative correlation that was not significant was found ($r(71) = -.200, p > .05$). Health attitudes were not related to reality television reception. A second Pearson correlation coefficient was calculated for the relationship between participants' health attitudes and ratings of television dramas starring Black women. A weak negative correlation was found ($r(85) = -.240, p > .05$), indicating a significant relationship between the two variables. Positive health attitudes result in negative reception of television dramas. Overall, we find that Black women do not buy in to the images of Black women living unhealthy lifestyles in the media. In fact, Black women reported having wellness-centered health attitudes and did not relate to the images in the media.

A COMMITMENT TO HEALTHY
BLACK FAMILIES

African American cultural values reflect an appreciation for family and community. Within this communal system of interdependence, women are highly valued, elders are respected, and child-rearing serves as an essential function of the Black family system (R. Hill, 2003; McAdoo, 2007; Nobles, 1974). This framework is derived from African cultures and heritage (Nobles, 1974) and informs the relational dynamics among African American families. For Black women, both motherhood and genuine sisterhood aid the family in its journey to liberation (Hudson-Weems, 1997), and they are essential in cultural traditions being sustained, as I discuss in *Challenging Misrepresentations of Black Womanhood: Media, Literature, and Theory* (M. Gammage, 2019):

> African women play an essential role in the process of life as child-bearers and in the sustainability of cultural traditions and values, as they groom and prepare new family members for active participation in society. In fact, African American women's role within the Black family system is modeled off of these same principles of womanhood. Thus, the Black woman operates as a central hub for her kinship. Therefore, it is not surprising to find Black women, especially elderly Black women, serving as the moral compass and wise sage of the family, and their homes operating as the "Big House" or "Main House," the central meeting place for family gatherings and discussions, for an entire family network. (p. 136)

Although misinterpreted as the matriarch, Black women work collectively and in partnership with Black men to preserve and maintain the Black family, community, and African American culture, in their shared struggle for justice and liberation (Hudson-Weems, 1997; Staples 1981). Marriage and partnerships still play a vital role in African American families, and Black women actively seek lifelong partners to build families and communities (Stewart, 2020). Black family scholars situate the Black family in communal extended family systems that are mutually beneficial and uplifting (Sudarkasa, 1997).

While media representations of Black womanhood have problematized Black women's romantic pursuits and have failed to unpack issues of systemic racism and oppression (Stewart, 2020), Black women desire healthy romantic relations. In the AAWHS, 88% (n = 86) of participants reported that they "prefer to be in a committed relationship." They also did not find media images to promote healthy dating. Less than 1% of participants (n = 2) believe that Black women in television dramas have healthy dating relationships (see Figure 6.1) and respect other women's romantic relationships (n = 4). Embedded within the media are stereotyped messages of Black womanhood that they revert back to myths and stereotypes of Black women being sexually promiscuous, as in the case of the jezebel stereotype. Black women in the study reported observing similar messages. For instance, almost 80% of participants (N = 89) reported that Black women are overly (n = 36) or very (n = 34) sexual in television dramas (see Figure 6.3). Media racism continues to frame the public narrative of Black women's lives, yet Black women prove to be resilient and work collectively to resist marginalization and to advance their families and communities. It is imperative that media and society in general engage Black women's diverse experiences and authentic lives.

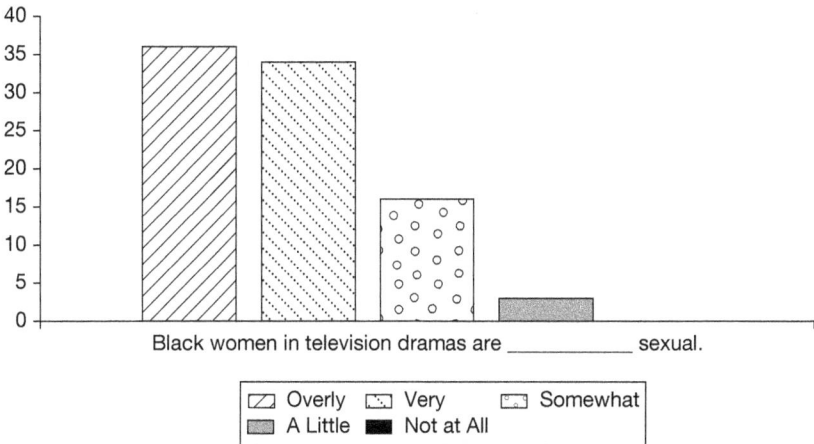

Black women in television dramas are _____ sexual.

Overly   Very   Somewhat   A Little   Not at All

Figure 6.3 Black Women's Perceptions of Sexual Representations in Television Dramas

CONTEXTUALIZING BLACK
WOMEN'S REALITY

Media representations of Black women have methodically portrayed them as chronically unhealthy both physically and socially, which has largely incited fear that Black women's unhealthy lifestyles will lead to negative outcomes for the general public. These concerns have not been based on evidence, yet media have unapologetically sensationalized messages of Black women as social degenerates and threats to public safety and social programs. However, this research questions the legitimacy of these assumptions about Black women. Results from this study indicate that Black women possess healthy concepts of both their physical and social well-being. The participants demonstrated a positive commitment to personal and preventive care. Despite the increased media presence of Black women as abusers of alcohol, Black females in this study disagree with this behavior. They also disagree with the idea of using street drugs. When evaluating the depictions of Black women in the media, Black women in this study found the media illustrations of Black womanhood to be inaccurate. Comparison of their health attitudes and reviews of media signifies a noteworthy difference. Not only are the representations rated negatively, but they also do not mirror Black women's thoughts about their own health and their lifestyles and advocacy work.

Although media representations of Black women have consistently framed Black women as pathologically dysfunctional and irresponsible in their romantic relationships, results from this study counter those misjudgments. Black females in this study expressed positive attitudes about dating relationships. Ninety percent of Black women in this study prefer to be in a committed monogamous relationship. Also, the great majority (98%) believe that it is unacceptable to date married men. However, in all three of the television dramas starring Black women discussed throughout this text (*Scandal* [Rhimes et al., 2012–2018], *Being Mary Jane* [Akil et al., 2013–2019], and *How to Get Away With Murder* [Rhimes et al., 2014–2020]), the lead Black female characters have engaged in extramarital affairs and have not been able to sustain exclusive committed relationships. Therefore, it is not surprising to find that Black females perceive the romantic relationships of Black women in both television dramas and reality television shows as problematic. The Black women in this study rated the romantic relationships of Black women in television dramas and reality television shows very negatively.

Reality television shows market themselves as accurate reflections of real people. Yet, the overwhelming majority of Black women in this study do not identify with the women in reality television shows. Almost 90% of

Black women participants reported that they do not act like the women in reality television shows. Also, most (88%) of the Black women in this study disagree with acting like the women in reality television shows, and the majority believe that modeling their behaviors after women in reality television shows will impact their health.

While this research is revealing of the disparity between Black women's health attitudes and social initiatives, and media representations of Black women's health and wellness, further research is suggested to more comprehensively investigate this phenomenon. A limitation of this study is the small sample size of participants and the limited regional span. Larger populations of Black women should be studied to assess the health attitudes of Black women on a national level. This will allow for a greater generalizability of the findings. Another limitation of this study is the use of an online survey platform. Varied platforms are recommended to reach a diverse population of Black women in the United States.

CONCLUSION

Establishing Culturally Conscious Media Ownership and Production[1]

The public imagination of Black bodies has skyrocketed on screen, in social media, and in music. Unfortunately, the representations of Blackness in the media have been inundated with anti-Black ideologies that marginalize the humanity and cultures of Africana women, men, and children (Allison, 2016; M. Gammage, 2015). Mass media has systematically reflected a White male patriarchal gaze, which is not surprising, given that the majority of the media industry in America is owned by wealthy White men. Within this lens, Blackness has been viewed on a spectrum as inferior to Whiteness, whereby Eurocentric ideologies define the human experience and juxtapose Black reality to White beliefs, values, and practices (Entman & Rojecki, 2000; M. Gammage, 2015; Gray, 1995; Parenti, 1992). The resulting racist mythology of Africanness has yielded inaccurate caricatures and stereotypes that have maintained a stronghold on the public perception of Black culture and Black families. Indeed, the persistent arrogance of Whites has corroded the framing of Blackness while seducing the public into accepting the superiority of Whiteness.

One very important fact surrounding the incomplete and, thus, inaccurate presentations and portrayals of Blacks and Black life in the media is that Whites predominate, not only as major financers and, thus, financial benefactors of the productions, but more important, they monopolize the key positions in the making of films, including Black films, wherein lies why affirming messages of Blackness are not present in certain productions. Consider the following facts relative to the 1998 film adaptation, directed by Jonathan Demme, of the 1987 Pulitzer Prize–winning novel,

Beloved, by the 1993 Nobel laureate Toni Morrison: Only 1 out of 5 producers was Black; the associate producer, the director, and the executive producer were all White; 1 out of the 4 screenplay writers was African; both film editors were White; the cinematographer was Asian; the casting director was White; and virtually all of the other key crew members were White. Other than Oprah Winfrey, African Americans were absent among this production crew. Hence, an authentic African American perspective was missing from the production of the film, which by and large may have compromised the genuineness of the storyline and the portrayals of the Black characters' experiences and their cultural phenomena. Authenticity is a major cornerstone in the theory of Africana Womanism; thus the incorporation of Black cultural perspectives in film production of Black stories is necessary.

In a 1999 review of the movie in *The Western Journal of Black Studies* by Dr. Clenora Hudson-Weems, conceptualizer of Africana Womanism (Hudson-Weems, 2010) and coauthor, with Dr. Wilfred D. Samuels, of the first full-length critical study of the works of the Nobel laureate, titled *Toni Morrison* (Samuels & Hudson-Weems, 1990),

> Morrison had stated years ago that her intention in writing the book was to "rip that veil" to tell the whole story of slave life and to present the interior lives of the enslaved themselves. Together, these issues communicate the bigger picture, which unfortunately the movie sorely misses. (Hudson-Weems, 1999, p. 204)

Indeed, what is missing is the perspective and defining issues, cares, and concerns of Black people, including our lifestyle and unique talent—that is, the art of dancing, which the title character lacks in the movie. In the novel, however, she has mastered that talent, for her sister asks, "Where'd you learn to dance?" Moreover, the character Sixo is grossly misrepresented in the movie, whereas we have a fuller presentation of him in the novel:

> Sixo, too, who represents in the novel the profound love of Black men for Black women in his relationship with his "thirty-mile woman"—for whom he has to travel thirty miles to another plantation just to spend an hour with her—appears [in the movie] in a quick flash, with barely a name, barely a history. (Hudson-Weems, 1999, p. 204)

In the movie, we witness only a quick snap of a man hanging with a noose around his neck, assumed to be that of Sixo, denied in the movie real presence as the recipient of an important part of life in general—*love*. Black movies, on the whole, do not emphasize Black love.

Finally, there is the absolute omission of the poignant experience of another key character in this slave saga, Paul D, the significant other of

Sethe, the mother of Beloved, after she is left without her husband, the father of her five children. Here again we witness the denial of the fuller picture of Paul D, his recounting of his sexual exploitation during his time on a Georgia chain gang, which "made him tremble." Hudson-Weems (1999) offers a possible explanation for this omission, stating "that experience, the sexual exploitation of Black men by white men (guards), forces us to appreciate the commonality of the sexual exploitation of both Black men and Black women, used as receptacles for white pleasures during slavery" (p. 204). Certainly, a conscious commitment to broadcasting the internal underpinnings of Blackness and how we experience our reality has been rejected from the movie-making process.

For Black women's portrayals in particular, standards of womanhood have been restricted to White feminist systems that further subjugate Black women to a marginal existence. That is, the Black woman's image in the media has by and large existed within a racist and sexist context, limiting her possibilities and distorting her truths (Allison, 2016; Collins, 2005; M. Gammage, 2015; hooks, 1992). Nonetheless, the media industry's control and ownership of the Black image have not gone uncontested. In fact, Black media creators and producers have purposely rebelled against this monopolization of Black stories, by calling for antiracist policies and practices in the industry and society in general, and by systematically constructing more authentic representations of Black reality and culture.

Pushing back against the disenfranchisement of Black media producers, Black women's artistry reimagines the possibilities of Black individuals, families, and communities. Fundamentally, the intentionality of culturally conscious representations is designed to sensitize the public to images more germane to Africana people's cultures and lived realities and move the public perception away from anti-Black ideologies of criminality and hypersexuality. Through the use of television and film media, independent media, and social media, the Africana woman media producers are reinvigorating media content with our stories told from our perspectives, serving as a fundamental precept to the reclamation of the Africana image in the media.

Black women's investment in the ownership of Africana media undertakes the activism and advocacy needed to dismantle the racist patriarchal dominance of the media. A new path of independence has been plotted and has allowed for Black artists to control their creation and production of images of Blackness in the media. Black-women-owned media corporations, such as Harpo Productions—founded by Oprah Winfrey; ARRAY—inaugurated by Ava DuVernay; Issa Rae Productions, now known as Hoorae Media—established by Issa Rae; and Cleo TV—owned by Urban One and founded by Cathy Hughes, all have elevated the voices of Black storytellers from conception to marketing and distribution. These Africana women have been able to establish safe production spaces for creators of media content who seek to tell authentic Black stories. Shows including *Black Love* (C. Oliver, 2017–2022), *Cleo Speaks* (Holland & Charles, 2019–present), and *Queen Sugar* (DuVernay, 2016–2022) offer viewers diverse representations that explore the complexities of the Black experience.

Black women media producers, creators, and performers, such as Issa Rae, are able to bring to life the experiences of Africana people in a way that is authentic and true to their current lives. Through Hoorae Media and ColorCreative, founded by Rae and Deniese Davis, Rae has been able to establish new categories of Black media and generate opportunities for other artists, which has paid off significantly. *Insecure* (Rae & Wilmore, 2016–2020), a comedy-drama centering on the experiences of young Black women as they navigate life, love, friendships, and careers, is highly acclaimed and has received over 20 industry awards, including both 2019 and 2020 Outstanding Comedy Series Awards from Black Reel Awards for Television.

The success of these Black women has catapulted the desire of the American public to see more holistic and multidimensional representations of Black women and Black families in the media. These media productions have yielded high dividends and have been exceedingly awarded and applauded by audiences globally. Now, media broadcasting companies are more compelled to produce media content that speaks to Black media consumers. However, Black women are not waiting on affirmation and buy-in from major production companies. Rather, Black women are reclaiming ownership of the creative and production process, thereby ensuring the advancement of Black stories from Black perspectives. In an interview at the Obama Foundation Summit with Theaster Gates on November 8, 2019, Ava DuVernay advanced this agenda in her discussion of her film distribution and resource collective company ARRAY:

> You know, we tried to build our own systems of distribution and amplifying things so that we can rely on people valuing our stories a lot less, because they may value it today and not value it tomorrow; and that's not what we are building. We are building something that allows us to be prioritized and centered in every moment in every day of our lives. That's the institution building that I am working on . . . and building our own pipeline. (Obama Foundation, 2019)

DuVernay, like other Black female media producers, emerges like a breath of fresh air, restoring and proclaiming the beauty and value of Black stories. Through their ownership, Africana media creators have successfully distributed authentic narratives that reclaim Black family heritage, promote social-justice-driven counternarratives, and broadcast celebrations of Blackness.

AUTHENTIC NARRATIVES THAT RECLAIM BLACK FAMILY HERITAGE

Political figures, governmental agencies, literature, and media have consistently unfairly represented Black families as nonexistent and dysfunctional (M. Gammage & Alameen-Shavers, 2019; Staples, 1997; Sudarkasa, 1997). The leading literature in the 20th century on Black families relied predominantly on research applying Eurocentric methodological frameworks, such as the pathological paradigm that assessed the Black family using a middle-class White family model. This treatment of Black families ignored Black family cultural characteristics and instead penalized the Black woman for her role within the Black family system. White patriarchy and its byproduct, female subordination, were standard rubrics applied when discussing Black families, despite the fact that White American families differed significantly from Black families in America.

A classic example of this can be noted in Daniel P. Moynihan's 1965 report to the U.S. Department of Labor titled *The Negro Family: The Case for National Action*. In Chapter 4, "The Tangle of Pathology," he applies a normative cultural approach whereby the Black family is evaluated in comparison to the middle-class White family. Here, Moynihan concludes that the Black family is pathologically dysfunctional because it fails to mirror the White male-dominated family system. As a result, he classifies the Black woman as a burden to the Black family's ability to ascend into the American dream as she stands in direct opposition to the Black male assuming a position of dominance and control over the family. Unaffirming of the White patriarchal order, the Black woman in particular in the Black family was miscategorized as a matriarch and single-handedly blamed for the social and economic challenges faced by Black families in America, without a single account for the institutional racism that marginalized Black social, political, and economic mobility.

This racist miscategorization of the Black family has been used to rationalize the systemic public policy attack on Black women, which has framed the Black woman as an illegitimate criminally unfit "baby mama" or "welfare queen" and the Black man as a superpredatory absentee "baby daddy." And the media has primarily reflected these same stereotyped sentiments. From impoverished welfare-dependent portrayals to drug-addicted caricatures, media has overwhelmingly perpetuated racist typecasts of Blackness. The myths surrounding Black families were overly sensationalized in the media for centuries (Bennett, 2010); however, culturally grounded Black media producers have endeavored to reclaim and take ownership of the Black family representations in media as a form of restorative justice and Black cultural pride.

Recentering the authentic cultural practices of Africana families has served as a priority among Africana media owners and producers. In particular, Black women in the media have intentionally devoted their creative works to producing culturally conscious Black-family-centered media content that both celebrates the beauty of African cultures and simultaneously challenges century-old racist narratives of the dysfunctional Black family and community. Contemporary media imagery by Africana women engenders continuity between the cultural practices of African Americans and their aspirations, while at the same time highlighting the voices of Black media creators and artists.

Africana women such as Ava DuVernay, Issa Rae, Codie Elaine Oliver, and Stella Meghie use the power of the media to transform the way Black family stories are communicated. In 2019, DuVernay contended that there exists a need to decompose the negative and problematic images in the media:

> At ARRAY we focus on the image, we focus on the cinematic image and the way in which the telling of story in a distorted way about all of us and who we are have really diminished us as people. The storytelling is such a part, it's the crux of our belief about each other. The stories we've been told about each other. Right. And not just the stories passed along and whispered between families and generations, but the way that the image has been used to really harm. To really portray certain people as thugs, certain people as lazy, certain people as frivolous, certain people as sinister; it's the stories that have done that, that have been kind of beaten into us through repetition over the years. And so, that's what we try to deconstruct and disrupt at ARRAY. All of the systems around the story. (Obama Foundation, 2019)

In abandoning the anti-Black racist ideologies that engulf the media, Black women are envisioning a newer, more complete multifaceted depiction of Blackness for now and the future.

A noteworthy genre that illustrates the revolutionary stance applied in Black women's media is in the area of romantic love. New Black media chronicles Africana people's commitments to love and the interdependence of community while existing in a racist dehumanizing society. Previously, stories of Black love in the media were predominantly limited to unhealthy unconsummated hopes for love. Joyous love was difficult if not impossible to imagine in media among Black romantic couples. Many romantic storylines would end with hopes of sweet fulfilling love; yet characters would spend the majority of their screen time drowning in grief and sorrow with sprinkles of passionate love scenes. In their completed form, films such as *Baby Boy* (Singleton, 2001), *Love Jones* (Witcher, 1997), and *Jason's Lyric* (McHenry, 1994) were unable to fully actualize the establishment of Black love in a healthy and long-standing relationship. While each of the films is entitled to its own accolades within Black cinematic productions, the characters' potential for mature love is underdeveloped, given that they lack personal traits to be a healthy partner in a relationship. For instance, Jody in *Baby Boy*—a drama detailing the immature romantic entanglements of a 20-year-old Black male, Jody—is portrayed as a self-centered childish male incapable of socioemotional, financial, sexual, or spiritual commitment to a single partner. Yet, by the end of the film, he commits to Yvette, one of the mothers of his children, and their family. Ironically, the film does not allow time for the viewer to witness the carrying out of their new union. Prior to his revelation and commitment to his family, Jody does not display signs of fidelity, trust, or commitment. Thus, the audience is left to wonder if Jody actually possesses the ability to maintain the relationship in a healthy and mutually fulfilling state. Similarly, in *Love Jones*—a romantic drama depicting the romance of two young African Americans, Darius and Nina—the characters are not represented as having the attributes of honesty, selflessness, and commitment. Both Darius and Nina allow their pride and personal insecurities to override their willingness to love each other, and it is only when they momentarily put their egos aside that they choose love—and then the story ends. In both films, the characters' display of selfishness compromises their ability to be committed partners in healthy relationships. Therefore, when they make the choice at the end of each movie to pursue love, we must question if love is actually possible and can be sustained.

Not only are viable character traits missing in each of the storylines, but each character must make major personal sacrifices in relation to family and/or career, as in the case of *Love Jones*. An illustration of this can be found in *Jason's Lyric*, a Black romantic drama set in an economically devasted community engulfed in violence that tells the love story of Jason and Lyric. Both are surrounded by family drama and crimes that challenge the potential of their romantic relationship. For example, in order to pursue their relationship, both must sacrifice their relationships with their immediate family members, and both of their brothers are involved in violent crimes. Essentially, they must abandon the African cultural values of family and community in order to achieve love. While Jason struggles to commit to both love and family, he is torn and forced to decide to relinquish one, the family. In this struggle, he jeopardizes his safety and freedom and that of the woman he loves. In the end, Jason and Lyric lose their relationships with their families and must leave their community in an to attempt to build their own union. In each of these films, the characters are fractured, lacking essential qualities needed for healthy relationships.

Another important aspect of romantic relationships and marriage among Africana people is the role of family and models of marriage (Chapman, 1997; Franklin, 1997). Illustrated in all three films is the lack of sustained healthy marriages. In *Love Jones*, one of Darius's friendship stories includes a married couple; however, their relationship is a struggle and leads to the wife leaving their family home. Additionally, the sage advice of elders from the family and community is generally missing from the storylines. Lyric (*Jason's Lyric*) is left to solicit relationship advice from a friend who is in a toxic and dangerous love affair. Jody (*Baby Boy*) has his mother to turn to; however, he does not value her advice, as she has struggled to establish a lasting romantic relationship. The thread of tragic and unhealthy love has been woven throughout the representations of Black romantic couples, yet increasingly there has been an investment in transforming the narratives of Black love. Now, the possibilities of Black love are being reimagined outside of the racialized tropes of Black hypersexuality, violence, and poverty. Alternatively, Black love is being imagined with depth and width, spanning beyond the confines of two wounded souls hoping for real love.

The 2020 romance drama *The Photograph*, directed by Stella Meghie, who is also credited for the screenplay, conceptualized Black love among two mature, multifaceted adults, Mae Morton and Michael Block. The couple consciously step into love despite fears and uncertainty, and their hopefulness for love is realistic as its possibility is displayed in the film through another couple, Kyle and Asia. The established long-standing romantic relationship among two Black adults as a model for genuine healthy love serves as a reference point for the potential of genuine love. This is especially important for Mae, given that her immediate reference point for romantic love unfolds through her discovery of her mother and father's past romance. Mae worries that, like her mother, she will allow her own fear to override her ability to love. To combat their doubts, both Mae and Michael seek the advice of family, friends, and elders to guide them in their journey for love. It is these examples, advice, and both Mae and Michael's willingness to step outside of their own comfort zone that allow them to experience love with each other.

In terms of television shows, in both *Queen Sugar* (2016–2022) and *Cherish the Day* (2020), Ava DuVernay unpacks the burdens of racism and classism and their impact on Black families and Black love. While her characters are not without flaws, it is the complexities of each character and their interactions with others that provide a richness to their relational experiences. These shows also have embedded within their storylines examples of committed loving relationships. *Queen Sugar* chronicles the family reunion of the Bordelon siblings—Charley, Nova, and Ralph Angel—after the unsuspected tragic loss of their father. Within the television series, there is a plethora of varying romantic entanglements that are explored and flushed out, and then reimagined. Violet, the aunt to the Bordelon siblings, and Hollywood's relationships serve as a grounding anchor for the younger adults and couples around them. While the characters Violet and Hollywood have their own insecurities and flaws, the maturity of their love allows them to commit to marriage and a lifetime together. Both are willing to make personal sacrifices that do not compromise their own families and desires but instead help fulfill each other's needs and aspirations. Ralph Angel and Darla's relationship comes full circle in its unfolding of the many layers of love—and by the end of the series in 2022, it was not surprising to see their relationship take a full 360 again, which helped them and their relationship mature. As for Charley, Nova, and Ralph Angel, they are constantly challenged by each other and their family and friends to develop healthy loving relationships based on honesty and respect. While these relationships are not perfect, they do not need to be; instead, they offer endless possibilities of love.

Apparent in both *Queen Sugar* and *Cherish the Day* is the presence of family and community, each demonstrating their investment in the romantic couples' journey for love. *Cherish the Day* (2020) is a television series on the OWN network, created and produced by Ava DuVernay. The show uses single-day storylines, for each episode, to disentangle the process of love for Gently and Evan. After a chance encounter at a library, Gently and Evan journey together on a rocky yet inspiring romance. Gently relies on the advice and support of the elders in her life, including her adoptive father, uncles, and mentor, Miss Luma Lee. Their advice coaches her into making informed decisions that lead to her relationship and marriage to Evan. Likewise, Evan has the support and advice of his family and friends to aid him in his pursuit of love with Gently, although the advice he receives is discouraging at times. When the couple fails to heed the advice of their loved ones, it is then that the couple's relationship comes to an end. When the couple reunites at a birthday party, it is clear that they still love each other, and the prospect of a rekindled love is presented. The series reimagines the struggles of love among Black couples and the endless opportunities for romance, love, and devotion, while incorporating Black cultural values of communalism and familyhood (Staples, 1997; Sudarkasa, 1997).

Presently, Black love has been overwhelmingly displayed through scripted and semiscripted reality television shows. Through this medium, Black love has been showcased as dangerous and toxic (Alameen-Shavers, 2016a; M. Gammage, 2015). Departing from these unhealthy representations of Black relationships, Black women, using a culturally authentic lens, seek to project truth to the lived realities of Black romantic couples. *Black Love* (2017–2022), created by Codie Elaine Oliver, highlights the unscripted honest and complex love stories of real Black couples. This docuseries sheds light on the intricacies of marriage among Blacks and the couples' willingness to be vulnerable and committed to love. Fantasy and toxic narratives of love are put aside for authentic discussions of healthy Black relationships, which have proven to be of interest to Black media consumers, as the show aired for six seasons.

Indeed, the shifting projections of Black families and Black male–female relations by Black women media creators have changed the trajectory of the unidimensional narrative of Blackness, as they have clearly opted for the last of the "three distinct reactions to the dominant standard— acceptance, adjustment, and rejection"—which is *rejection* (Hudson-Withers, 1986, p. 132). While racial tropes of Black families and Black love continue to be broadcasted in the mass media, these are no longer the singular narrative for consumers. Diversifying the media portrayals of Black families is proven to be viable and sustainable. The telling of our stories from our varied perspectives enhances the significance of our culture in our lives and affirms the need for the media to be more inclusive of Black voices and ideas. This is what Africana Womanism promotes—the prioritization of race and class, and gender, too, coupled with family centrality and positive male–female relationships, which truly need to be reflected in authentic Black love films as evidenced in life.

SOCIAL-JUSTICE-DRIVEN COUNTERNARRATIVES

For decades, the experiences of African Americans with the criminal justice system have predominantly been told from the vantage point of the American justice system, which has historically viewed and treated Blacks in America as criminal and as a threat to the American sovereignty. These media images have largely been created and produced by White Americans who have used the media to perpetuate America's racist views of Blacks. Early film productions such as *Birth of a Nation* (1915), produced by D. W. Griffith and adopted from Thomas Dixon Jr.'s novel *The Clansman: An Historical Romance of the Ku Klux Klan* (1905), depicted racist ideas about Black Americans that framed Blacks as unintelligent, criminal, and hypersexual, which helped rationalize the public brutality and attack on Blackness. This film set the stage for the cinematic criminal mistreatment of Blackness on screen and is still applauded today.

Over the next two centuries, images of Blacks in American television and film continued to reinforce racist White supremacist propaganda that advanced anti-Blackness as the inherent culture of America. However, as Black media producers entered the industry, they began to challenge the stereotypes by generating more robust representations of Blackness. Unfortunately, many of these films and shows were drowned out by the industry, which was almost exclusively controlled by White men. While there was some marketing to Black media consumers, media representations in the late 20th century diverged very little from the stereotypical portrayals of the early 1900s. Instead, modernized images of Black criminality and hypersexuality emerged in the form of thugs, pimps, bitches, and whores (Allison, 2016; M. Gammage, 2015; hooks, 1992).

The current demand for a more just and inclusive society in America has given way for Africana media producers to create imagery that reflects the call for social justice. Black women have taken up this challenge and have invested their creative energies in sharing and retelling the stories of Blacks in America who have been victimized and terrorized by law enforcement and the American criminal justice system. Ava DuVernay's Law Enforcement Accountability Project (LEAP) focuses on changing the lens of the narrative through which police misconduct and brutality is framed, shifting the media discourse to unearthing genuine narratives of Black experiences. Fighting systematic racism in the media, especially as it pertains to the representations of African Americans' encounters with the criminal justice system, works in conjunction with the social and political movements aiming to dismantle the inherent racial injustice in America and affirm the rights and freedoms of Black people. The problematic White-centric depictions of Blacks as criminals in news media and mass media in general have bolstered the anti-Black perceptions that are deeply rooted in the American psyche. Self-representations, which depict the intimate human experiences of Black Americans with the cruel and unjust systems in America, directly interrogate the myth of justice in America and reposition how we think about justice for African Americans.

One such attempt can be observed in the revolutionary film *When They See Us* (2019) created by Ava DuVernay. The film retells the story of five Black and Latinx teens from the Harlem community in New York City, known as the Central Park Five, and their grotesque entrapment in the criminal justice system in America. Antron McCray, Kevin Richardson, Raymond Santana, Yusef Salaam, and Korey Wise were wrongfully convicted in 1989 for the assault of a White woman in Central Park. The politics and media coverage of the case applied the same racist tropes of the Black male, as pathologically hypersexual and criminal and a threat to White womanhood, as broadcasted in the film *The Birth of a Nation* (Griffith, 1915).

After the exoneration of the Central Park Five, DuVernay (2019) challenged herself and the media to retell the stories of each man and produce a counternarrative of their experiences with a social justice lens. The film shows the interconnectedness of the justice process and racial indifference for the rights and lives of Black Americans. The systemic process of racism is unpacked to reveal how the justice system and its gatekeepers—the offices, attorneys, judges, and juries—work collectively in upholding racist ideologies and disenfranchising the rights of the vulnerable Black population. In the film, the false assumptions about the youth's guilt are exposed through the lack of physical evidence connecting the youth to the case, and how they were forcibly coerced into admitting their involvement in a crime of which they were completely innocent. Let me be clear: The film does not apply a fantasy-based portrayal of the youth and their fight for freedom. It applies a historical and ethnographic assessment of evidence and experiences, including the autobiographic stories of the youth and their families. Truth-telling in media-making elevates *When They See Us* from a simple biopic to a much-needed social justice counternarrative. Following the release and success of the film, calls for further justice for the now adult men ensued. They received a settlement in the sum of $41 million ("Central Park Five," 2019).

Counternarratives rooted in social justice more accurately contextualize the everyday inequalities and discrimination experienced by Black Americans. Often the voices and stories of Black women and men are eclipsed by racist practices and policies carried out by all levels of law enforcement. Capturing the historic legacy of African Americans and the American justice system, the documentary *13th* (2016) by Ava DuVernay chronicles the deeply embedded racism of the criminal justice system and its predatory nature that forces Blacks into the prison industrial complex. Evidence-based social and political commentary guides the viewer through the long-standing racial targeting used to disenfranchise Blacks' rights, and how these systems of oppression are commonplace in American law enforcement and the entire criminal justice system. The film's release in 2016 came at a time when social movements on the part of the Black community, demanding justice in a system that has proven itself to be incapable of delivering justice for all Americans, particularly African Americans, were on a rise. The film echoed the concerns and critiques of the American criminal justice system as championed by the Black Lives Matter movement; therefore, the film became a form of media advocacy.

As noted in Chapter 1, the hashtag #BlackLivesMatter was created in 2013 by Alicia Garza, Patrisse Cullors, and Opal (Ayọ) Tometi as a conscious Black affirmation movement designed to expose and dismantle systems of oppression that marginalize the lives of Blacks globally. The momentum of the movement has led to local and national protest and legislative reform agendas.

The discourse and public sentiment surrounding the Black Lives Matter protest questions the legitimacy of African American social movements and direct-action protest. Sparked after the murder of George Floyd, recorded on video, and the failure to bring criminal charges against the civilians who murdered Ahmaud Arbery and the officers who murdered Breonna Taylor, the Black Lives Matter global protest demands for the deconstruction of systemic racism in the criminal justice system by calling for the abolishment of state funding for police and the systematic restructuring of the criminal proceedings process. However, these protests have been accused of threatening the sovereignty of the nation. Former U.S. president Donald Trump has attacked Black Lives Matter, calling it anti-American and destructive. As president, Trump operated as the national voice of America; thus, his rendering of the Black Lives Matter movement as illegitimate, counterproductive, and disillusioned discredits and dismisses its perceived purpose, thus validating public institutions and officials' failure to enact justice for the countless number of Black lives unjustly taken by America.

Black media producers have published counternarratives that attempt to disrupt this line of thinking about Black social movements and protest. *Selma* (2014), directed by Ava DuVernay, took a humanistic view of African Americans' struggles for equality during the civil rights movement and the 1965 voting rights march, led by Dr. Martin Luther King Jr., from Selma to Montgomery, Alabama. The biopic demonstrates the great personal sacrifices, both physical and socioemotional, taken by African Americans in an attempt to improve and advance America as a nation. The patriotic nature of the march, as represented in the film, challenges the American perception of Black protest. The film grounds Black social movements in the duty and responsibility of citizenship to enhance the country.

Television dramas such as *Shots Fired* (2017), whose executive producer is Gina Prince-Bythewood, attempt to explore the civil unrest and cry for justice surrounding the unjust killings of Black men, women, and children in America by police officers and the resulting failure of the criminal justice system to hold its law enforcement officials accountable. The one-season series portrays African Americans' legitimate distrust in the criminal justice system, still with their continued hopefulness for an equal, more just institution and nation. Thus, in the film we see the convergence of the legacy of institutional racism, as well as African Americans' desire for justice and equality as citizens.

Likewise, *Queen & Slim* (2019), an American drama film shadowing the pursuit of freedom by Slim and Queen after they protect themselves from the violence of a police officer, which results in their being considered cop killers, represents the fears and legacy of trauma experienced by African Americans every time they are pulled over by a police officer. Directed by Melina Matsoukas, *Queen & Slim* encompasses an empathic look at the vulnerability of Black bodies in America. Songs such as "I Can't Breathe" by H.E.R. (2020) speak to this same terrifying existence for African Americans. The lyrics state:

> Started a war screaming "Peace" at the same time
>
> All the corruption, injustice, the same crimes
>
> Always a problem if we do or don't fight
>
> And we die, we don't have the same rights
>
> What is a gun to a man that surrenders?
>
> What's it gonna take for someone to defend us?
>
> If we all agree that we're equal as people
>
> Then why can't we see what is evil? (H.E.R., 2020)

The criminalization of innocent beautiful Black bodies through the lens of law enforcement takes a haunting toll on African Americans and restricts their ability to enjoy the privileges and liberties of citizenship, which is yet to be fully granted. Paradoxically, White America is disconnected from this fear that entraps the African American. Therefore, media such as *Queen & Slim* demonstrates the impact of racism in American society on the African American experience and the responsibility of the nation to address these gross injustices.

Undeniably, social-justice-driven counternarratives serve to challenge and transform institutional racism and aim to dismantle the racist tropes and ideologies that cripple the American psyche, practices, and culture. Through socially conscious revolutionary media, Black women are painting masterpieces that point us to the justice that African Americans seek daily and have been pursuing for centuries. These storytelling platforms give credence to the voices of Black women writers who seek to create authentic thought-provoking media that helps move the nation forward.

BROADCASTING CELEBRATIONS OF BLACKNESS

Combating the predominance of negative images of Blackness in the mass media, Black women's celebrations of Blackness in the media serve as a form of Black racial pride, while at the same time operating as advocates of Black cultural values as a means to empower Africana people globally. Implicit in the construction of celebratory images of Africana women and families in the media is the embracing of historical legacies, cultural phenomena, and the African worldview system, working together to construct media that authentically reflects what it means to be African or of African descent. Moreover, how we are authentically identified as Africana Womanists, rather than being named outside of our cultural reality, demonstrates the power of restorative justice in the media via recognizing the long-standing practice of authentic existence for the advancement of the Africana family (Hudson-Weems, 1993, 2019; M. Gammage, 2015).

Highlighting the historic legacies of Black women through the media, biographical cinematic productions aspire to recount the lived experiences, struggles, and triumphs of extraordinary Black women. Black women have often had to experience life in America as the first and at times the only ones of their race and gender. From entry into colleges, to traveling to space, to heading governmental agencies and major corporations, Black women have embarked on journeys that have placed them as the first African American woman, and often first woman, to achieve accomplishments of these magnitudes. These women's stories have made their way onto the screen over the years, with films like *Hidden Figures* (Melfi, 2016), *Harriet* (Lemmons, 2019), and *The Rosa Parks Story* (Dash, 2002) that chronicle social advocacy and activism among Black women. Most recently, *Self Made: Inspired by the Life of Madam C. J. Walker*, directed by DeMane Davis and Kasi Lemmons, debuted on Netflix in February 2020 and narrates how a Black woman, whose parents were enslaved, became the first female African American self-made millionaire in the early 1900s. The film reinforces Black cultural and political principles of self-reliance and Black economic mobility that have been practiced by African Americans for decades. These were the exact principles promoted by the Black Panther Party and the Black Power movement in the 1960s and 1970s and are part of the current Black Lives Matter movement.

Although met with controversy over its accuracy, the film nevertheless was able to broadcast these principles as natural and necessary for Black Americans. The timing and relevance of the movie is what makes it even more important. Hence, its release came at a time when Black activists were advancing the economic support for Black-owned businesses by Black consumers. In fact, in the summer of 2020, the Black community advocated for a month-long #BuyBlack campaign. Promotions of Black consumers' boycotts from shopping seasons and companies that fail to respect the humanity of Africana people are a part of the historic trajectory to uplift the Black community and the race. Thus, what *Self Made: Inspired by the Life of Madam C. J. Walker* provides is validation for Black economic self-reliance, and the film reinforces the cultural values that have strengthened African Americans and have built Black wealth. The genius of the film is embedded in its indirect achievement of these very principles. While some have focused on the accuracy of Madam C. J. Walker's business practices, others have been able to gain knowledge of the usefulness and power of the Black dollar and Black businesses.

In an attempt to reinforce and fortify the significance of our contributions to the world and the human experience, Black women media producers tell the stories of themselves, their mothers and grandmothers, and their sisters and girlfriends. These self-representations unmistakably culminate in the affirmation of our humanity, cultures, and experiences. Thus, storytelling is in and of itself a celebration of Blackness, for too long have Black women's stories gone unheard of by the general public and the world. African people are of an oral tradition, a storytelling tradition, which has served to pass down family histories from generation to generation. Therefore, it makes sense that we use the media to tell our stories on a grand scale, becoming imprinted on the fabric of America and thus having the potential to become eternal.

Emboldened with the knowledge and strength of her heritage, Beyoncé has launched celebrations of her Blackness as a reclamation of her identity. As the most acclaimed Black female performing artist of the 21st century, Beyoncé (2020a) has chosen to use the power of her celebrity to advocate for the just and humane treatment of Blacks through her art. In July 2020, she released *Black Is King*, a musical film celebrating the wonders of Blackness globally and its impact on the world. In a 2020 interview on ET Canada Live, Beyoncé explained the significance and purpose of *Black Is King*:

> My hope for this film is that it shifts the global perception of the word *Black*, which has always meant inspiration, and love, and strength and beauty to me. But *Black Is King* means Black is regal and rich in history, in purpose and lineage.

The visual album illuminates the diversity of Blackness, its beauty and strength. From African clothing, hairstyles, and dance moves to African cultural and spiritual phenomena, the musical film marvels at the uniqueness and power of that which is Black. With songs like "Nile," "Brown Skin Girl," and "My Power," Beyoncé invokes the spirit of Africanness in a way that unapologetically affirms Blackness. In her song "Black Parade," Beyoncé (2020b) weaves together Black heritage, cultural pride, injustice, and the power of social movements. She successfully promotes Black ownership, African spiritual systems, and social justice advocacy. The story that unfolds is the story of the Black experience.

Empowering and motivating media that celebrates Black pride, beauty, resistance, and resilience is increasingly transforming how the world perceives Blackness. Advancing the multidimensional layers of Blackness as glorious, Black women have also used social media hashtags like #MelaninPoppin, #BlackGirlMagic, and #BlackGirlsRock to advance the brilliance of Blackness. This new wave of publicly displaying Black pride through media puts rich diverse representations of African people at the world's fingertips. Thus, African Americans are beginning to transform the media into a tool that can be used for social justice advocacy and racial upliftment.

NOTE

1. The conclusion of this book is published with the permission of Cambridge Scholars Publishing. "Reclaiming Africana-Melanated Women: The Future of Africana Family/The Power of Media" first appeared in *Africana-Melanated Womanism: In It Together* by Dr. Clenora Hudson-Weems (2022).

References

ABC7. (2015, June 23). *Cops bought Burger King for Dylann Roof following his arrest.* https://abc7.com/news/cops-bought-burger-king-for-dylann-roof-following-his-arrest/801013/

Abramson, B., Scott-Young, M., Gelfand, D., Diaz, N. L., Springman, S., Gayle, S. R., Barraud, T., & Dorsey, D. (Executive Producers). (2012–present). *Love and hip hop: Atlanta* [TV series]. Monami Productions; Eastern TV; Big Fish Entertainment; New Group Productions; MTV Entertainment Studios.

Abrego, C., Cronin, M., & Samek, B. (Executive Producers). (2007–2008). *I love New York* [TV series]. VH1 Television.

Akil, M. B. (Writer), & Akil, S. (Director). (2013, July 2). Pilot (Season 1, Episode 1) [TV series episode]. In M. B. Akil, S. Akil, & G. Union (Executive Producers), *Being Mary Jane.* Akil Productions; Breakdown Productions; Schoolcraft Productions; Will Packer Productions.

Akil, M. B. (Writer), & Akil, S. (Director). (2015a, February 3). People in glass houses shouldn't throw fish (Season 2, Episode 1) [TV series episode]. In M. B. Akil, S. Akil, & G. Union (Executive Producers), *Being Mary Jane.* Akil Productions; Breakdown Productions; Schoolcraft Productions; Will Packer Productions.

Akil, M. B. (Writer), & Akil, S. (Director). (2015b, April 14). Signing off (Season 2, Episode 12) [TV series episode]. In M. B. Akil, S. Akil, & G. Union (Executive Producers), *Being Mary Jane.* Akil Productions; Breakdown Productions; Schoolcraft Productions; Will Packer Productions.

Akil, M. B. (Writer), & Akil, S. (Director). (2015c, October 20). Facing fears (Season 3, Episode 1) [TV series episode]. In M. B. Akil, S. Akil, & G. Union (Executive Producers), *Being Mary Jane.* Akil Productions; Breakdown Productions; Schoolcraft Productions; Will Packer Productions.

Akil, M. B., Akil, S., & Union, G. (Executive Producers). (2013–2019). *Being Mary Jane* [TV series]. Akil Productions; Breakdown Productions; Schoolcraft Productions; Will Packer Productions.

Akil, M. B., Anderson, E. L. (Writers), & King, R. (Director). (2015, February 24). Mary Jane knows best (Season 2, Episode 3) [TV series episode]. In M. B. Akil, S. Akil, & G. Union (Executive Producers), *Being Mary Jane.* Akil Productions; Breakdown Productions; Schoolcraft Productions; Will Packer Productions.

Akil, M. B., Andries, L. (Writers), & Akil, S. (Director). (2015, February 10). Freedom (Season 2, Episode 2) [TV series episode]. In M. B. Akil, S. Akil, & G. Union (Executive Producers), *Being Mary Jane*. Akil Productions; Breakdown Productions; Schoolcraft Productions; Will Packer Productions.

Akil, M. B., Fisher, D. J. (Writers), & Rubio, N. (Director). (2017, September 15). Feeling destined (Season 4, Episode 18 [TV series episode]). In M. B. Akil, S. Akil, & G. Union (Executive Producers), *Being Mary Jane*. Akil Productions; Breakdown Productions; Schoolcraft Productions; Will Packer Productions.

Akil, M. B., Goff, K., Turner, J. (Writers), & Akil, S. (Director). (2015, October 27). Sparrow (Season 3, Episode 3) [TV series episode]. In M. B. Akil, S. Akil, & G. Union (Executive Producers), *Being Mary Jane*. Akil Productions; Breakdown Productions; Schoolcraft Productions; Will Packer Productions.

Akil, M. B. (Writer), & King, R. (Director). (2015, March 17). Let's go crazy (Season 2, Episode 7) [TV series episode]. In M. B. Akil, S. Akil, & G. Union (Executive Producers), *Being Mary Jane*. Akil Productions; Breakdown Productions; Schoolcraft Productions; Will Packer Productions.

Akil, M. B. (Writer), & Scott, O. (Director). (2015, December 15). Some things are black and white (Season 3, Episode 10) [TV series episode]. In M. B. Akil, S. Akil, & G. Union (Executive Producers), *Being Mary Jane*. Akil Productions; Breakdown Productions; Schoolcraft Productions; Will Packer Productions.

Alameen-Shavers, A. (2016a). The "down ass bitch" in the reality television show *Love and Hip Hop*: The image of the enduring Black woman and her unwavering support of the Black man. In D. C. Allison (Ed.), *Black women's portrayals on reality television: The new sapphire* (pp. 191–212). Lexington Books.

Alameen-Shavers, A. (2016b). The Woman Question: Gender dynamics within the Black Panther Party. *Spectrum: A Journal on Black Men, 5*(1), 33–62.

Alang, S., McAlpine, D., McCreedy, E., & Hardeman, R. (2017). Police brutality and Black health: Setting the agenda for public health scholars. *American Journal of Public Health, 107*(5), 662–665. https://www.ncbi.nlm.nih.gov/pmc/articles/PMC5388955/pdf/AJPH.2017.303691.pdf

Aldrich, M. (1979). Progressive economists and scientific racism: Walter Willcox and Black Americans, 1895–1910. *Phylon, 40*(1), 1–14. https://doi.org/10.2307/274418

Alexander, M. (2010). *The new Jim Crow: Mass incarceration in the age of colorblindness*. The New Press.

Allen, V., & Anderson, M. (2014). *One nation underemployed: Jobs rebuild America: 2014 state of Black America*. National Urban League/Publications Unit.

Allison, D. C. (2016). *Black women's portrayals on reality television: The new sapphire*. Lexington Books.

Anderson, M., Green, N., Crowe, H., Rankine, S., & Smith-Hill, J. (Executive Producers). (2019, March 6–2020, July 12). *Married to medicine: Los Angeles* [TV series]. FremantleMedia North America; Purveyors of Pop.

Anderson, M., Green, N., & Fraenkel, J. (Executive Producers). (2016, November 11–December 30). *Married to medicine: Houston* [TV series]. FremantleMedia North America; Purveyors of Pop.

Andreeva, N. (2022, August 12). VH1 logs best Monday primetime demo rating & share in over 2 years with "Love & hip hop" duo. *Deadline*. https://deadline .com/2022/08/vh1-monday-ratings-love-hip-hop-atlanta-miami-1235090620/

Bachman, R. (1994). *Violence against women: A national crime victimization survey report* (Vol. 106). Washington, DC: U.S. Department of Justice, Office of Justice Programs, Bureau of Justice Statistics. https://www.ojp.gov/library/pub lications/violence-against-women-national-crime-victimization-survey-report

Balkaran, S. (1999). Mass media and racism: An analysis of the role of the mass media in the formation of Whites' beliefs and attitudes towards African-Americans. *Yale Political Quarterly, 21*(1), 15.

Balogun, M., Thompson, S. L. (Writers), & Fuentes, Z. (Director). (2018, March 1). *Lahey v. Commonwealth of Pennsylvania* (Season 4, Episode 13) [TV series episode]. In S. Rhimes, B. Beers, B. D'Elia, & P. Nowak (Executive Producers), *How to get away with murder*. Shondaland; NoWalk Entertainment; ABC Studios.

Balogun, M. (Writer), & Wilkinson, J. (Director). (2016, November 10). No more blood (Season 3, Episode 8) [TV series episode]. In S. Rhimes, B. Beers, B. D'Elia, & P. Nowak (Executive Producers), *How to get away with murder*. Shondaland; NoWalk Entertainment; ABC Studios.

Bauldwin, P., Chase, L., Hurtado, B., Jaeger, T., Shelton, J., Swan, A., Ciaccio, T., & Jackson, L. N. (Executive Producers). (2017). *Xscape: Still kickin' it* [TV series]. Truly Original; Monami Entertainment.

Bennett, D. (2010). Looking for the 'hood and finding community: South Central, race, and media. In D. Hunt & A. C. Ramon (Eds.), *Black Los Angeles: American dreams and racial realities* (pp. 215–231). New York University Press.

Berry, M. F. (1995). *Black resistance/White law: A history of constitutional racism in America*. Penguin.

Beyoncé. (Co-writer, Executive Producer, & Director). (2020a). *Black is king* [Film]. Walt Disney Pictures; Parkwood Entertainment; Hamlet.

Beyoncé. (2020b). Black parade [Song]. On *The lion king: The gift* [Album]. Parkwood; Columbia.

The Black Dot. (2005). *Hip hop decoded: From its ancient origins to its modern day matrix*. MOME Publishing.

Black, W. R. (2014, December 8). How watermelons became a racist trope: Before its subversion in the Jim Crow era, the fruit symbolized Black self-sufficiency. *The Atlantic*. https://www.theatlantic.com/national/archive/2014/ 12/how-watermelons-became-a-racist-trope/383529/

Black Lives Matter Global Network Foundation. (n.d.). *Herstory*. https://black livesmatter.com/about/herstory/

Black Women for Wellness. (2022). *About us*. https://bwwla.org/about/

Black Women's Health Imperative. (2023). *Eliminating barriers to wellness for Black women and girls*. https://bwhi.org/

Blackmon, D. A. (2009). *Slavery by another name: The re-enslavement of Black Americans from the Civil War to World War II*. Anchor.

Blankenship, K. M., Smoyer, A. B., Bray, S. J., & Mattocks, K. (2005). Black-White disparities in HIV/AIDS: The role of drug policy and the corrections system. *Journal of Health Care for the Poor and Underserved, 16*(4 Suppl. B), 140–156.

Blythewood, R. R., & Prince-Blythewood, G. (Creators). (2017). *Shots fired* [TV series]. Undisputed Cinema; Imagine Television; 20th Century Fox Television.

Boardman, J. D., & Alexander, K. B. (2011). Stress trajectories, health behaviors, and the mental health of Black and White young adults. *Social Science & Medicine, 72*(10), 1659–1666.

Boyer, C. B., Shafer, M. B., Pollack, L. M., Canchola, J., Moncada, J., & Schachter, J. (2006). Sociodemographic markers and behavioral correlates of sexually transmitted infections in a nonclinical sample of adolescent and young adult women. *The Journal of Infectious Diseases, 194*(3), 307–315.

Bravo Media. (2023). *About Bravo TV.* http://www.bravotv.com/about-us

B-Rock and the Bizz. (1997). My baby daddy [Song]. On *Porkin' beans and weanies*. LaFace; Arista.

Brown v. Board of Education, 347 U.S. 483 (1954). https://www.oyez.org/cases/1940-1955/347us483

Browne-Marshall, G. J. (2012). A cautionary tale: Black women, criminal justice, and HIV. *Duke Journal of Gender Law & Policy, 19*, 407. https://scholarship.law.duke.edu/cgi/viewcontent.cgi?article=1233&context=djglp

Brownstein, H. (1996). *Rise and fall of a violent crime wave: Crack cocaine and the social construction of a crime problem.* Harrow and Heston.

Buck v. Bell, 274 U.S. 200 (1927). https://www.oyez.org/cases/1900-1940/274us200

Burke, T. (2021). *Unbound: My story of liberation and the birth of the Me Too movement.* Flatiron Books: An Oprah Book.

Burruss, K., Hersh, G., Lopez, K., Ford, M., & Weinstock, S. (Executive Producers). (2013, April 9–May 26). *The Kandi factory* [TV series]. True Entertainment; Kandi Koated Entertainment.

Burruss, K., & Tucker, T. (Executive Producers). (2018). *Kandi koated nights* [TV series]. Embassy Row; T. Tucker Productions.

Bynoe, Y. (2004). *Stand and deliver: Political activism, leadership, and hip hop culture.* Soft Skull Press.

Byrne, M. (Writer), & McCrane, P. (Director). (2015, March 19). It's good to be kink (Season 4, Episode 16) [TV series episode]. In S. Rhimes, B. Beers, M. Wilding, T. Verica, & M. Fish (Executive Producers), *Scandal*. ABC Studios; Shondaland.

Carpenter, T. R. (2012). Construction of the crack mother icon. *The Western Journal of Black Studies, 36*(4), 264–275.

Castellanos, D. (2012, March 23). Geraldo Rivera: Hoodie responsible for Trayvon Martin's death. *Los Angeles Times.* https://www.latimes.com/nation/la-xpm-2012-mar-23-la-na-nn-geraldo-rivera-hoodie-trayvon-martin-2012 0323-story.html

Centers for Disease Control and Prevention. (2011). *30 years of AIDS in Black America: An overview.* https://www.cdc.gov/nchhstp/newsroom/docs/30-years-aids-in-black-america-508.pdf

Centers for Disease Control and Prevention. (2022, March 3). *Leading causes of death—females—non-Hispanic Black—United States, 2018.* https://www.cdc.gov/women/lcod/2018/nonhispanic-black/index.htm

The Central Park Five. (2019, September 23). *History.* https://www.history.com/topics/1980s/central-park-five

Chapman, A. B. (1997). The Black search for love and devotion. In H. Pipes-McAdoo (Ed.), *Black families* (3rd ed., pp. 273–283). Sage.

Chen, M., Miller, B. A., Grube, J. W., & Waiters, E. D. (2006). Music, substance use, and aggression. *Prevention Research Center, Pacific Institute for Research and Evaluation, 67*(3), 373–381. https://doi.org/10.15288/jsa.2006.67.373

Chermak, S. (1997). The presentation of drugs in the news media: The news sources involved in the construction of social problems. *Justice Quarterly, 14,* 687–718.

Collins, P. H. (1999). Will the real mother please stand up. In A. E. Clarke & V. L. Olesen (Eds.), *Revisioning women, health and healing: Feminist, cultural, and technoscience perspectives* (pp. 266–282). Routledge.

Collins, P. H. (2005). *Black sexual politics: African Americans, gender, and the new racism.* Routledge.

Collins, P. H. (2006). *From Black power to hip hop: Racism, nationalism, and feminism.* Temple University Press.

Comcast. (n.d.). *Our company.* https://corporate.comcast.com/company

Conway, D. M. (2021). Black women's suffrage, the Nineteenth Amendment, and the duality of a movement. *Alabama Civil Rights & Civil Liberties Law Review, 13*(1). https://ideas.dickinsonlaw.psu.edu/cgi/viewcontent.cgi?article=1274&context=fac-works

Crawford, C. L. (2005). *Race, social construction, and the policy process: The case of the ADAA* (Publication No. 3191444) [Doctoral dissertation, Purdue University]. ProQuest.

Dash, J. (Director). (2002). *The Rosa Parks story* [Film]. CBS; Chotzen/Jenner Productions; Come Sunday; Jaffe/Braunstein Films.

Davenport, C. (2009). *Media bias, perspective, and state repression: The Black Panther Party.* Cambridge University Press.

Davis, D., & Lemmons, K. (Directors). (2020). *Self made: Inspired by the life of Madam C. J. Walker* [Film]. SpringHill Entertainment; Orit Entertainment; Wonder Street; Warner Bros. Television; Netflix.

Demme, J. (Director). (1998). *Beloved* [Film]. Touchstone Pictures; Harpo Films; Clinica Estetico.

Despres, E., Steinberg, E., & Kriegman, J. (Executive Producers). (2019, September 6–present). *Couples therapy* [TV series]. Edgeline Films.

Dixon, T., Jr. (1905). *The clansman: A historical romance of the Ku Klux Klan.* A. Wessels.

The Dogs (featuring Disco Rick). (1991). Your mama's on crack rock [Song]. On *Beware of the dogs.* Joey Boy Records.

Dominick, R., Wilkos, R., & Shannon, K. (Executive Producers). (1991–2008). *Jerry Springer* [TV series]. List.

Dougall, D. (2020, October 28). "Real housewives of Atlanta" breaks ratings records. *Essence*. https://www.essence.com/news/real-housewives-of-atlanta-breaks-ratings-records/

Dred Scott v. Sandford, 60 U.S. 393 (1857). https://www.oyez.org/cases/1850-1900/60us393

Drumright, L. N., Gorbach, P. M., & Holmes, K. K. (2004). Do people really know their sex partners? Concurrency, knowledge of partner behavior, and sexually transmitted infections within partnerships. *Sexually Transmitted Diseases, 31*(7), 437–442.

Du Bois, W. E. B. (1999). *Darkwater: Voices from within the veil*. Dover Publications.

Dukes, K. N., & Gaither, S. E. (2017). Black racial stereotypes and victim blaming: Implications for media coverage and criminal proceedings in cases of police violence against racial and ethnic minorities. *Journal of Social Issues, 73*(4), 789–807. https://doi.org/10.1111/josi.12248

DuVernay, A. (Director). (2014). *Selma* [Film]. Plan B Entertainment; Harpo Productions; Ingenious Media; Pathé; Cloud Eight Films.

DuVernay, A. (Director). (2016). *13th* [Film]. Kandoo Films.

DuVernay, A. (Executive Producer). (2016–2022). *Queen sugar* [TV series]. ARRAY Filmworks: Harpo Films; Harpo Productions.

DuVernay, A. (Director). (2019). *When they see us* [Film]. Harpo Films; Tribeca Productions; ARRAY; Participant Media.

DuVernay, A. (Executive Producer). (2020). *Cherish the day* [TV series]. Warner Horizon Scripted Television; Harpo Films; ARRAY Filmworks.

Emmerson, N., Demyanenko, A., O'Neal, S., Holmes, J., Huffman, T., & Rankine, S. (Executive Producers). (2017, April 17–August 14). *Basketball wives* (Season 6) [TV series]. Shed Media US.

Enouen, S. W. (2017, February 14). *Investigation: Planned Parenthood speeds targeting of minorities*. Life Issues Institute. https://www.lifeissues.org/2017/02/investigation-planned-parenthood-speeds-targeting-minorities/

Entman, R. M., & Rojecki, A. (2000). *The Black image in the White mind: Media and race in America*. University of Chicago Press.

Ericksen, K. P., & Trocki, K. F. (1994). Sex, alcohol and sexually transmitted diseases: A national survey. *Family Planning Perspectives, 26*(6), 257–263.

ET Canada. (2020, July 30). *Beyoncé talks "Black is king" release* [Video]. YouTube. https://www.youtube.com/watch?v=MoaGOHMMiY4

Faulhaber, P., & Povich, M. (Executive Producers). (1991–2022). *Maury* [TV series]. MoPo Productions.

Fish, M. (Writer), & Fuentes, Z. (Director). (2015, October 15). Dog-whistle politics (Season 5, Episode 4) [TV series episode]. In S. Rhimes, B. Beers, M. Wilding, T. Verica, & M. Fish (Executive Producers), *Scandal*. ABC Studios; Shondaland.

Fish, M. (Writer), & Liddi-Brown, A. (Director). (2015, March 12). The testimony of Diego Muñoz (Season 4, Episode 15) [TV series episode]. In S. Rhimes, B. Beers, M. Wilding, T. Verica, & M. Fish (Executive Producers), *Scandal*. ABC Studios; Shondaland.

Fisher, D. J. (Writer), & Green, R. E. (Director). (2017, August 8). Feeling friendless (Season 4, Episode 14) [TV series episode]. In M. B. Akil, S. Akil, & G. Union (Executive Producers), *Being Mary Jane*. Akil Productions; Breakdown Productions; Schoolcraft Productions; Will Packer Productions.

Fisher, D. J., Polk, P.-I. (Writers), & Green, R. E. (Director). (2017, February 14). Getting served (Season 4, Episode 5) [TV series episode]. In M. B. Akil, S. Akil, & G. Union (Executive Producers), *Being Mary Jane*. Akil Productions; Breakdown Productions; Schoolcraft Productions; Will Packer Productions.

Foley, M. (Writer), & D'Elia, B. (Director). (2016, November 17). Who's dead? (Season 3, Episode 9) [TV series episode]. In S. Rhimes, B. Beers, B. D'Elia, & P. Nowak (Executive Producers), *How to get away with murder*. Shondaland; NoWalk Entertainment; ABC Studios.

Foley, M., Swafford, E. G. (Writers), & D'Elia, B. (Director). (2015, November 19). What did we do? (Season 2, Episode 9) [TV series episode]. In S. Rhimes, B. Beers, B. D'Elia, & P. Nowak (Executive Producers), *How to get away with murder*. Shondaland; NoWalk Entertainment; ABC Studios.

Foley, M., Swafford, E. G. (Writers), & Williams, S. (Director). (2014, November 20). Kill me, kill me, kill me (Season 1, Episode 9) [TV series episode]. In S. Rhimes, B. Beers, B. D'Elia, & P. Nowak (Executive Producers), *How to get away with murder*. Shondaland; NoWalk Entertainment; ABC Studios.

Foster, W. A., IV. (2012, October 17). From 500 to 1: The death of the African-American owned hospital. *HBCU Money*. https://hbcumoney.com/2012/10/17/from-500-to-1-the-death-of-the-african-american-owned-hospital/

Franklin, J. H. (1997). African American families. In H. Pipes-McAdoo (Ed.), *Black families* (3rd ed., pp. 5–8). Sage.

Friedman, E. (2014, June 3). U.S. hospitals and the Civil Rights Act of 1964. *Hospitals & Health Networks Daily*. http://www.fvfs.org/emilyfriedman.com/columns/2014-06-03-civil-rights.html

Gammage, J. (2017). Black power and the power of protest: Re-examining approaches for radical economic development. *The Review of Black Political Economy*, 44(1–2), 23–36.

Gammage, J. (2018). Professional athletes and their protests during the National Anthem: Dominant narratives as a form of agency reduction. In V. Grim, S. McDougal III, & M. Tillotson (Eds.), *International Journal of African Studies* (pp. 54–76, Vol. 19). National Council of Black Studies U.S. in cooperation with Alabama State University.

Gammage, M. M. (2015). *Representations of Black women in the media: The damnation of Black womanhood*. Routledge.

Gammage, M. (2017). Pop culture without culture: Examining the public back-lash to Beyoncé's Super Bowl 50 performance. *Journal of Black Studies*, 48(8). https://doi.org/10.1177/0021934717729504

Gammage, M. M. (2018). Stereotyped representations of the Black mother-in-law in reality television shows. In J. Parnell (Ed.), *Representations of the mother-in-law in literature, film, drama, and television* (pp. 53–70). Rowman & Littlefield.

Gammage, M. M. (2019). Representing the Black woman as immoral and abandoning the Black family: A cultural analysis of 21st century television dramas starring Black women. In M. M. Gammage & A. Alameen-Shavers (Eds.), *Challenging misrepresentations of Black womanhood: Media, literature and theory* (Vol. 1, pp. 135–154). Anthem Press.

Gammage, M., & Alameen-Shavers, A. (2019). *Challenging misrepresentations of Black womanhood: Media, literature, and theory.* Anthem Press.

Gan, S., Zillmann, D., & Mitrook, M. (1997). Stereotyping effect of Black women's sexual rap on White audiences. *Basic and Applied Social Psychology*, 19(3), 381–399.

Gandy, O. H., Jr. (1998). *Communication and race: A structural perspective.* Arnold.

Garcia, J. M., Batchelor, J., & Mixon, R. (Directors). (2015). *72%: A baby mama crisis* [Film]. Moguldum Studios.

Garza, A. (2014). A herstory of the #BlackLivesMatter movement. In J. Hobson (Ed.), *Are all the women still White? Rethinking race, expanding feminisms* (pp. 23–28). State University of New York Press.

Giaudrone, A. (Writer), & Akil, S. (Director). (2015, March 10). Pulling the trigger (Season 2, Episode 6) [TV series episode]. In M. B. Akil, S. Akil, & G. Union (Executive Producers), *Being Mary Jane*. Akil Productions; Breakdown Productions; Schoolcraft Productions; Will Packer Productions.

Gilens, M. (2003). How the poor became Black: The racialization of American poverty in the mass media. In S. F. Schram, J. Soss, & R. C. Fording (Eds.), *Race and the politics of welfare reform* (pp. 101–130). University of Michigan Press.

Gill, G. (2020, July 9). *Tarana Burke: Me Too founder says "Black women are a target."* BBC Newsbeat. https://www.bbc.com/news/av/newsbeat-53345945

Goldsmith, M. (Writer), & Barclay, P. (Director). (2017, October 5). I'm not her (Season 4, Episode 2) [TV series episode]. In S. Rhimes, B. Beers, B. D'Elia, & P. Nowak (Executive Producers), *How to get away with murder*. Shondaland; NoWalk Entertainment; ABC Studios.

Graham, E. (Writer), & King, R. (Director). (2015, February 24). Sleepless in Atlanta (Season 2, Episode 4) [TV series episode]. In M. B. Akil, S. Akil, & G. Union (Executive Producers), *Being Mary Jane*. Akil Productions; Breakdown Productions; Schoolcraft Productions; Will Packer Productions.

Graham, E., Quinn, C. (Writers), & Hardy, R. (Director). (2015, April 7). Primetime (Season 2, Episode 10) [TV series episode]. In M. B. Akil, S. Akil, & G. Union (Executive Producers), *Being Mary Jane*. Akil Productions; Breakdown Productions; Schoolcraft Productions; Will Packer Productions.

Gray, H. (1995). *Watching race: Television and the struggle for "Blackness."* University of Minnesota Press.

Griffith, D. W. (Director). (1915). *The birth of a nation* [Film]. David W. Griffith Corp.

Gyant, L. (1996). Passing the torch: African American women in the civil rights movement. *Journal of Black Studies, 26*(5), 629–647.

Gyllenhaal, N. F. (Director). (1995). *Losing Isaiah* [Film]. Paramount Pictures.

Hall, S., Critcher, C., Jefferson, T., Clarke, J., & Roberts, B. (1978). *Policing the crisis: Mugging, the state, and law and order*. Macmillan.

Hardeman, R. R., Medina, E. M., & Kozhimannil, K. B. (2016). Structural racism and supporting Black lives: The role of health professionals. *The New England Journal of Medicine, 375*(22), 2113–2115. https://www.ncbi.nlm.nih.gov/pmc/articles/PMC5588700/pdf/nihms867337.pdf

Harrison, E. (Writer), & D'Elia, B. (Director). (2015, February 12). She's a murderer (Season 1, Episode 12) [TV series episode]. In S. Rhimes, B. Beers, B. D'Elia, & P. Nowak (Executive Producers), *How to get away with murder*. Shondaland; NoWalk Entertainment; ABC Studios.

Harrison, E. (Writer), & Rubio, N. (Director). (2017, October 12). It's for the greater good (Season 4, Episode 3) [TV series episode]. In S. Rhimes, B. Beers, B. D'Elia, & P. Nowak (Executive Producers), *How to get away with murder*. Shondaland; NoWalk Entertainment; ABC Studios.

H.E.R. (2020). I can't breathe [Song]. On *I can't breathe*. RCA Records.

Hersh, G., Eskelin, L., Haughton-Lawson, L., Sylvester, A., Neslage, L., Swan, A., King, C., Cohen, A., & Weinstock, S. (Executive Producers). (2008–present). *The real housewives of Atlanta* [TV series]. Truly Original.

Hikes, Z. L. (2004). Hip-hop viewed through the prisms of race and gender. *Black Issues in Higher Education, 21*(13), 40.

Hill, J. (2008, March 21). *LeBron should be more careful with his image*. ESPN. https://www.espn.com/espn/page2/story?page=hill/080320

Hill, R. B. (2003). *The strengths of Black families*. University Press of America.

Hill, R. B. (2007). The impact of welfare reform on Black families. In H. P. McAdoo (Ed.), *Black families* (3rd ed., pp. 328–338). Sage.

Holland, G., & Charles, M. (Executive Producers). (2019–present). *Cleo speaks* [TV series]. Cleo TV.

hooks, b. (1981). *Ain't I a woman: Black women and feminism*. South End Press.

hooks, b. (1992). *Black looks: Race and representation*. South End Press.

Hoops, H. R. (1918). *Destroy this mad brute: Enlist U.S. Army*. Library of Congress. https://www.loc.gov/pictures/item/2010652057/

Hudson, C. (1993). *Africana womanism: Reclaiming ourselves*. Bedford Publishers.

Hudson, C. (2019). *Africana womanism: Reclaiming ourselves* (5th ed.). Routledge.

Hudson-Weems, C. (1997). Africana womanism and the critical need for Africana theory and thought. *The Western Journal of Black Studies, 21*(2), 79–84.

Hudson-Weems, C. (1999). *Beloved*: From novel to movie. *The Western Journal of Black Studies, 23*(3), 203–204.

Hudson-Weems, C. (2010). *Africana womanism: Reclaiming ourselves* (5th ed.). Routledge.

Hudson-Weems, C. (Ed.). (2022). *Africana-melanated womanism: In it together*. Cambridge Scholars Publishing.

Hudson-Withers, C. (1986). Toni Morrison's world of topsy-turvydom: A methodological explication of new black literary criticism. *The Western Journal of Black Studies, 23*(3), 132–136.

Hughes, A., & Hughes, A. (Directors). *Menace II society* [Film]. New Line Cinema.

Hunkele, K. L. (2014). Segregation in United States healthcare: From Reconstruction to deluxe Jim Crow. *Honors Theses and Capstones, 188.* https://scholars.unh.edu/honors/188

Hunt, D., & Ramon, A. C. (2010). Killing "Killer King": The *Los Angeles Times* and a "troubled" hospital in the hood. In D. Hunt & A. C. Ramon (Eds.), *Black Los Angeles: American dreams and racial realities* (pp. 283–322). New York University Press.

Huq, M., Anderson, M., & Green, N. (Executive Producers). (2013–present). *Married to medicine* [TV series]. Fremantle North America; Purveyors of Pop.

IMDb. (1990–2023). *Basketball wives: TV series, 2010–.* https://www.imdb.com/title/tt1637756/

Jacobson v. Massachusetts, 197 U.S. 11 (1905). https://www.oyez.org/cases/1900-1940/197us11

Jefferson, T. (1787). *Notes on the state of Virginia, query XIV.* University of Massachusetts Lowell. http://faculty.uml.edu/sgallagher/thomasjefferson.htm

Jones, J., & Schmitt, J. (2014, May). *A college degree is no guarantee.* Center for Economic and Policy Research. http://cepr.net/documents/black-coll-grads-2014-05.pdf

Joseph Burstyn, Inc. v. Wilson, 343 U.S. 495 (1952). https://supreme.justia.com/cases/federal/us/343/495/

Kalof, L. (1999). The effects of gender and music video imagery on sexual attitudes. *The Journal of Social Psychology, 139*(3), 378–385.

Kelley, S. S., Borawski, E. A., Flocke, S. A., & Keen, K. J. (2003). The role of sequential and concurrent sexual relationships in the risk of sexually transmitted diseases among adolescents. *Journal of Adolescent Health, 32*(4), 296–305. https://doi.org/10.1016/S1054-139X(02)00710-3

Kendi, I. X. (2012). *The Black campus movement: Black students and the racial reconstitution of higher education, 1965–1972.* Springer.

Kids Count Data Center. (n.d.). *Children in single-parent families by race* [Data set]. https://datacenter.kidscount.org/data/tables/107-children-in-single-parent-familiesby#detailed/1/any/false/870,573,869,36,868,867,133,38,35,18/10,11,9,12,1,185,13/432,431

King, C., Hersh, G., Eskelin, L., Sanchez-Warner, M., Leakes, N., & Weinstock, S. (Executive Producers). (2013, September 17–October 27). *I dream of NeNe: The wedding* [TV series]. NeNe Leakes Entertainment; True Entertainment.

Kissell, R. (2014, November 11). "Real housewives of Atlanta" has biggest Bravo bow ever as it kicks off Season 7. *Variety.* https://variety.com/2014/tv/ratings/real-housewives-of-atlanta-has-biggest-bravo-bow-ever-as-it-kicks-off-season-7-1201353624/

Krantz, G., & Garcia-Moreno, C. (2005). Violence against women. *Journal of Epidemiology & Community Health, 59*(10), 818–821.

Krazy. (1998). I hate my baby mama [Song]. On *My krazy world*. Hit Em Up Records.

Krieger, N., Chen, J. T., Waterman, P. D., Kiang, M. V., & Feldman, J. (2015). Police killings and police deaths are public health data and can be counted. *PLoS Medicine, 12*(12), e1001915. https://doi.org/10.1371/journal.pmed.1001915

Leary, G. Alcohol addiction and abuse. *Black Women's Health*. http://www.blackwomenshealth.com/blog/alcohol-addiction-and-abuse/

Lee, J. C., Harrison, E. (Writers), & Williams, S. (Director). (2016, March 10). There's my baby (Season 2, Episode 14) [TV series episode]. In S. Rhimes, B. Beers, B. D'Elia, & P. Nowak (Executive Producers), *How to get away with murder*. Shondaland; NoWalk Entertainment; ABC Studios.

Lee, J. C. (Writer), & Innes, L. (Director). (2016, February 11). What happened to you, Annalise? (Season 2, Episode 10) [TV series episode]. In S. Rhimes, B. Beers, B. D'Elia, & P. Nowak (Executive Producers), *How to get away with murder*. Shondaland; NoWalk Entertainment; ABC Studios.

Lee, J. C. (Writer), & Turner, J. (Director). (2016, October 20). It's about Frank (Season 3, Episode 5) [TV series episode]. In S. Rhimes, B. Beers, B. D'Elia, & P. Nowak (Executive Producers), *How to get away with murder*. Shondaland; NoWalk Entertainment; ABC Studios.

Lee, S. (Director). (2006). *When the levees broke: A requiem in four acts* [TV series]. HBO Studios.

Lemmons, K. (Director). (2019). *Harriet* [Film]. Perfect World Pictures; New Balloon; Stay Gold Features.

Lincoln, A. (1858, September 18). Fourth debate with Stephen A. Douglas at Charleston, Illinois. In *Collected Works of Abraham Lincoln* (Vol. 3). The Abraham Lincoln Association. https://quod.lib.umich.edu/l/lincoln/lincoln3/1:20.1?rgn=div2;view=fulltext

Livingston, G. (2018, April 27). *About one-third of U.S. children are living with an unmarried parent*. Pew Research Center. http://www.pewresearch.org/fact-tank/2018/04/27/about-one-third-of-u-s-children-are-living-with-an-unmarried-parent/

Mangan, K. (2018, May 10). A White student called the police on a Black student who was napping. Yale says it's "deeply troubled." *The Chronicle of Higher Education*. https://www.chronicle.com/article/A-White-Student-Called-the/243395?cid=rclink

Mapping Police Violence. (2021). *Police violence report*. https://policeviolencereport.org/policeviolencereport2021.pdf

Mapping Police Violence. (2022). *Police violence report*. https://policeviolencereport.org/?swcfpc=1

Matsoukas, M. (Director). (2020). *Queen & slim* [Film]. 3BlackDot; Bron Creative; Makeready; De La Revolución Films; Hillman Grad Productions.

McAdoo, H. P. (Ed.). (2007). *Black families*. Sage.

McCullers, M. (Director). (2008). *Baby mama* [Film]. Relativity Media.

McGee, G., Johnson, L., & Bell, P. (1985). *Black, beautiful, and recovering.* Hazelden.

McGee, Z. (Writer), & Verica, T. (Director). (2015, March 5). The lawn chair (Season 4, Episode 14) [TV series episode]. In S. Rhimes, B. Beers, M. Wilding, T. Verica, & M. Fish (Executive Producers), *Scandal.* ABC Studios; Shondaland.

McHenry, D. (Director). (1994). *Jason's lyric* [Film]. Polygram Film Entertainment.

Meghie, S. (Director). (2020). *The photograph* [Film]. Perfect World Pictures; Will Packer Productions.

Melfi, T. (Director). (2016). *Hidden figures* [Film]. Fox 2000 Pictures; Chernin Entertainment; Levantine Films.

Melton, N. M. (2020, October 28). "Single ladies" and "Basketball wives" set records. *Essence.* https://www.essence.com/news/single-ladies-basketball-wives-set-records-highest-ratings-vh1/

Mitchell, H. (Writer), & Zisk, R. (Director). (2015, February 19). No more blood (Season 4, Episode 13) [TV series episode]. In S. Rhimes, B. Beers, M. Wilding, T. Verica, & M. Fish (Executive Producers), *Scandal.* ABC Studios; Shondaland.

Mohamed, R. (Writer), & Allen, D. (Director). (2015, April 16). I'm just a bill (Season 4, Episode 19) [TV series episode]. In S. Rhimes, B. Beers, M. Wilding, T. Verica, & M. Fish (Executive Producers), *Scandal.* ABC Studios; Shondaland.

Montgomery, B., Self, C., George, D., Pupa, D., & Gamboa, T. (Executive Producers). (2014–2015). *Blood, sweat and heels* [TV series]. Leftfield Pictures.

Morrison, T. (1987). *Beloved.* Knopf.

Motion Picture Association of America. (2018, November). *G is for golden: The MPAA film ratings at 50.* https://www.mpaa.org/wp-content/uploads/2018/11/G-is-for-Golden.pdf

Moynihan, D. P. (1965). Chapter IV. The tangle of pathology. In *The Negro family: The case for national action.* U.S. Department of Labor. https://www.dol.gov/general/aboutdol/history/webid-moynihan/moynchapter4

Mutual Film Corporation v. Industrial Commission of Ohio, 236 U.S. 230 (1915). https://supreme.justia.com/cases/federal/us/236/230/

National Advisory Commission on Civil Disorders. (1967). *Kerner Commission report on the causes, events, and aftermaths of the civil disorders of 1967* [NCJ 8073]. U.S. Department of Justice, Office of Justice Programs. https://www.ojp.gov/ncjrs/virtual-library/abstracts/national-advisory-commission-civil-disorders-report

National Association for the Advancement of Colored People. (2023). *Criminal justice fact sheet.* https://www.naacp.org/criminal-justice-fact-sheet/

National Partnership for Women and Families. (2022, October). *Fact sheet: Black women and the wage gap.* http://www.nationalpartnership.org/wp-content/uploads/2023/02/african-american-women-wage-gap.pdf

Ng, P. (2011, November 8). "Real housewives of Atlanta" draws biggest premiere ratings for franchise. *The Hollywood Reporter.* https://www.hollywoodreporter.com/live-feed/real-housewives-of-atlanta-premiere-ratings-258771

Nielsen. (2017). *For us by us? The mainstream appeal of Black content*. https:// www.nielsen.com/us/en/insights/news/2017/for-us-by-us-the-mainstream-appeal-of-black-content.html

Nobles, W. W. (1974). Africanity: Its role in Black families. *The Black Scholar, 5*(9), 10–17.

Nowalk, P. (Writer), & D'Elia, B. (Director). (2016, September 22). We're good people now (Season 3, Episode 1) [TV series episode]. In S. Rhimes, B. Beers, B. D'Elia, & P. Nowak (Executive Producers), *How to get away with murder*. Shondaland; NoWalk Entertainment; ABC Studios.

Nowalk, P. (Writer), & Offer, M. (Director). (2014, September 15). Pilot (Season 1, Episode 1) [TV series episode]. In S. Rhimes, B. Beers, B. D'Elia, & P. Nowak (Executive Producers), *How to get away with murder*. Shondaland; NoWalk Entertainment; ABC Studios.

N.W.A. (1987). Dope man [Song]. On *N.W.A. and the posse*. Ruthless; Priority.

Obama Foundation. (2019). *Places too often hidden: Ava DuVernay in conversation with Theaster Gates* [Video]. YouTube. https://m.youtube.com/watch?v=4ly9Jp6RHhI

Oliver, C. E. (Director). (2017–2022). *Black love* [TV series]. Confluential Films.

Oliver, M. B. (2003). African American men as "criminal and dangerous": Implications of media portrayals of crime on the "criminalization" of African American men. *Journal of African American Studies, 7*(2), 3–18. http://www.jstor.org/stable/41819017

O'Neal, S., Weinstock, S., Hersh, G., Eskelin, L., Haughton-Lawson, L., Lombardi, J. B., Arnada, P., Aguirre, J., Loeliger-Myers, K., Seliga, M., Horowitz, A., Garcia, Y., & Sole, K. (Executive Producers). (2010–present). *Basketball wives* [TV series]. Shed Media; Truly Original; MTV Entertainment Studios.

Onwuachi-Willig, A. (2018, June 18). What about #UsToo? The invisibility of race in the #MeToo movement. *Yale Law Journal, 128*. https://www.yalelawjournal.org/forum/what-about-ustoo

Paramount. (2022). *Global brands: Making and marking culture*. https://www.paramount.com/brands

Parenti, M. (1992). *Make-believe media: The politics of entertainment*. St. Martin's Press.

Pazol, K., Gamble, S. B., Parker, W. Y., Cook, D. A., Zane, S. B., & Hamdan, S. (2009, November 27). *Abortion surveillance: United States, 2006*. Centers for Disease Control and Prevention, National Center for Chronic Disease Prevention and Health Promotion, Division of Reproductive Health. https://www.cdc.gov/mmwr/preview/mmwrhtml/ss5808a1.htm?s_cid=ss5808a1_e#tab10

Peeling, R. W. (2006). Testing for sexually transmitted infections: A brave new world? *Sexually Transmitted Infections, 82*(6), 425–430.

Pellerin, M. M. (2011). *Perceptions of African American females: An examination of Black women's images in rap music videos* [Doctoral dissertation, Temple University]. Temple University Libraries.

Pinsky, D., Irwin, J., Lapides, H., Sullivan, D., & Kuhlman, B. (Executive Producers). (2008, January 10–2012, November 18). *Celebrity rehab with Dr. Drew* [TV series]. Irwin Entertainment, Inc.; VH1.

Pitman, J. (Creator). (2018). *To Rome for love* [TV series]. Asylum Entertainment.

Prince-Bythewood, G. (Executive Producer). (2017). *Shots fired* [TV series]. Undisputed Cinema; Imagine Television; 20th Century Fox Television.

Public Enemy. (1988). Night of the living baseheads [Song]. On *It takes a nation of millions to hold us back*. Def Jam.

Quigley, J. M. (1965). Hospitals and the Civil Rights Act of 1964. *Journal of the National Medical Association, 57*(6), 455–459.

Rae, I., & Wilmore, L. (Creators). (2016–2021). *Insecure* [TV series]. 3 Arts Entertainment.

Ratchford, J. L. (2012). Black fists and fool's gold: The 1960s Black athletic revolt reconsidered: The LeBron James decision and self-determination in post-racial America. *The Black Scholar, 42*(1), 49–59.

Reinarman, C., & Levine, H. (1989). Crack in context: Politics and media in the making of a drug scare. *Contemporary Drug Problems, 16*, 535–577.

Reinarman, C., & Levine, H. (1997). The crack attack: Politics and media in the crack scare. In C. Reinarman & H. Levin (Eds.), *Crack in America: Demon drugs and social justice* (pp. 18–56). University of California Press.

Rhimes, S., Beers, B., D'Elia, B., & Nowak, P. (Executive Producers). (2014–2020). *How to get away with murder* [TV series]. Shondaland; NoWalk Entertainment; ABC Studios.

Rhimes, S., Beers, B., Wilding, M., Verica, T., & Fish, M. (Executive Producers). (2012–2018). *Scandal* [TV series]. ABC Studios; Shondaland.

Rhimes, S., Canales, S., Brownell, J. (Writers), & Bokelberg, O. (Director). (2015, May 7). A few good women (Season 4, Episode 21) [TV series episode]. In S. Rhimes, B. Beers, M. Wilding, T. Verica, & M. Fish (Executive Producers), *Scandal*. ABC Studios; Shondaland.

Rhimes, S., Mohamed, R. (Writers), & Allen, D. (Director). (2015, April 16). I'm just a bill (Season 4, Episode 19) [TV series episode]. In S. Rhimes, B. Beers, M. Wilding, T. Verica, & M. Fish (Executive Producers), *Scandal*. ABC Studios; Shondaland.

Rhimes, S. (Writer), & Verica, T. (Director). (2015, January 29). Run (Season 4, Episode 10) [TV series episode]. In S. Rhimes, B. Beers, M. Wilding, T. Verica, & M. Fish (Executive Producers), *Scandal*. ABC Studios; Shondaland.

Rhimes, S., Wilding, M. (Writers), & Verica, T. (Director). (2015, May 14). You can't take command (Season 4, Episode 22) [TV series episode]. In S. Rhimes, B. Beers, M. Wilding, T. Verica, & M. Fish (Executive Producers), *Scandal*. ABC Studios; Shondaland.

Rivera, M. (Writer), & Barnette, N. (Director). (2015, November 17). Don't call it a comeback (Season 3, Episode 6) [TV series episode]. In M. B. Akil, S. Akil, & G. Union (Executive Producers), *Being Mary Jane*. Akil Productions; Breakdown Productions; Schoolcraft Productions; Will Packer Productions.

Roberts, D. E. (1997). *Killing the Black body: Race, reproduction, and the meaning of liberty*. Pantheon Books.

Roberts, D. E. (1997). Unshackling Black motherhood. *Michigan Law Review, 95*(4), Symposium: Representing Race, 938–964. https://doi.org/10.2307/1290050

Roberts, D. E. (2012). Prison, foster care, and the systemic punishment of Black mothers. *UCLA Law Review*, *59*, 1474–1500.

Rose, T. (1994). *Black noise: Rap music and Black culture in contemporary America*. Wesleyan University Press.

Rotten Tomatoes. (n.d.a). *About Rotten Tomatoes*. https://www.rottentomatoes.com/about#whatisthetomatometer

Rotten Tomatoes. (n.d.b). *The birth of a nation (1915)*. https://www.rottentomatoes.com/m/birth_of_a_nation/

Rudman, L. A., & Lee, M. R. (2002). Implicit and explicit consequences of exposure to violent and misogynous rap music. *Group Processes Intergroup Relations*, *5*, 133–150.

Russo, M. (Writer), & Smith, M. (Director). (2017, October 19). Was she ever good at her job? (Season 4, Episode 4) [TV series episode]. In S. Rhimes, B. Beers, B. D'Elia, & P. Nowak (Executive Producers), *How to get away with murder*. Shondaland; NoWalk Entertainment; ABC Studios.

Sales, J., Brown, J. L., Vissman, A. T., & DiClemente, R. J. (2012). The association between alcohol use and sexual risk behaviors among African American women across three developmental periods: A review. *Current Drug Abuse Reviews*, *5*(2), 117–128.

Samuels, W. D., & Hudson-Weems, C. (1990). *Toni Morrison*. Twayne Publishers.

Sanger, M. (1921). The eugenic value of birth control propaganda. *Birth Control Review*, *5*(10), 5.

Scott-Young, M., Barraud, T., Springman, S., Gayle, S. R., Diaz, N. L., Gomez, V., Dorsey, D. (Executive Producers). (2014–2019). *Love and hip hop: Hollywood* [TV series]. Monami Productions; Eastern TV; Big Fish Entertainment.

Scott-Young, M., Gayle, S. R., Barraud, T., Springman, S., Chapple, M., DiGangi, D., Veteri, L., Carrozza, M., Diaz, N. L., Fine, L., & Gomez, V. (Executive Producers). (2017, October 30–2018, March 12). *Love and hip hop: New York* (Season 8) [TV series]. Monami Productions; Eastern TV; VH1.

Scott-Young, M., Gayle, S. R., Browning, L., Edge-Rachell, D., Bauldwin, P., Wiener, D., Schornak, B., Cyphers, E., Burns, M., Pendelton, S., & Collins, P. (Executive Producers). (2018–present). *Love and hip hop: Miami* [TV series]. Monami Productions; Eastern TV; Big Fish Entertainment; New Group Productions.

Scott-Young, M., Gayle, S., Williams, T., Barraud, T., Springman, S., DiGangi, D., Browning, L., Edge-Rachell, D., Diaz, N. L., Fine, L., & Gomez, V. (Executive Producers). (2018a, March 9–July 16). *Love and hip hop: Atlanta* (Season 7) [TV series]. Monami Entertainment: Eastern TV; VH1.

Scott-Young, M., Gayle, S., Williams, T., Barraud, T., Springman, S., Patry, D., DiGangi, D., Allen, R., Lang, M., Diaz, N. L., Fine, L., Gomez, V., & Zun, J. (Executive Producers). (2018b, July 23–November 19). *Love and hip hop: Hollywood* (Season 5) [TV series]. Monami Entertainment: Eastern TV; VH1.

Scott-Young, M., Springman, S., Gayle, S., DiGangi, D., Gomez, V., Diaz, N. L., Richards, J., Osorio, K., Barraud, T., Chapple, M., & Young, D. R. (Executive Producers). (2011–2020). *Love and hip hop: New York* [TV series]. Monami Productions; Eastern TV; Big Fish Entertainment.

Seliga, M., Healey, P., O'Neal, S., Scott, A., & Rankine, S. (Executive Producers). (2018, May 14–September 16). *Basketball wives* (Season 7) [TV series]. Shed Media US.

The Sentencing Project. (2018). *Incarcerated women and girls*. https://www .sentencingproject.org/publications/incarcerated-women-and-girls/

Sewell, A. A., & Jefferson, K. A. (2016). Collateral damage: The health effects of invasive police encounters in New York City. *Journal of Urban Health: Bulletin of the New York Academy of Medicine, 93*(Suppl. 1), 42–67.

Shakur, T. (1995). Dear Mama [Song]. On *Me against the world*. Interscope; Jive.

Shelton, E. K. (Writer), & Van Peebles, M. (Director). (2017, January 10). Getting nekkid (Season 4, Episode 1) [TV series episode]. In M. B. Akil, S. Akil, & G. Union (Executive Producers), *Being Mary Jane*. Akil Productions; Breakdown Productions; Schoolcraft Productions; Will Packer Productions.

Simmons, T. (2018). The effects of the war on drugs on Black women: From early legislation to incarceration. *The American University Journal of Gender, Social Policy & the Law, 26*(2), 719–739.

Singleton, J. (Director). (1991). *Boyz n the hood* [Film]. Columbia Pictures.

Singleton, J. (Director). (2001). *Baby boy* [Film]. Columbia Pictures.

Small, D. (2001). The war on drugs is a war on racial justice. *Social Research, 68*(3), 896–903.

Smiley, C. J., & Fakunle, D. (2016). From "brute" to "thug": The demonization and criminalization of unarmed Black male victims in America. *Journal of Human Behavior in the Social Environment, 26*(3–4), 350–366. https://doi .org/10.1080/10911359.2015.1129256

Smith, T. A. (Executive Producer). (2015, September 7–2021, November 29). *For my man* [TV series]. Sirens Media.

Sommers, S. R., Apfelbaum, E. P., Dukes, K. N., Toosi, N., & Wang, E. J. (2006). Race and media coverage of Hurricane Katrina: Analysis, implications, and future research questions. *Analyses of Social Issues and Public Policy, 6*(1), 1–17. https://ase.tufts.edu/psychology/sommersLab/documents/ raceRealSommers2006.pdf

Staples, R. (1981). The myth of the black matriarchy. *The Black Scholar, 12*(6), 26–34.

Staples, R. (1997). An overview of race and marital status. In H. Pipes-McAdoo (Ed.), *Black families* (3rd ed., pp. 269–272). Sage.

Stevens, M. (2018, April 15). Starbucks C.E.O. apologizes after arrests of 2 Black men. *The New York Times*. https://www.nytimes.com/2018/04/15/us/star bucks-philadelphia-black-men-arrest.html

Stewart, D. M. (2020). *Black women, Black love: America's war on African American marriage*. Seal Press.

Substance Abuse and Mental Health Services Administration. (2009). Chapter 6: Substance abuse among specific population groups and settings. In *Substance abuse treatment: Addressing the specific needs of women*. Treatment Improvement Protocol (TIP) Series, no. 51. https://www.ncbi.nlm.nih.gov/ books/NBK83240/

Sud, V. (Creator). (2018). *Seven seconds* [TV series]. East 2 West Entertainment; Fox 21; Netflix; Rock Films.

Sudarkasa, N. (1997). African American families and family values. In H. P. McAdoo (Ed.), *Black Families* (3rd ed., pp. 9–40). Sage.

Swafford, E. G. (Writer), & Sullivan, K. R. (Director). (2016, October 13). Don't tell Annalise (Season 3, Episode 4) [TV series episode]. In S. Rhimes, B. Beers, B. D'Elia, & P. Nowak (Executive Producers), *How to get away with murder*. Shondaland; NoWalk Entertainment; ABC Studios.

Taylor, D. B. (2020, October 29). "RHoA" season finale breaks ratings records. *Essence*. https://www.essence.com/news/rhoa-season-three-finale-breaks-bravo-ratings-record/

Terman, L. M. (1916). *The measurement of intelligence: An explanation of and a complete guide for the use of the Stanford revision and extension of the Binet-Simon intelligence scale.* Houghton Mifflin.

Thornton, S. (2022, May 19). Wild things: A short article on the dangers of owning exotic animals as pets. *National Geographic*. https://education.nationalgeographic.org/resource/wild-things/

Tillotson, M. (2011). *Invisible Jim Crow: Contemporary ideological threats to the internal security of African Americans.* African World Press.

USDA Forest Service. (n.d.). *Wildlife safety in the South.* https://www.fs.usda.gov/detail/r8/recreation/safety-ethics/?cid=fsbdev3_066388

Van Peebles, M. (Director). (1991). *New jack city* [Film]. The Jackson/McHenry Company; JacMac Films.

Vanzant, I., & Harrison, P. (Executive Producers). (2012, June 2–2021, May 22). *Iyanla: Fix my life* [TV series]. Pigeon, Inc.

VH1. (2019, August 29). *Evelyn, Shaunie & Jackie clap back at their haters: Fandemonium: Basketball wives* [Video]. YouTube. https://www.youtube.com/watch?v=tPysldoMGlo&ab_channel=VH1

Viacom International. (2023). *Basketball wives.* VH1. http://www.vh1.com/shows/basketball-wives

Washington, H. A. (2006). *Medical apartheid: The dark history of medical experimentation on Black Americans from colonial times to the present.* Doubleday Books.

Weinstock, S., Hersh, G., Eskelin, L., Haughton-Lawson, L., Bassaragh, K., Barnes-Williams, B., McFarlin Buie, A., & Cohen, A. (Executive Producers). (2016–present). *The real housewives of Potomac* [TV series]. True Entertainment.

Weinstock, S., Hersh, G., Eskelin, L., Haughton-Lawson, L., Neslage, L., Swan, A., Sylvester, A., & Cohen, A. (Executive Producers). (2017, November 5–April 29, 2018). *The real housewives of Atlanta* (Season 10) [TV series]. True Entertainment.

Weinstock, S., Hersh, G., Eskelin, L., VanderHeyden, T., Schiefen, M., Zolciak-Biermann, K., & Biermann, K. (Executive Producers). (2012, April 26–2020, December 29). *Don't be tardy* [TV series]. Truly Original.

Welch, A. (2018, June 25). *Monday cable ratings: "Basketball wives" holds steady, "Love & hip hop: Atlanta" ticks up.* TV by the Numbers.

https://tvbythenumbers.zap2it.com/daily-ratings/monday-cable-ratings-june-25-2018/

Wesley, N., Jr. (2010). *Black hospitals in America: History, contributions, and demise.* NRW Publications.

West, C. M. (2008). Battered, black and blue. *Women and Therapy, 25*(3–4), 5–27.

Wilding, M. (Writer), & Verica, T. (Director). (2015, November 19). Baby, it's cold outside (Season 5, Episode 9) [TV series episode]. In S. Rhimes, B. Beers, M. Wilding, T. Verica, & M. Fish (Executive Producers), *Scandal.* ABC Studios; Shondaland.

Willcox, W. F. (1911). Negro. In *The Encyclopedia Britannica: A dictionary of arts, sciences, literature and general information* (11th ed., Vol. 19, pp. 344–349). Encyclopedia Britannica, Inc.

Wingood, G. M., DiClemente, R. J., Bernhardt, J. M., Harrington, K., Davies, S. L., Robillard, A., & Hook, E. W., III. (2003). A prospective study of exposure to rap music videos and African American female adolescents' health. *American Journal of Public Health, 93*(3), 437–439.

Witcher, T. (Director). (1997). *Love Jones* [Film]. New Line Cinema.

Witte, S. S., El-Bassel, N., Gilbert, L., Wu, E., & Chang, M. (2010). Lack of awareness of partner STD risk among heterosexual couples. *Perspectives on Sexual and Reproductive Health, 42*(1), 49–55.

Young, J. (1973). The amplification of drug use. In S. Cohen & J. Young (Eds.), *The manufacture of news: Deviance, social problems and the mass media* (pp. 350–360). Constable.

Zhang, Y., Miller, L. E., & Harrison, K. (2008). The relationship between exposure to sexual music videos and young adults' sexual attitudes. *Journal of Broadcasting & Electronic Media, 52*(3), 368–386.

Zwane, S. (Director). (2018). *Baby mamas* [Film]. Sorele Media.

Index